YUI 2.8 Learning the Library

Develop your next-generation web applications with the
YUI JavaScript development library

Daniel Barreiro

Dan Wellman

BIRMINGHAM - MUMBAI

YUI 2.8 Learning the Library

First published: July 2010

Production Reference: 1080710

Published by Packt Publishing Ltd.
32 Lincoln Road
Olton
Birmingham, B27 6PA, UK.

ISBN 978-1-849510-70-7

www.packtpub.com

Cover Image by Gavin Doremus (gdoremus24@gmail.com)

Credits

Authors

Daniel Barreiro

Dan Wellman

Reviewers

Iliyan Peychev

Glenn Stephens

Acquisition Editor

Douglas Paterson

Development Editors

Ved Prakash Jha

Tarun Singh

Technical Editors

Kavita Iyer

Tariq Rakhange

Indexer

Hemangini Bari

Editorial Team Leader

Mithun Sehgal

Project Team Leader

Priya Mukherji

Project Coordinator

Vincila Colaco

Proofreader

Chris Smith

Production Coordinator

Arvindkumar Gupta

Cover Work

Arvindkumar Gupta

About the Authors

Daniel Barreiro (screen name Satyam) has been around for quite some time. The ENIAC was turned off the day before he was born, so he missed that—but he hasn't missed much since. He's had a chance to punch cards, program 6502 chips (remember the Apple II?), own a TRS-80, and see some fantastic pieces of operating equipment in his native Argentina, which might have been in museums elsewhere.

When globalization opened the doors to the world, his then barely usable English (plus an Electrical Engineering degree) put him on the career path that ended in a 5-year job in the Bay Area back in the days of NCSA Mosaic. Totally intrigued by the funny squiggles a friend of his wrote in his plain text editor, full of <'s and >'s, he ended up learning quite a lot about the world of frontend engineering.

It's been a long journey since COBOL and Fortran. Now he lives quite happily semi-retired in the Mediterranean coast close to Barcelona, Spain. When he's not basking in the Mediterranean sun, Satyam can be found among the most prolific and knowledgeable participants in the YUI community on the YUI developer forum. He has also authored the ProgressBar component and took over responsibility for the TreeView component of the YUI Library.

This book wouldn't exist had the guys in the YUI Team not done and continued doing such a magnificent work. Thanks to them for sharing their work with the community and for having invited me to participate; this has taught me lots about good programming practices.

Dan Wellman is an author and web developer from the UK. He works full-time for Design Haus, a local family-run digital agency, and specializes in creating fast, effective frontends using the latest technologies and solutions. In the evenings he writes books and tutorials on many aspects of web development, and spends time with his wife and four children. This is his fourth book.

Many thanks to Eamon O'Donoghue for the use of his stunning artwork that helped bring several of the examples in this book to life.

About the Reviewers

Iliyan Peychev is a Software Engineer with more than 10 years experience in different areas such as GPS tracking systems, map applications, security and Smart Cards, PKI, and X.509 Certificates. He started his career developing Win32 and GNU/Linux applications, then Java Enterprise Applications and now he is devoted to ECMAScript and Web developing. He has been using YUI library since 2006.

Iliyan has participated in many different projects concerning security, data control, and access to information. During the years he has developed many applications in multiple different areas—from a Java EE-based Smart Card management system to ECMAScript libraries like Windowing and SVG/VML drawing library, both built on top on YUI.

He spends his free time creating Open Source software. He has created some YUI Gallery modules like YUI Accordion.

At the moment, Iliyan is developing a large web-based system, which allows remote management and control of different kinds of devices, built on top of the YUI library.

Glenn Stephens is a developer, architect, and manager of software solutions and has been involved in numerous industries from education, security, finance and the health industry. Glenn has written numerous publications, has one Delphi/Kylix book under his belt and is the developer of the Monarch BPM Business Process Management software (www.monarchbpm.com). He is intrigued by many aspects of the software process such as architecture, operations and marketing, the roles of the user, and more. Glenn's weaknesses include all musical instruments, snowboarding and comedy clubs. Glenn can be contacted at glenn@glennstephens.com.au

He has also written the *Tomes of Kylix – The Linux API* many years ago (http://www.amazon.com/Tomes-Kylix-Linux-API-CD-ROM/dp/1556228236/ref=sr_1_1?ie=UTF8&s=books&qid=1273985360&sr=8-1).

Table of Contents

Preface

The YUI Library has grown and improved since the first edition of this book. Several components came out of beta or experimental status and most of them will be covered in new chapters or added to related chapters, which will now have more than the two components originally presented.

The coding style has changed and that will be reflected in the examples, which have been modified accordingly.

New developer tools have appeared to make code more reliant, to reduce loading time, to debug, test, and do performance profiling and we will take a look at them.

The biggest change is the release of version 3 of the YUI Library. YUI3 has recently had its first General Availability (GA) release which includes the most basic components, the infrastructure of the whole library. The Widget component, the basis for all the components that will have a User Interface (UI) is still Beta so there are no visual components in GA. YUI3 still has some way to go to achieve the variety of UI components of YUI2 and, above all, the maturity and reliability of its code base. Thus, this book will be based on the current YUI 2.8 release of the library. YUI2 is not dead by any measure; development continues and future releases will come when and if any significant number of changes warrant it.

Loading YUI2 components in YUI3

JavaScript programming is not what it used to be. As we ventured into more complex client-side applications and learned more about the language and the environment it lives in, the programming style has changed. All the examples in the first edition of this book have been updated to the new coding style.

The components in the YUI Library show that same change in style, though some of the original ones now feel aged and the newer ones are more flexible and capable. However, for the sake of the innumerable applications out there, the old components cannot be upgraded as backward compatibility must be preserved. To get out of this tight spot, the YUI team decided to branch off with YUI3, incorporating all the techniques learned over these years. However, YUI3 is not backward compatible with YUI2. Version 2 of the library will still be maintained and upgraded and, in fact, since the two versions branched, there have been as many releases in the YUI2 branch as in the YUI3 branch.

Although YUI3 is a much better programming environment than YUI2 and it has a more consistent and capable interface, it still lacks components such as "widgets", that is, those that have a visual interface. Recently, however, the YUI3 loader (and at this point it is not necessary to go deep into what the loader does) has been enabled to load YUI2 components as well. YUI2 can and regularly does coexist with other non-YUI library components and so does YUI3; there was no reason for them to not coexist with each other. Now, this has been made much easier with the ability of the YUI3 environment to load YUI2 components.

This means two things. First, YUI2 still has a long life. By ensuring that they can run in the YUI3 environment, we can mix and match both versions. All the complex visual components in YUI2 that had no equivalent yet in YUI3 can be used in the YUI3 environment. And second, it means that the YUI team can relax and take their time migrating the YUI2 components, ensuring that when they do get released as YUI3 native, they will be high quality, as per our expectations.

WAI-ARIA

The Web Accessibility Initiative's committee of the World Wide Web Consortium has developed the ARIA (Accessible Rich Internet Application) suite of documents to make the rich applications we can build with YUI accessible to people with disabilities. The degree of support for ARIA is not even across all YUI components. Only components with a visual interface the visitor can interact with need ARIA support. Of those, most YUI components do support ARIA — some have it built-in, others need extra subcomponents, and some do not support ARIA at all. Those that do support ARIA often have a few configuration options, though the defaults rarely need any change. In other words, we as programmers usually don't need to concern ourselves with ARIA besides loading the required subcomponents, if any. We won't cover WAI-ARIA in this book just as we don't cover "beta" components, they are both a work-in-progress with its state still changing and, even when it is available, we rarely need to concern ourselves with it beyond activating it.

What this book covers

In *Chapter 1, Getting Started with YUI*, we look at the library as a whole covering subjects such as how it can be obtained, how it can be used, its structure and composition, and the license it has been released under. We also look at a coding example featuring the Calendar control.

In *Chapter 2, Creating Consistency with the CSS Tools*, we cover the extensive CSS tools that come with the library, specifically the Reset and Base Tools, the Fonts Tool, and the extremely capable Grids Tool. Examples on the use of each tool are covered. We also see how skinning works in the YUI Library.

In *Chapter 3, DOM Manipulation and Event Handling,* we look at the all-important DOM and Event utilities. These two comprehensive utilities can often form the backbone of any modern web application and are described in detail. We look at the differences between traditional and YUI methods of DOM manipulation and how the Event Utility unites the conflicting Event models of different browsers. Examples in this chapter include how the basic functions of the DOM Utility are used. We also look at the Element Utility, which is the basis of most of the new UI components and any a developer might build.

In *Chapter 4, Calling Back Home,* client-server communication is the subject, where we look at how the Connection Manager handles all of our XHR requirements. Then we look at the JSON data interchange format, which is becoming a popular alternative to XML, and at the Get Utility, which allows us to break out of the same-origin policy that limits XHR. Examples include obtaining remote data from external domains and the sending and receiving of data asynchronously to and from our own servers.

In *Chapter 5, Animation, the Browser History Manager, and Cookies,* we first look at how the Animation Utility can be used to add professional effects to your web pages. The chapter then moves on to cover how the Browser History Manager re-enables the back and forward buttons and book marking functionality of the browser when used with dynamic web applications. Finally, we take a brief look at the Cookies Utility, which allows us to persist information at the browser, helping us save user preferences across our site and in between visits.

In *Chapter 6, Content Containers and Tabs*, we look at the Container family of controls as well as the TabView control. Each member of the Container family is investigated and implemented in the coding examples. We also look at and implement the visually engaging and highly interactive TabView control.

In *Chapter 7, Menus*, we look at one of the most common parts of any website — the navigation structure. The example looks with the ease at which the Menu control can be implemented.

In *Chapter 8, Buttons and Trees*, the focus is on the Button family of controls and the TreeView control. We first cover each of the different buttons and look at examples of their use. We then implement a TreeView control and investigate the methods and properties made available by its classes.

In *Chapter 9, DataSource and AutoComplete*, we deal with the DataSource Utility, which allows us to fetch and parse tabular data from various sources, both local and remote and in various formats and deliver it to other components in a consistent manner. We will then look at one of those components, AutoComplete.

In *Chapter 10, DataTable*, we will see another user of DataSource, the DataTable control that allows us to display tabular information and efficiently operate on it on the client side with minimal server intervention.

In *Chapter 11, Rich Text Editor*, we see the Rich Text Editor, which allows our users to create enhanced text as one of the most popular forms of user interaction over the Internet is user-created content.

In *Chapter 12, Drag-and-Drop with the YUI*, the first part is Drag-and-Drop, one of DHTML's crowning achievements wrapped up in an easy-to-use utility. In the second part of this chapter we look at the related Slider control and how this basic but useful control can be added to pages with ease. We also briefly mention the Resizer and Layout components that allow us to move and resize dynamic panels within the browser.

In *Chapter 13, Everyday Tools*, we cover several developer tools. We see how the Logger Control is used to view the event execution of other controls and how it can be used to debug existing controls and custom classes. We also look at other resources such as JSLint and the YUI Compressor. We briefly mention other more advanced tools such as YUI Test, Performance Analyzer, and YSlow.

What you need for this book

This book expects and requires you to have a prior knowledge and understanding of at least JavaScript, HTML, and CSS. While the use of the utilities, controls, and CSS tools will be explained in detail throughout the book, any HTML, CSS, or PHP code that is featured in any of the examples may not be explained in detail. Other skills, such as the ability to install and configure a web server, are required. A PC or Mac, a browser, text editor, the YUI, and a web server are also required.

Who this book is for

This book is for web developers comfortable with JavaScript and CSS, who want to use the YUI Library to easily put together rich, responsive web interfaces. No knowledge of the YUI Library is presumed.

Conventions

In this book, you will find a number of styles of text that distinguish between different kinds of information. Here are some examples of these styles, and an explanation of their meaning.

Code words in text are shown as follows: "In a capable, supported browser the library can transform the `<textarea>` element into the full Rich Text Editor control."

A block of code is set as follows:

```
<script type="text/javascript" src="http://yui.yahooapis.com/
        2.8.0/build/yahoo-dom-event/yahoo-dom-event.js">
</script>
<script type="text/javascript" src="http://yui.yahooapis.com/
              2.8.0/build/animation/animation-min.js">
</script>
```

When we wish to draw your attention to a particular part of a code block, the relevant lines or items are set in bold:

```
<div id="hd">This is your Header</div>
    <div id="bd">This is the body
        <div class="yui-b">This is the secondary block</div>
        <div class="yui-main">
          <div class="yui-b">This is the main block</div>
        </div>
    </div>
    <div id="ft">This is your footer</div>
```

New terms and **important words** are shown in bold. Words that you see on the screen, in menus or dialog boxes for example, appear in the text like this: "The **Collapse** button will reduce it to the title bar itself".

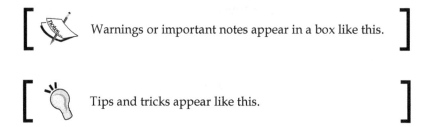

Warnings or important notes appear in a box like this.

Tips and tricks appear like this.

Reader feedback

Feedback from our readers is always welcome. Let us know what you think about this book—what you liked or may have disliked. Reader feedback is important for us to develop titles that you really get the most out of.

To send us general feedback, simply send an e-mail to feedback@packtpub.com, and mention the book title via the subject of your message.

If there is a book that you need and would like to see us publish, please send us a note in the **SUGGEST A TITLE** form on www.packtpub.com or e-mail suggest@packtpub.com.

If there is a topic that you have expertise in and you are interested in either writing or contributing to a book on, see our author guide on www.packtpub.com/authors.

Customer support

Now that you are the proud owner of a Packt book, we have a number of things to help you to get the most from your purchase.

Downloading the example code for the book

You can download the example code files for all Packt books you have purchased from your account at http://www.PacktPub.com. If you purchased this book elsewhere, you can visit http://www.PacktPub.com/support and register to have the files e-mailed directly to you.

Errata

Although we have taken every care to ensure the accuracy of our content, mistakes do happen. If you find a mistake in one of our books—maybe a mistake in the text or the code—we would be grateful if you would report this to us. By doing so, you can save other readers from frustration and help us improve subsequent versions of this book. If you find any errata, please report them by visiting http://www.packtpub.com/support, selecting your book, clicking on the **let us know** link, and entering the details of your errata. Once your errata are verified, your submission will be accepted and the errata will be uploaded on our website, or added to any list of existing errata, under the Errata section of that title. Any existing errata can be viewed by selecting your title from http://www.packtpub.com/support.

Piracy

Piracy of copyright material on the Internet is an ongoing problem across all media. At Packt, we take the protection of our copyright and licenses very seriously. If you come across any illegal copies of our works, in any form, on the Internet, please provide us with the location address or website name immediately so that we can pursue a remedy.

Please contact us at copyright@packtpub.com with a link to the suspected pirated material.

We appreciate your help in protecting our authors, and our ability to bring you valuable content.

Questions

You can contact us at questions@packtpub.com if you are having a problem with any aspect of the book, and we will do our best to address it.

Getting Started with YUI

Welcome to the first chapter of *YUI 2.8: Learning the Library*. Throughout this book, we'll be exploring what makes up the library and what it can do for you. By implementing a selection of the available utilities and controls, we can see exactly how each one works and what functionality and tools it leaves at your disposal.

In this chapter we're going to introduce ourselves to the library by taking an overall view of it. The topics that we are going to cover include:

- How to get the library, where to get it from, how to install it, and how to work with it in your own web pages
- Where it came from, what inspired its creation, who made it, and the core ideas behind it
- Exploring the library and investigating what components form its constituent parts
- Where we can find important information and news about the library and places where we can go to for help if we need it
- The licensing issues that surround its legal use
- Who is likely to make the most of it

We'll also go over a brief coding example where you will get down to some proper scripting and find out for yourself just how easy it is to get up and running with the components themselves. This is where you will see the power provided by the library at first-hand.

What is the YUI?

The **Yahoo! User Interface** (**YUI**) Library is a free collection of utilities and controls, written primarily in JavaScript, which has been produced by the expert developers at Yahoo! to make your life easier as a web developer or frontend user interface designer.

It consists of a series of JavaScript and CSS components that can be used to quickly and easily build the rich and highly interactive applications that today's web consumer expects and demands.

The premise of the library is simple; often when writing JavaScript, you'll come up with a function that works perfectly in one browser, yet badly (or worse, not at all) in alternative browsers. This means that you'll often need a set of different functions to do exactly the same thing in different browsers.

This can be done for some of the major browsers without too much difficulty using standard object detection methods within `if` statements. However, this can lead to massively increased script files and unwieldy code that takes longer to debug and troubleshoot, and longer to write in the first place.

The YUI wraps both sets of code up into one object that can be used programmatically with one class, so instead of dealing with different sets of code for different browsers, you deal with the library and it makes the different calls depending on the browser in use.

Another important aspect of the library that I should mention at this point is its respect for the Global Namespace. All objects created by the library and its entire code run within, and can only be accessed through, the YAHOO Global Namespace object. This means that the entire library, including every utility and every control, and its numerous classes, create just one namespace object within the Global Namespace.

The Global Namespace is the global collection of JavaScript object names, and it is very easy to litter it with potentially conflicting objects, which can become a problem when code is shared between applications. The YUI library minimizes its impact on the Global Namespace while at the same time remains globally accessible by occupying a single name, YAHOO. However, for application code *sandboxing* is preferred and we shall show both techniques and mostly use the latter.

Essentially, the YUI is a toolkit packed full of powerful objects that enables rapid frontend GUI design for richly interactive web-based applications. The utilities provide an advanced layer of functionality and logic to your applications, while the controls are attractive pre-packed objects that we can drop onto a page and begin using with little customization.

Who is it for and who will it benefit the most?

The YUI is aimed at and can be used by just about anyone and everyone, from single site hobbyists to creators of the biggest and best web applications around. Developers of any caliber can use as much or as little of it as they like to improve their site and to help with debugging.

It's simple enough to use for those of you that have just a rudimentary working knowledge of JavaScript and the associated web design technologies, but powerful and robust enough to satisfy the needs of the most aspiring and demanding developers amongst you.

The library will be of interest primarily to frontend developers, as the main aim of the YUI is to provide a framework within which robust and attractive interfaces can be quickly and easily designed and built. It can help you to side-step what can otherwise be insurmountable compatibility issues.

There is no set standard that says you must know this much or that much before you can begin to use the YUI. However, the more you know and understand about JavaScript, the more the library will make sense to you and the more you will be able to gain from using it.

Trying to learn how to make use of the YUI without first knowing about the JavaScript language itself, at least to a basic working standard, is an endeavor likely to end in frustration and disappointment. It would be a great shame if a lack of understanding prevented you from enjoying the benefits that using the library can bring to both your creativity and creations.

So to get the most out of the YUI, you do need to have at least a basic understanding of JavaScript and the principles of object oriented programming. However, a basic working understanding is all that is required and those developers who have less knowledge of scripting will undoubtedly find that they come out of the experience of developing with the YUI knowing a whole lot more than they did to begin with.

The YUI can teach you advanced JavaScript scripting methods, coding, and security best practices, and more efficient ways of doing what you want to do. It will even help more advanced programmers streamline their code and dramatically reduce their development time, so everyone can get something from it.

For some, the YUI is also a challenge; it's an excellent opportunity for developers to get involved in a growing community that is creating something inspiring. The Firefox browser is a great example of an open source, community-driven, collaborative effort of separate but like-minded individuals. Some people may not want to develop web pages or web applications using the library: they may just want to be involved in evolving it to an even greater accomplishment.

I should also point out at this stage that like the library itself, this book expects you to have a prior knowledge and understanding of JavaScript, HTML, and CSS. While the use of the utilities, controls, and CSS tools will be explained in detail throughout the book, any HTML, CSS, or PHP code that is featured in any of the examples may not be explained in detail. Other skills, such as the ability to install and configure a web server, are also required.

Why the Yahoo! User Interface Library?

Using any JavaScript library can save you great amounts of time and frustration when coding by hand, and can allow you to implement features that you may not have the knowledge or skill to make use of. But why should you use the YUI rather than the many other libraries available?

To start with, as I'm sure you already know, Yahoo! is extremely well established, and at the forefront of cutting-edge web technology and frontend design principles. The utilities and controls provided by the library have already been tried and tested in their world-class service provision environment. Hence you know that the components are going to work, and work in the way that you expect them to work and that Yahoo! says that they will. The YUI Library is not a second-rate product, it is what Yahoo! uses.

The YUI library is not the only developer-centric offering to come from these world-class leaders and to achieve high levels of accomplishment and a following amongst developers. Apart from this, other very successful projects include the extensive Design Pattern library, Yahoo! Widgets, and the Yahoo! Query Language. They also have a wide range of APIs for you to experiment and work with, so they have already shown a commitment to providing open source tools designed to succeed.

Additionally, the library has already been publicly available for over three years and in this time has undergone rapid and extensive improvement in the form of bug fixes and additional functionality. Like the Mozilla and Firefox browsers, it has a huge, world-wide following of developers, all seeking to further enhance and improve it.

Other libraries seek to alter the JavaScript language itself, by building capabilities into the language that the developers felt should already have been present and extending the language in new and interesting ways. While these libraries can provide additional functionality at a deeper and more integrated level, their use can often be hampered by technical implementation difficulties. These will be too difficult to overcome for all but the most advanced and seasoned developers.

The YUI is not like this; it is extremely well documented, stuffed full of examples, and is extremely easy to use. It doesn't get bogged down in trying to alter the JavaScript language at a fundamental level, and instead sits on top of it as a complementary extension.

There's also no reason why you can't use the YUI library in conjunction with other JavaScript libraries if a particular feature, such as the rounding of box corners as provided by MochiKit for example, is required in your application but not provided by the YUI.

Graded browser support

Whichever browser you prefer, there's one thing that I think we can all agree on; all browsers are not created equal. Differing support and a lack of common standards implementation are things that have confounded web developers for as long as there have been web developers.

Although the situation is improving with agreed standards from the W3C, and we have better and more consistent support for these standards, yet we are far from being in a position where we can write a bit of code and know that it is going to function on any of the many browsers in use.

There may never come a time when this can be said by developers, but with the YUI, you can already count on the fact that the most popular browsers in use, on all types of operating systems, are going to be able to take full advantage of the features and functionality you wish to implement.

It doesn't, and can't be expected to support every single web browser that exists, but it does group together common browsers with common capabilities into a graded support framework that provides as much as it can to visitors no matter which browser they happen to be using.

Every single browser in existence falls into one of the defined grades; the most common class of browser are the A-grade variety of browsers, which the creators of the library actively support. These are modern, generally standards compliant and are capable of rendering in full the enhanced visual fidelity, and advanced interface functionality provided by the library as well as the inner core of content.

Though the number of browsers in this category is small, more than 95% of users regularly accessing Yahoo's sites use one of these. The YUI development team continually checks Yahoo's own statistics so that new browsers may be incorporated into or dropped from this category accordingly.

C-grade browsers are able to access the base or core content and functionality of the library components, but cannot handle the enhanced content. They are basically old, less capable versions of current browsers, or discontinued ones. These are browsers that are simply not supported by the library.

X-grade browsers are the ones that do not fall in the previous two categories. They are most likely to provide the full, enhanced experience. The most frequent cause for a browser to be in the X-grade list is that it does not have enough market share to justify devoting much time to test the YUI on it. A current example is Safari, which works fine in Windows, but it is not tested because it is an uncommon combination. Any browser that has not been extensively tested by the YUI development team is automatically an X-grade browser regardless of its capabilities.

Currently (in 2010 Q1), the complete spectrum of A-grade browsers supported by the library includes the following combinations of browser and platform configurations:

Browsers	Platforms
IE6, IE7, and IE8	Windows XP
IE8	Windows Vista
Firefox 3.0	Windows XP
Firefox 3.6	Windows XP, Vista and Mac OS 10.6
Safari 4.0	Mac OS 10.5 and 10.6
Google Chrome 4.0	Windows XP

These common configurations are able to make use of not just the core content of any applications we create with the YUI, but also all of the enhanced functionality brought on by the library. Any browser not on this list will still receive either an A or C-grade experience, but may be classed as an X-grade browser if it has not been extensively tested.

The graded browser support strategy is based on the notion of progressive enhancement as opposed to graceful degradation. **Graceful degradation** is a term that I'm sure you've heard at some point and involves designing content such that when it breaks in older browsers, it retains some semblance of order.

This method involves designing a page with presentation in your supported browsers as your main priority while still allowing unsupported browsers to view at least some kind of representation of your content.

Progressive enhancement approaches the problem of supporting browsers with different capabilities from the other direction by providing a core of accessible content and then building successive layers of presentation and enhanced functionality on top of this inner core of generalized support.

The following screenshot shows how the Rich Text Editor control appears in a C-grade browser. Older readers may recognize the browser used in this experiment as Netscape Navigator version 4—a browser popular approximately a decade ago.

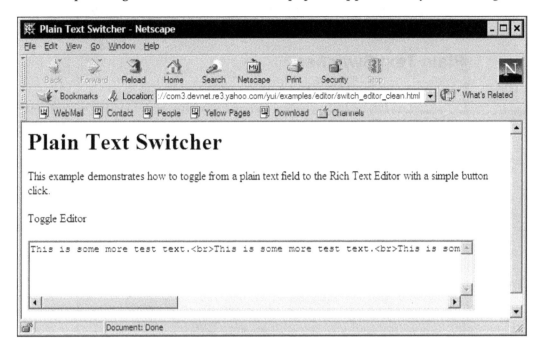

As you can see from this example, the inner core of the page content is a standard HTML `<textarea>` element, which is displayed completely normally. The page doesn't break, but the high-fidelity content is not displayed. Using graceful degradation techniques, the browser would probably attempt to display the editor, but it would probably look very poor and would certainly not function.

The following screenshot shows how the editor appears in an A-grade browser:

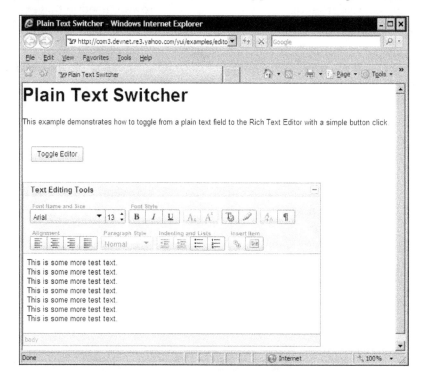

In a capable, supported browser the library can transform the `<textarea>` element into the full Rich Text Editor control. Now the following screenshot shows exactly the same page in exactly the same browser but with JavaScript switched off:

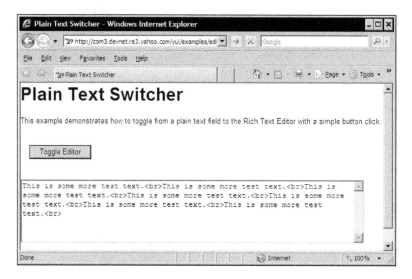

Notice the similarity between a C-grade browser and an A-grade browser with JavaScript switched off.

The knowledge that has enabled Yahoo! to use the concept of graded browser support has been gained from the wide variety of user agents that hit their site every single day. They've been accessed by over 10,000 different software and platform configurations since they began focusing on by whom and how their portal is accessed. Approximately 96% of this total has received an A-grade experience when using the Yahoo! site.

What comes with the YUI?

Some JavaScript libraries are condensed into a single script file, such as the jQuery library. While this can make linking to them easier, it can be inefficient depending on how much of the library you actually use.

The YUI Library is split into its constituent components, making it easy to pick and mix which utilities and controls are used, and making it much more efficient to implement. In addition to the large collection of JavaScript files the library provides a great deal more.

The library topography

The library is currently divided into four distinct sections; the library core files, a series of utilities, a set of controls, and some excellent CSS tools. These are complemented by a series of tools that assist in the development process. There are also three versions of most of the library's utilities and controls, including a full version of the underlying JavaScript file that powers each component, complete with whitespace and comments for better readability and understanding that can help your learning and development.

Along with the full versions, there are also -min.js and -debug.js versions of all the utilities and controls. The -min (for *minified*) files have had all whitespace and comments removed, and variable names have been shortened where possible to cut down drastically on file size. The tool used to produce the -min version, the YUI Compressor is available for downloading at the YUI site so you can use it on your own pages.

The `-min` versions of each component are perfect for production-release applications. These are the ones that you would include in your own pages. Once all development and testing is done, you should minify your own code. Your development code should be well commented and nicely formatted and spaced; you shouldn't scrimp on the code you write for the sake of reducing the file size, the YUI Compressor can take care of doing that for you.

The `-debug` version of each component is designed to be used in conjunction with the Logger Control rather than presented to your visitors. Along with whitespace and comments, these files also contain additional code that logs messages to the Logger console during key interactions within the components. In fact, the `-debug` version is the original source; the other two are automatically generated from this one by first stripping the logging messages for the full version and then compress for the minified one.

The differences between the full and `-min` versions of each file can be quite large, with the `-min` versions often being less than half the size of the full version. The only comment in each of the `-min` files is the copyright notice, which has to stay intact in every file. Other than that, these files are pretty much solid chunks of hard code and readability is therefore very poor.

To further improve the loading time of the library, several combinations of files often used together are provided as **aggregates**. Thus the core files can be loaded in just one go. These are provided only in minified form even though they lack the `-min` suffix.

Once the application is ready to be deployed, Yahoo provides two more performance enhancements. You may load the library files from your own servers, but you can also load them either from Yahoo's **Content Delivery Network (CDN)** or from Google's CDN. These ensure that the user of your application, anywhere in the world, can retrieve the YUI components from the closest server farm available, the very same servers that the Yahoo! site pages use.

Finally, Yahoo's CDN accepts combination requests. Browsers can only have a certain number of active communications channels open at once. When there are more requests for included files than it can handle, the rest will be queued. A combination request is one where the names of several components are concatenated into the same URL and requested all at once, thus avoiding getting later requests delayed in the queue.

If we try to load the Calendar component as well as the Base CSS Tools, this is how it translates into actual numbers:

Method	Number of connections	Download Size (KB)	Delay (ms)
Raw	9	93.9	2365
Minified	9	34.2	1662
Aggregates	5	33.1	1277
Combo	2	32.1	115

Combination requests are different from aggregate files. The latter are produced in the build process of the library and are available from both CDNs as well as in the developer download. The combination requests are completely dynamic and have to be produced on the fly with an application running on the CDN; the combined components do not exist as files in the CDN as the aggregates do. You cannot do a combination request from Google CDN nor when developing in your own machine. However, a first beta release of the application that serves these requests has been released as the YUI PHP Loader and an external contributor has already done an experimental port to Java.

To assist the developer in building the `<script>` and `<style>` tags required to retrieve the library components, the YUI site provides the Dependency Configurator. It lets you select the components you need, the version (`-debug`, full, or `-min`) you want, and which CDN you want to download it from. It will produce a listing that you can simply copy and paste into your page. All mandatory dependencies will be there in the proper order.

There are also three different file designations that each component can be classed as; fully released components are termed **GA (General Availability)**. GA components are typically the oldest, have been tested extensively, and had most of the bugs weeded out. They are reliable and have been considerably refined.

Beta designated utilities and controls are still in the process of being ironed out, but they have been released to the development community for wider testing, bug highlighting, and feature suggestion.

Any component termed experimental is still in the conceptual phase of its design and may or may not be promoted to Beta or GA status.

The core files

The core of the library consists of the following three files:

- YAHOO Global Object
- Dom utilities
- Event Utility

The Global Object sets up the Global YUI namespace and provides other core services to the rest of the utilities and controls. It's the foundational base of the library and is a dependency for all other library components (except for the CSS tools). It also contains the `YAHOO.Lang` object which is made of a series of static methods that add functionality that the language, JavaScript, should have, such as a `.trim()` function for strings.

The Dom utilities provides a series of convenient methods that make working with the Document Object Model much easier and quicker. It adds useful selection tools, such as those for obtaining elements based on their class instead of an ID, and smoothes out the inconsistencies between different browsers to make interacting with the DOM programmatically a much more agreeable experience.

The Event Utility provides a unified event model that co-exists peacefully with all of the A-grade browsers in use today and offers a consistent method of accessing the event object. Most of the other utilities and controls also rely heavily upon the Event Utility to function correctly.

As the core files are required in most YUI implementations, they have been aggregated into a single file: `yahoo-dom-event.js`. Using this one file instead of three individual files helps to minimize the number of HTTP requests that are made by your application.

The Utilities

The utilities provide you with different sets of user-interface functionality that you can implement within your web pages. They provide programming logic and deal specifically with the behavior and interactions between your visitors and the different objects and elements on your pages.

They are a concept that you begin with and then build upon, and they provide the foundation from which you create your vision. They provide unseen behavior; for example, the Animation Utility isn't something your visitors will see directly, but its effects on the element being animated will of course be visible. They are the backstage hands of your application.

Like the core files of the library, several utilities have all been rolled up into one easy-to-link-to aggregate file: utilities.js. Again, this can be used to make your application run more efficiently when using all of the utilities together. The Dependency Configurator will automatically offer to load this file instead of its individual components if it proves smaller.

The set of utilities included in the current release of the library (which is constantly changing and growing) are as follows:

- Animation Utility
- Browser History Manager
- Connection Manager (core and full)
- Cookie Utility
- DataSource Utility
- Drag & Drop Utility
- Element Utility
- Event plugins
- Get Utility
- ImageLoader Utility
- JSON Utility
- Resize Utility
- Selector Utility
- Storage Utility [beta]
- StyleSheet Utility [beta]
- SWF Utility and related components [beta]
- YUILoader Utility

The Connection Manager is provided in the minimal, core, and the full–featured version. So, if you need the very basic set of features, you are not loading the extras. Likewise, the basic Event Utility, part of the core utilities, is supplemented by an extra set of optionals. This pattern is repeated, as we will see in the next section.

The Controls

The controls, on the other hand, are a collection of pre-packaged objects that can be placed directly on the page as they are, with very little customization. Your visitors can then interact with them.

These are objects on the page that have properties that you can adjust and control, and are the cornerstone of any web-based user interface.

These controls will be highly recognizable to most visitors to your site and will require little or no learning in order to use. The complete suite of controls currently included with the library is:

- AutoComplete Control
- Button Control
- Calendar Control
- Carousel Control [beta]
- Charts Control [beta]
- Color Picker Control
- Container Family (core and full)
- DataTable Control
- ImageCropper [beta]
- Layout Manager
- Menu Control
- Paginator
- ProgressBar Control [beta]
- Rich Text Editor Control (simple and full)
- Slider Control
- TabView Control
- TreeView Control
- Uploader [experimental]

The CSS Tools

The CSS Tools form the smallest, but by no means the least useful, component of the library. The utilities and controls are designed to be used almost independently (although some of the files do depend on other files in the library to function properly), but the CSS tools are designed to be used together (although they can also be used separately if desired) and provide a framework for standardizing the visual representation of elements on the page.

The following four tools make up the current CSS section of the library:

- Reset CSS
- Fonts CSS
- Grids CSS
- Base CSS

The CSS tools have just two versions of each CSS file instead of three: a full version and a minimum version; there are no debug versions in this section of the library. As with the `yahoo-dom-event` utility, some of the CSS files have also been combined into one file for your convenience. You can use `reset-fonts-grids.css` or `reset-fonts.css` depending on your requirements.

The developer tools

These files are meant to assist you in the process of developing or deploying the application; they are not expected to ever reach the final user. They are:

- Profiler
- Profiler Viewer
- Logger
- YUI Test
- YUI Compressor
- YUI PHP Loader [beta]
- YUI Doc
- YUI Builder

The first four are JavaScript files that can be loaded along with your application to test or evaluate it. The others are external utilities written in different languages that need to be installed into your development machine or deployment server. These and other utilities developed by others will be covered towards the end of this book.

The library's structure

Once the library has been unpacked, you'll see that there are a series of folders within it; the `build` folder contains production-ready code that you can use immediately on your website. This is where the code that makes each component work and all of its associated resources, such as images and stylesheets can be found.

The `docs` directory contains the complete API documentation for every library component. This is where you can find the classes that make up each component, look at the underlying code, and review the properties and methods available to you.

The `examples` folder contains a series of demonstrative web pages that highlight the key functionality or behavior of each library component and mirror the example space found online. They are often a good place to start testing a new idea: find an example close to what you want and start changing it.

The `tests` folder contains a series of pages that use the YUI Test tool and the Logger Control to check that each component is functioning correctly for the platform on which it is being run. Each method for the component being tested is called, and the results are logged for you to examine. Any change or patch to the library should be tested to ensure it doesn't break existing functionality. These are the very same tests run on all A-grade browsers at Yahoo! before any new release.

The `assets` folder contains extras used either by the examples, the API docs, or index files in the library pack; they are not used by the YUI components. Finally, an `as-docs` folder contains the documentation for the interface to the SWF flash components, which are beta at this stage.

Another set of folders that you'll need frequently when using the library controls are the `assets` folders under each of the component folders in the `build` directory. Each of the controls has its own `assets` folder, which contains things like supporting images and stylesheets, as well as the `sam` skin files (if applicable) for display purposes.

There are some other files and folders within the library, such as an `index` for the library so that you can easily look for documentation or examples and release notes.

Due to the changing nature of the beta, and the experimental utilities and controls, we will not be looking at them in any great detail in this book. For information regarding any of these components, see the YUI site and API guides.

What else does Yahoo! provide?

There are some additional resources that are available courtesy of Yahoo! to help you use the library to its maximum potential. There is a series of very helpful "Cheat Sheets" for each component at its developer guide page in a PDF file, which can be printed each on a single page.

These resources provide a useful and centralized reference manual, which lists the key methods, properties, and syntax patterns of each of the fully released components and gives some basic examples of their implementation.

There is a discussion forum, which developers can use to discuss their projects and get help from experts. The old Yahoo! Group for YUI developers, with 13,600 members and an average of 1000 messages a month until half a year ago, is still active but it has been steadily declining since then in favor of the new forum at `http://yuilibrary.com/forum/`. Both are fully searchable and they are a good place to start if you've got a problem with getting a utility or control to do what you want it to or to submit a question if there is no information listed.

The forum is home to a growing community of developers that have been brought together by the YUI; community involvement is an excellent way to connect with developers and can take a project in new and impressive directions.

For those of you who want to join the YUI development community and give something back to the Yahoo! Developers who have bestowed this awesome tool upon us, besides helping your fellow developers in the forum, there is also the facility to submit bug reports or feature requests. This is an excellent channel of feedback and as the YUI team points out, many useful features have been added to the library following a feature request. It also allows the team to remove errors and refine the features of existing components.

To file a ticket for a bug fix or an enhancement suggestion you can go to `http://yuilibrary.com/projects/yui2/newticket`. A year ago this tracking system resided in `SourceForge.net`, but it didn't have all the features the YUI team needed and, in fact, internally they used another system to track their progress so the two systems were often out of sync. Now, the bug tracker we see is the one the YUI team sees. Though all the members of the YUI team participate in the forum, if you find a bug don't just comment it in the forum, as forum posts cannot be tracked; the bug tracker is the place to ensure that a bug gets fixed.

Once a bug is fixed, you no longer need to wait until the next release to get your hands on the fix. The YUI Library and many of its tools are now saved into GitHub at `http://github.com/yui` so, as soon as you see a bug fixed, you can retrieve the latest build from the very same place the YUI team uses. This is a live development repository, so not all the files are in a stable state; any file retrieved from this repository has to be used with caution and generally not in a production environment.

To keep up-to-date on developments in the YUI and read associated news statements and technical articles about the library and the Yahoo! Developer Network in general, or to watch screencasts from the development team and other experts, you can visit the YUI blog at `http://yuiblog.com`.

This is a companion blog not just for the YUI Library but also for the Yahoo! Design Pattern Library. This is separate from the YUI and is not something that we'll be looking at in this book, but it is worth mentioning because the two resources can be used together in many situations.

The entire selection of different video screencasts and podcasts are brought together in one place for easy searching in the YUI Theater. Both the blog and the theater are subscribable via RSS, so that you can have up-to-date news and announcements surrounding the library.

Finally, you can go further: sign a **Contributor License Agreement (CLA)** and help with the YUI code itself. The CLA basically ensures that you agree to provide your contributions under the same license as the YUI and that you are not violating other people's rights when offering this code. This prevents any individual contributor from forcing exceptions to the general terms of the license used with the YUI.

Are there any licensing restrictions?

All of the utilities, controls, and CSS resources that make up the YUI have been publicly released, completely for free, under the open source BSD license. This is a very unrestrictive license in general and is popular amongst the open source community.

For those of you who don't know anything about what the license stands for and what it allows you to do, I'll give you quick overview now so that you need not worry about it again. Consider these next few paragraphs your education in open source software licensing!

BSD stands for **Berkeley Software Distribution** and was originally designed and used by a team of developers who created an open source operating system of the same name that was similar in many ways to the UNIX platform (and even shared part of its code base with it). Many of today's most popular operating systems, including Windows and Mac OS X are derived from or contain code from the original BSD operating system.

The current BSD version, sometimes known as the New BSD license, differs from the original. It has had the restrictive UC Berkeley advertising clause removed, making it almost equivalent to the MIT license, but with the addition of a brief final clause prohibiting the use of the copyright owner's name for endorsement without obtaining prior consent.

This means that you can pretty much do whatever you want to do with the library source code; you can use it as it is, you can modify it as you wish, add to it, or even remove bits. You can use the files in the format in which they are provided, or you can use the code within them in the distribution of a compiled, closed-source application. Thus, the code belongs to the community and should Yahoo! ever drop it, the community can carry on.

You can use it in your own personal projects, as part of a commercial venture or even within an educational framework. You can do all of this provided that you retain the copyright notice in your source code, or the copyright notice present on each of the library files remains intact.

If you're using the library files as they come in the library, all you need to do is make sure that the existing copyright notice is left at the top of every file that you use. In a compiled application, it should be clearly visible in the help section or user manual.

Installing the YUI

The YUI is not an application in its own right, and it doesn't need to be installed as such. Getting started with the YUI is extremely simple; you first choose whether to download all of the source files from Yahoo! and use them locally as part of your websites' hierarchy, or whether to use the URLs provided on the YUI developer pages to reference the library files stored on Yahoo's web servers.

These are the exact same files that are used in many different interface implementations across the Yahoo! websites and as such can be depended on for being almost continuously available.

Another benefit of using Yahoo's or Google's CDN is that their networks are global in nature, with servers running in many geographically distinct parts of the world. Being able to serve library files from a location closer to your visitors' location results in a better response from your application; this is good news for your visitors and therefore good news for your business.

Additionally, as I mentioned earlier, there are different versions of each of the working files in the library including a "minified" file that has been stripped of whitespace and comment blocks. The Yahoo! servers provide these minified versions of the files, but in addition, they also serve the files in a GZIP format, making the files up to 90% smaller and therefore, much more efficient for transportation across the Internet. Finally, Yahoo! also helps the cache hit rates by issuing `expires` headers with expiration dates set far in the future. But best of all, these benefits are all provided for free.

If you've decided that you want to download the YUI in its entirety, you'll find a link on the YUI home page at `http://developer.yahoo.com/yui/2/`. The files were formerly stored at `SourceForge.net` and you might find references pointing there, including in the first edition of this book, but the project has been migrated away from SourceForge.

So as far as installing the library goes, the most that you'll need to do is to download the library to your computer and unpack it to a local directory where you can easily find the files, assets, and resources that you require for your current project, and if you choose to let Yahoo! host the files for you, you won't even need to do that.

Creating an offline library repository

All the examples in this book fetch the library components from the Yahoo servers. If you are unable to access those you may create your own repository. So you will need to create a new folder on your hard drive called `yuisite`. This folder is where all of our examples will reside.

Just as some of the examples included in the downloaded files do, we will use PHP for server-side scripting, thus this folder needs to be created somewhere under your web server root and where PHP scripts can be executed. It is worth mentioning that YUI is not tied to PHP in any way. Every sample PHP script in this book as well as any provided with the examples in the YUI library download can be replaced by equivalent files in any other server platform. We use PHP simply because it is popular, simple and, most important, free, but any other server platform would do just as well.

Inside this folder, create another new folder called `yui`. When you unpack the library, you will see a folder called `build` inside it. You will need to copy and paste the entire `build` directory into the `yui` folder that you have just created. You may, if you wish, copy the whole library to the `yui` folder, but our examples only require the `build` directory.

To use the examples with this offline repository, the code for the examples needs to be changed. All the `<script>` and `<style>` tags that point to the Yahoo! servers need to be changed to point to the location of the offline repository, whichever it might be. While the examples in the code bundle point to the Yahoo servers, the printed version of them might point to this off-line repository just to keep the URLs short.

It is important that this structure is correct; otherwise none of the examples that we create as we progress through this book will work. A common indicator that library files are not accessible is a JavaScript error message stating that **YAHOO is undefined**.

Using the library files in your own web pages

One thing that you need to check when using different controls and utilities from the library is which, if any, of the other utilities will be needed by the component that you wish to use; fortunately the online documentation and cheat sheets will list out any dependencies of any component that you choose and the Dependency Configurator will assist you in finding out the best combination.

There is only one file that must be used in every implementation of any of the various components: the YAHOO Global Object. This utility creates the namespaces within which all of the YUI library code resides, and contains some additional methods that are used by other files throughout the library.

It must appear before any of the other library files because if references to other component files appear before the Global Object, none of the namespaces used will be recognized by your script. This will cause a JavaScript error message stating that **YAHOO is undefined**.

The CSS files should be linked to in the `<head>` section of your page, as any other CSS file would be. For performance reasons, the code that invokes and customizes the library components should be as close to the bottom of the page as possible. Also, you can easily separate your JavaScript from your HTML altogether and keep your scripts in separate files.

To use the current version of the Animation Utility from the Yahoo! servers for example, the following `script` tags would be required:

```
<script type="text/javascript" src="http://yui.yahooapis.com/
          2.8.0/build/yahoo-dom-event/yahoo-dom-event.js">
</script>
<script type="text/javascript" src="http://yui.yahooapis.com/
                2.8.0/build/animation/animation-min.js">
</script>
```

All code components depend on the YAHOO Global Object, which should always go first. As the Animation Utility also depends on the Event and Dom utilities, we can use the `yahoo-dom-event` aggregate instead of individual files.

Once these `script` tags have been added to your page, the code required to animate your object or element would go into its own `script` tag in the `<body>` section of the page.

Now, we'll take our first look at one of the library components in detail: the Calendar Control. We can take a quick look at its supporting classes to see what methods and properties are available to us, and can then move on to implement the control in the first of our coding examples.

Code placement

Good coding practice should always be adhered to, whether designing with the YUI or not. Keeping your JavaScript and CSS code in separate files helps to minimize the initial size of the page so it shows up earlier and also increases the chances of finding the external, common files in the cache. But it does have its downsides too; every file that your page links to adds another HTTP request to the interaction between your visitor and your server, which can result in slower performance. However, as they change far less than the HTML page that uses them, repeated visitors are more likely to have them in their caches.

In real-world implementations, we would always keep as much of our JavaScript and CSS in separate files as possible, keeping a clear distinction between content, behavior, and presentation layers. For the purpose of this book, however, we will be keeping the HTML and JavaScript code in one file. I stress that this is not the correct way to do things and is done purely so that the examples do not become bloated with numerous files.

Perfect date selection with the Calendar Control

For our first coding example, we'll take a quick look at the Calendar Control. The YUI Calendar allows you to easily create a variety of attractive and highly functional calendar interfaces that can allow your visitors to quickly and easily select single dates or range of dates.

It's an easy component to master, making it ideal for our very first coding example. Not much coding is required for a basic calendar implementation, and the control can easily be customized using the Calendar classes' extensive range of properties or by overriding the default styling.

There is also a range of different formats of Calendar that we can create; there's the basic, single select, one-page calendar control, which displays one month at a time, or there's a larger, multi-page calendar, which allows multiple months to be displayed at once. Multi-select calendars can come in either single or multiple month display formats.

The rendered calendar is instinctively intuitive to use and is presented in a very attractive manner. Almost anyone being presented with it will instantly know how to use it. By default, it features a clear and sensible interface for selecting a date, arranging the dates of the current or starting month in a grid headed by the day of the week.

It also features automatic rollovers for valid or selectable dates, automatic current date selection, and an infinite date range both forwards and backwards in time that the visitor can move through to select the date of their choice. When navigating between months, the individual days automatically reorder themselves so that the correct date appears in the correct day of the week.

Several classes make up the Calendar Control; two separate classes represent the two different types of calendar that can be rendered and another class contains math utilities that allow you to add, subtract, or compare different dates. We will take a look at the classes that make up this control to see what is available and exactly how it works before we begin coding.

The basic Calendar class

The most basic type of calendar is the single-panel Calendar, which is created with the YAHOO.widget.Calendar class. To display a calendar, an HTML element is required to act as a container for the calendar. The following screenshot shows a basic Calendar Control:

The constructor can be called specifying, at the very least, a reference to the HTML element that will contain the calendar. This can either be an actual DOM reference or it can be its id attribute.

You can also specify an additional argument that can accept a literal object containing various configuration properties. The configuration object is defined within curly braces within the class constructor. This is a pattern frequently used in YUI components.

When the constructor for an object might take many optional arguments, instead of reserving a slot in the argument list for each possible one, a configuration object is accepted instead, which is nothing more than a regular JavaScript object literal or an expression that returns an object. This object should have properties corresponding to the configuration attributes that you want to set different from the default.

For the Calendar Control you would set attributes such as its title, a comma-delimited range of pre-selected dates or a close button shown on the calendar.

There are many methods defined in the basic Calendar caliber class. Some of the more useful methods are:

- A method for determining whether a date is outside of the current month: isDateOOM.

- Navigation methods such as nextMonth, nextYear, previousMonth, and previousYear that can be used to programmatically change the month or year displayed in the current panel.

- Operational methods such as addMonths, addYears, subtractMonths, and subtractYears, which are used to change the month and year shown in the current panel by the specified number of months or years.

- The render method is used to draw the calendar on the page and is called for every implementation of a calendar, after it has been configured. Without this method, no calendar appears on the page.

- Two reset methods: reset, which resets the calendar to the month and year originally selected, and resetRenderers, which resets the render stack of the calendar.

- Selection methods that select or deselect dates such as deselect, deselectAll, deselectCell, select, and selectCell.

As you can see, there are many methods that you can call to take advantage of the advanced features of the Calendar Control.

The CalendarGroup class

In addition to the basic calendar, you can also create a grouped calendar that displays two or more month panels at once using the YAHOO.widget. CalendarGroup class. The control automatically adjusts the calendar's UI so that the navigation arrows are only displayed on the first and last calendar panels, and so that each panel has its own heading indicating which month it refers to.

The `CalendarGroup` class contains additional built-in functionality for updating the calendar panels on display, automatically. If you have a two-panel calendar displaying, for example, January and February, clicking the right navigation arrow will move February to the left of the panel so that March will display as the right-hand panel. All of this is automatic and nothing needs to be configured by you.

Though showing two or more calendars in the page looks very different to the user, for the programmer it hardly makes any difference at all.

Implementing a Calendar

To complete this example, the only tool other than the YUI that you'll need is a basic text editor. Native support for the YUI is provided by some web authoring software packages, most notably Aptana, an open source application that has been dubbed "Dreamweaver Killer". However, I always find that writing code manually while learning something is much more beneficial.

It is very quick and easy to add the Calendar, as the basic default implementation requires very little configuration. It can be especially useful in forms where the visitor must enter a date. Checking that a date has been entered correctly and in the correct format takes valuable processing time, but using the YUI Calendar means that dates are always exactly as you expect them to be.

So far we've spent most of this chapter looking at a lot of the theoretical issues surrounding the library; I don't know about you, but I think it's definitely time to get on with some actual coding!

The initial HTML page

Our first example page contains a simple text field and an image that once clicked will display the Calendar control on the page, thereby allowing a date to be selected and added to the input. Begin with the following basic HTML page:

```
<!DOCTYPE HTML PUBLIC "-//W3C//DTD HTML 4.01//EN"
                    "http://www.w3.org/TR/html4/strict.dtd">
<html lang="en">
  <head>
    <meta http-equiv="content-type" content="text/html;
                                    charset=utf-8">
    <title>YUI Calendar Control Example</title>
    <script type="text/javascript"
        src="yui/build/yahoo-dom-event/yahoo-dom-event.js">
    </script>
```

```
      <script type="text/javascript"
             src="yui/build/calendar/calendar-min.js">
      </script>
      <link rel="stylesheet" type="text/css"
             href="yui/build/calendar/assets/skins/sam/calendar.css">
      <style type="text/css">
        input { margin:0px 10px 0px 10px;}
      </style>
   </head>
   <body class="yui-skin-sam">
      <div>
        <label>Please enter your date of birth:</label>
        <input type="text" name="dobfield" id="dobfield">
        <img id="calico" src="icons/cal.png"
             alt="Open the Calendar control">
      </div>
      <div id="mycal"></div>
   </body>
</html>
```

We begin with a valid DOCTYPE declaration, a must in any web page. A question that often pops up in the YUI forums is why HTML4 Strict? Experience has shown that it is the one more reliably implemented across all browsers. Support for XHTML is uneven across browsers and HTML5 is not yet a standard. Let us call HTML4 Strict the A-grade supported doc type; others might just work but are not tested and some are positively known not to work. Remember, Yahoo! collects an unbeatable quantity of statistics and this doc type is the one that they have found that provides the best and most consistent user experience to their millions of visitors per day.

For validity, we can also add the lang attribute to the opening <html> tag and for good measure, enforce the utf-8 character set. Nothing so far is YUI-specific, but coding in this way every time is a good habit.

We link to the stylesheet used to control the appearance of the Calendar Control, which is handled in this example by the sam skin within the <link> tag. Accordingly, we also need to add the appropriate class name to the <body> tag.

Following this, we link to the required library files with <script> tags; the Calendar Control is relatively simple and requires just the YAHOO, Dom, and Event utilities (using the aggregated yahoo-dom-event.js file for efficiency), as well as the component source file calendar-min.js.

A brief `<style>` tag finishes the `<head>` section of the page with some CSS relevant to this particular example, and the `<body>` of the page at this stage contains just two `<div>` elements: the first holds a `<label>`, the text field, and a calendar icon (which can be used to launch the control), while the second holds the calendar control. When viewed in a browser, the page at this point should appear like this:

 The calendar icon used in this example was taken, with gratitude from Mark Carson at `http://markcarson.com`.

We need to create a `<script>` tag to contain our code. As an HTML page loads many of its components asynchronously, we cannot be sure what HTML elements get loaded when and when they get appended to the DOM. In this case, we cannot be sure the calendar icon will be there by the time the script starts executing so right before the closing `</body>` tag, add the following code:

```
<script type="text/javascript">
    YAHOO.util.Event.onDOMReady(function () {
        var Dom = YAHOO.util.Dom,
            Event = YAHOO.util.Event,
            Lang = YAHOO.Lang;
    });
</script>
```

We first call the `.onDOMReady()` method of the Event Utility, which will call the function that is supplied as its argument when the DOM is ready to be used. We could even be more specific by using the method `.onAvailable()` to ask for our calendar icon but we would gain little by doing that.

Instead of supplying `.onDOMReady()` with a reference to a function to call, we are defining the function right on the spot. This is part of the flexibility that JavaScript has built-in: you can define a function anywhere you need it and you don't even need to give it a name. An anonymous function has a further advantage. We have already mentioned that the whole of the YUI Library takes a single name in the Global Namespace: YAHOO, which is a good thing because this namespace gets easily cluttered with variables and functions and what not. You might think that you control what goes into the Global Namespace. That is not the case.

All the members of both `window` and `document` have aliases in the Global Namespace. The properties `window.location`, `document.location`, `window.document.location` and plain `location` all point to the very same property. The property `window.name` can simply be called `name`; many programmers using the variable `name` don't even realize they are using a DOM property. Proprietary extensions in different browsers add extra members in this namespace. Worried enough already?

At some point someone decides to make some extra money by adding some paid banners, or provide directions by embedding some active map into the page and it will include some code. Some of this code is sloppy and further pollutes the Global Namespace.

The Global Namespace is not a comfortable place to be in.

An anonymous function takes no name at all in any namespace. We leave no litter behind; we get no pollution from outside.

Let's go back to the earlier code. Within that anonymous function we are declaring a set of three variables: `Dom`, `Event`, and `Lang`. We call these "shortcuts". They point to the most frequently used classes in the core utilities. Having the whole YUI stored under the single global name YAHOO has a cost: all its members have long names, all starting with YAHOO. We don't want to type those long names all the time so we create aliases for those we use more frequently. We might not use them all; in this example we won't use `Lang`. A tool we will see in the last chapter, JSLint, will tell us which variables went unused so we may well have this set of shortcuts as a template and let JSLint tell us if we overdid it. We may add additional shortcuts as needed. These shortcuts are not copies of the classes but additional references to the very same class; they don't waste time or memory, in fact, in the end they save on both.

The anonymous function provides another benefit, it creates a *sandbox*. Every variable or function declared in it will be local to that function and accessible to all functions within. The shortcuts we have created are visible to all the code contained in the sandbox, we can use them freely within, but are completely invisible outside the sandbox because they are local to the anonymous function. That is why we had to spell out the whole YAHOO.util.Event.onDOMReady outside the sandbox, because the Event shortcut is not visible there (and has not been executed yet, but we would not be able to even if it had been). If we declare a variable called name within the sandbox, we would not be using window.name accidentally, we would still be able to access that one by its full name if we need to, but if we refer to name it would be our very own variable.

The use of sandboxes has become the standard in YUI programming. In fact, YUI3 uses sandboxing extensively. The other alternative, creating your own namespace, which was the recommended way not long ago, is no longer used for most application code. Formerly you would piggyback your code in a branch under the YAHOO global variable. Most examples packed with the YUI library use the YAHOO. example namespace. The examples in the first edition of this book used YAHOO. yuibook. You did not take any space in the Global Namespace; you simply used some space you knew the YUI library did not use.

Creating your own namespace is still done for libraries. As anything created within the sandbox cannot be seen outside of it, you can't create libraries in sandboxes because they cannot be seen elsewhere. For application code, which is not called from anywhere outside of the sandbox itself, keeping everything hidden within is perfectly fine.

Now we can add the extremely brief code that's required to actually produce the calendar. Within the braces of our anonymous function, add the following code:

```
//create the calendar object, specifying the container
var myCal = new YAHOO.widget.Calendar("mycal");

//draw the calendar on screen
myCal.render();

//hide it again straight away
myCal.hide();
```

This is all that we need to create the Calendar; we simply define myCal as a new Calendar object, specifying the ID of the HTML element that will hold it as an argument of the constructor.

Once we have a `Calendar` object, we can call the `.render()` method on it to create the calendar and display it on the page. No arguments are required for this method. As we want the calendar to be displayed when its icon is clicked, we hide the calendar from view straight away.

To display the calendar when the icon for it is clicked, we'll need one more function. Add the following code beneath the `.hide()` method:

```
//define the showCal function which shows the calendar
var showCal = function() {

  //show the calendar
  myCal.show();
}
```

As we've said, JavaScript allows us to create functions anywhere. This function is contained within the anonymous function that is our sandbox; a function within a function. We can do this any number of levels deep. An inner function can access all the local variables of the functions it is contained in; thus we can refer to `myCal` from inside `showCal`.

Functions can be stored in variables; in fact, naming a function is nothing more than saying in what variable the function will be stored. Here we are storing the function that shows the calendar in a variable called `showCal`, effectively declaring a function named `showCal`. We prefer this notation to highlight where it is being stored.

The keyword `var` in front of the variable name is vital. JavaScript allows us to use variables without declaring them previously. Variables used without being declared are created automatically in the Global Namespace. We don't want this to happen. We want `showCal` to be in the sandbox, that is why we declare the variable `showCal` with the `var` keyword and initialize it to a function. But don't worry, if we forget the `var` keyword, the JSLint utility will warn us.

To have the `showCal` function executed when the icon for it is clicked, we'll need to listen for the `click` event. We can use method `YAHOO.util.Event.addListener()` but we already have a shortcut called `Event` and the YUI also gives us a shorter alias for `.addListener()` so we can add the following code beneath the `.hide()` method:

```
Event.on("calico", "click", showCal);
```

Save the file that we've just created as `calendar.html` or similar in your `yuisite` directory. If you view it in your browser now and click on the Calendar icon, you should see this:

The calendar is automatically configured to display the current date, although this is something that can be changed using the configuration object mentioned earlier.

Now that we can call up the Calendar Control by clicking on our Calendar icon, we need to customize it slightly. Unless the person completing the form is very young, they will need to navigate through a large number of calendar pages in order to find their date of birth. This is where the Calendar Navigator interface comes into play.

We can easily enable this feature using a configuration object passed into the `Calendar` constructor. Alter your code so that it appears as follows:

```
//create the calendar object, using container & config object
var myCal = new YAHOO.widget.Calendar("mycal", {navigator:true});
```

Clicking on the **Month** or **Year** label will now open an interface that allows your visitors to navigate directly to any given month and year:

The configuration object can be used to set a range of calendar configuration properties including the original month and year displayed by the Calendar, the minimum and maximum dates available to the calendar, a title for the calendar, a close button, and various other properties.

Let's update our `Calendar` instance so that it features a title and a close button. Add the following properties to the literal object in our constructor:

```
//create the calendar object, specifying the container and a literal
//configuration object
var myCal = new YAHOO.widget.Calendar("mycal",
     {navigator:true, title:"Choose your Date Of Birth",
     close:true});
```

This is what our Calendar should now look like:

Configuration properties like those we have just set can also be set outside of the constructor by using the `.setProperty()` method. Let's use these to alter our Calendar so that the first column header is set to Monday instead of Sunday. Add the following code directly before the call to the `.render()` method:

```
//configure the calendar to begin on Monday
myCal.cfg.setProperty("start_weekday", "1");
```

When the calendar is displayed now, Monday will be the first day instead of Sunday:

Finally, we need to add some additional code that will allow the date that is selected to be inserted into the text field. We can do this using some of the custom events defined by the calendar classes.

Highly eventful

Both the `Calendar` and `CalendarGroup` classes have a series of custom events defined for them that allow for easily listening and reacting to interesting moments during any calendar or calendar group interaction.

The two classes both have the same set of events defined for them, which include:

- `beforeDeselectEvent`: Fired before a cell is deselected
- `beforeHideEvent`: Fired just before the calendar is hidden
- `beforeHideNavEvent`: Fired just before the calendar navigator is hidden
- `beforeRenderEvent`: Fired before the calendar is drawn on screen
- `beforeSelectEvent`: Fired before a cell is selected
- `beforeShowEvent`: Fired just before the calendar is shown
- `beforeShowNavEvent`: Fired just before the calendar navigator is shown
- `changePageEvent`: Fired once the current calendar page has been changed
- `clearEvent`: Fired once the calendar has been cleared
- `deselectEvent`: Fired once the cell has been deselected

- `hideEvent`: Fired once the calendar has been hidden
- `hideNavEvent`: Fired once the calendar navigator has been hidden
- `renderEvent`: Fired once the calendar has been drawn on screen
- `resetEvent`: Fired once the calendar has been reset
- `selectEvent`: Fired once a cell, or range of cells, has been selected
- `showEvent`: Fired once the calendar has been shown
- `showNavEvent`: Fired once the calendar navigator has been shown

This rich event system allows you to easily watch for cells being selected or deselected, month panel changes, render events, or even the reset method being called, and add code to deal with these key moments effectively. As you can see, most of the events form pairs of before and after events, which allows you to easily cancel or abort an operation before it has any visual impact by returning `false` in the before event.

Let's now take a look at how these custom Calendar events can be used. First define the function that will handle the `select` event; add the following code directly after the `showCall()` function:

```
//attach listener for click event on calendar icon
Event.on("calico", "click", showCal);

//define the ripDate function which gets the selected date
var ripDate = function(type, args) {

}

//subscribe to the select event on Calendar cells
myCal.selectEvent.subscribe(ripDate);
```

Every time the `select` event is detected, our `ripDate` function will be executed. The `type` and `args` objects are automatically provided to us by the control; the `args` object is what we are interested in here, because it gives us easy access to an array of information about our Calendar.

Now, within the curly braces of the `ripDate()` function set the following variables:

```
//get the date components
var dates = args[0],
    date = dates[0],
    theYear = date[0],
    theMonth = date[1],
    theDay = date[2];
```

The first item in the `args` array is an array of selected dates, so we first save this to the variable `dates`. As this is a single-select calendar, only the first item of the `dates` array will contain data, so this is also saved to a variable: the `date` variable.

Each date is itself an array, with the first item corresponding to the year, the second item equaling the month, and the third item mapped to the individual date. All of these values are saved into variables.

```
var theDate = theMonth + "/" + theDay + "/" + theYear;
```

This part of the function uses standard concatenation techniques to build a string containing the individual date components in the format in which we want to present them (so that, for example, it would be extremely easy to express dates in UK format, where the date appears before the month):

```
//get a reference to the text field
var field = Dom.get("dobfield");

//insert the formatted date into the text field
field.value = theDate;

//hide the calendar once more
myCal.hide();
```

Finally, we use the very handy Dom utility's `.get()` method to grab a reference to the text field, set the value of the text field to our date string, and then hide the calendar once more.

Save the file once more and view it again in your browser of choice. After clicking the calendar icon and choosing a date, it should be displayed in the text field:

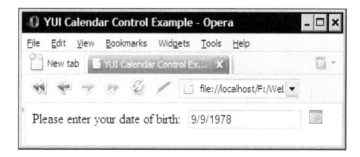

At this point, we can take a brief look at how we can override the default styling of the calendar. When we added the calendar navigator there was no visible clue for the user to show that the month and year could be clicked. When the cursor hovers over them, they change, but the user might never notice that. We might want to correct that so that the month and year have the same white background as the navigation arrows. This can be done with the following simple CSS rule, which should be inserted into the `<style>` tag in the `<head>` of our document:

```
.yui-skin-sam .yui-calendar a.calnav {
    border: thin solid silver;
    background: white;
}
```

Because we're using the default `sam` skin, we should begin the selector with the `yui-skin-sam` class name then the class name of the calendar container and finally that of the month and year. Other elements of the calendar, such as the navigation arrows, can easily be styled in this way. Using a DOM explorer to expose the names of other parts of the calendar is also an easy way to change other elements of the calendar. Our calendar should now appear like this:

 We should never change the original YUI files.

Changing the YUI files may seem harmless at first, but when a new version is released we find ourselves desperately trying to locate the changes we made in the old version to apply them to the new one, or we have to forgo updating. Besides, we preclude ourselves from using the CDNs to load the library files. There is always a way to override—as we just did—redefine or subclass the original CSS styles or JavaScript objects in our own, separate application code.

The DateMath class

In addition to the two classes catering for two different types of calendar, a class, `YAHOO.widget.DateMath`, defines a series of utilities for performing simple mathematical calculations or comparisons on dates. It has only a small number of static properties and a small set of methods. There are no events defined in this class and no configuration attributes. It is very much like JavaScript's own `Math` class that you can use without creating an instance.

All of its methods return either a Boolean value indicating whether the comparison was true or false, or a modified date object. Some of them will be used very frequently, while others will be used only rarely (but are still very useful).

Our date of birth calendar isn't really appropriate for seeing how the `DateMath` calls can be used. In order to examine some of the available methods, we should create a new calendar. In a blank page of your text editor, begin with the following HTML:

```
<!DOCTYPE HTML PUBLIC "-//W3C//DTD HTML 4.01//EN"
                      "http://www.w3.org/TR/html4/strict.dtd">
<html lang="en">
  <head>
    <meta http-equiv="content-type" content="text/html;
                                    charset=utf-8">
    <title>YUI MathDate Class Example</title>
    <link rel="stylesheet"
          type="text/css"
          href="yui/build/calendar/assets/skins/sam/calendar.css">
    <script type="text/javascript"
            src="yui/build/yahoo-dom-event/yahoo-dom-event.js">
    </script>
    <script type="text/javascript"
            src="yui/build/calendar/calendar-min.js">
    </script>
  </head>
  <body class="yui-skin-sam">
    <div id="mycal"></div>
    <div id="results"></div>
  </body>
</html>
```

This very simple page will form the basis of our example. It looks very much like the previous example; in fact, all our examples will look pretty much the same, so, from now on, we'll only point out the components we'll need to include—and we already know the many alternative ways of fetching them—the HTML that goes in the body and the script that always goes right before the closing `</body>` tag.

Formerly, the `DateMath` class was only available along the Calendar Control, whether you meant to show a calendar or not. Now, it can be loaded separately, but we will use the Calendar in this example so we load the bundle.

Next, add the following `<script>` tag to the `<body>` tag of the page, directly below the results `<div>` tag:

```
<script type="text/javascript">
    // create the sandbox when the DOM is ready
    YAHOO.util.Event.onDOMReady(function() {
        // shortcuts
        var Dom = YAHOO.util.Dom, Calendar = YAHOO.widget.Calendar,
            DateMath = YAHOO.widget.DateMath;
    });
</script>
```

As usual, we wait until the DOM is ready and then we create our sandbox. Within it, we create our shortcuts. Instead of the generic ones, we create shortcuts for the classes we will use in this example. Inside of our sandbox, we add:

```
  //create the calendar object, specifying the container
var myCal = new Calendar("mycal");

//draw the calendar on screen
myCal.render();

//we will find out things about today's date,
// which we get from the Calendar control.
var today = myCal.today;
```

We create the calendar in the same way as in the previous example and render it on the page. This time, we don't need to worry about hiding it again as it will be a permanent fixture of the page. As we do some math on today's date, we read it from the calendar and keep it handy. We keep adding:

```
//we will pile up the results here:
var results = "";

// ** Our code will go here **

//insert the results into the page
Dom.get("results").innerHTML = results;
```

Performance analysis still shows that inserting HTML markup into the `innerHTML` property of a DOM element is, by far, faster than creating and appending DOM elements one by one. So, we create a variable to hold our results and then insert it into the container we created for them.

We won't have much user interaction with the Calendar Control, but we will use several of its tables of strings to assemble our results. Insert the following code where indicated above:

```
//get and display today's date
var dayNum = today.getDay(),
    dayString = myCal.Locale.WEEKDAYS_LONG[dayNum],
    date = today.getDate(),
    monthNum = today.getMonth(),
    monthString = myCal.Locale.MONTHS_LONG[monthNum],
    year = today.getFullYear();
//put them all together
results += "<p>Today is " + dayString + ", " + date + " " +
        monthString + " " + year + "<\/p>";
```

Once we have this, we can get references to the date and month numerical representations and from these we can get the full day name and month name using `Locale.WEEKDAYS_LONG[dayNum]` and `Locale.MONTHS_LONG[monthNum]`.

The `Locale` object is automatically created by the control and contains localized day and month names. It is primarily used to add new locales and specify alternative day and month names. English is available by default so we can simply read the properties and pull out what we want.

We can see some all-uppercase property names in this code, a naming convention usually reserved for constants. JavaScript has no constants, every variable can be changed; however, we use this convention to indicate our intent: these variables are not meant to be changed in application code. In this case, we would change them if we added other locales, but that would be customizing the library. Our application code would never change them.

Another naming convention worth mentioning is that of variables or functions starting with an underscore. Those are meant to be private members. JavaScript has no provision for private members so using the underscore is the way for the developer to tell everybody to stay away. There are many reasons for the developer to do it and a big one for you to stay away from them: they are not part of the contract; if the developer finds a better way to do things, private variables might suddenly disappear. Many developers find those variables through a debugger and use them. That is not a good idea; there will always be a public, safe way of achieving the same.

Once we have the information we need, it is simple enough to concatenate everything into our result string. Your page should look similar to the following screenshot:

Now we can have some fun with a few of the DateMath methods. First, add the following directly beneath our last block of code:

```
//work out date in 10 days time
var futureDate = DateMath.add(today, DateMath.DAY, 10);

results += "<p>In ten days time it will be " + futureDate + "<\/p>";
```

We can use the .add() method of the YAHOO.widget.DateMath class to add a specified amount of time to a date object. The .add() method takes three arguments. The first is the date object on which the addition should be carried out, the second is one of the built-in constants representing the unit to be added (which could be days, weeks, months, or years), and the final argument is the actual amount to be added.

For the purposes of this example, I have left the futureDate field in full UTC format, but we could easily extract just the parts of the date that we want, just as we did to get the today's date.

Let's now look at the almost identical `.subtract()` method. Add the following code:

```
//work out date two months ago
var pastDate = DateMath.subtract(today, DateMath.MONTH, 2);
results += "<p>Two months ago the date was " + pastDate + "<\/p>";
```

You can see how easy the `DateMath` class makes addition and subtraction of date objects. The class has other useful methods such as the `.getDayOffset()` and `.getWeekNumber()` methods. We can expose the functionality of these two methods with the following code:

```
//work out day and week numbers of current date
var numberOfDays = DateMath.getDayOffset(today, year);
results += "<p>" + numberOfDays +
          " days have elapsed so far this year<\/p>";

var weekNumber = DateMath.getWeekNumber(today);
results += "<p>We are in week number "+ weekNumber + "<\/p>";
```

Save the file as `datemath.html` and view it in your browser of choice:

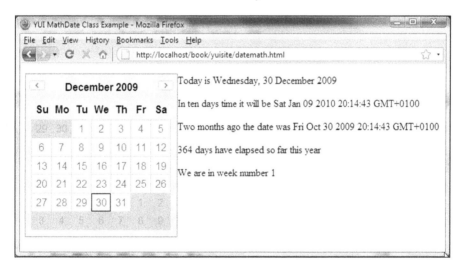

Summary

During the course of this chapter we have taken an in-depth view into what the YUI is, where it came from, and the things that spurred it into existence. We have seen everything that the license gives us permission to do and investigated the different ways of serving the files that power it. We've also looked at who can make the most of the library, how to install it, and how to use it in your own web pages.

Lastly, we finished off all the theory with a practical example that had you creating and customizing your first user interface control: a calendar, and working with one of its supporting classes: the `DateMath` class. I hope that this first example has made you eager to experiment with the library further and has shown you how easy it is to implement YUI components.

2
Creating Consistency with the CSS Tools

Not only does the library provide you with a rich selection of easily implemented utilities and UI controls that save you time and effort when developing and debugging, but it is also a gift that keeps on giving with a selection of CSS Tools that every developer should have to hand.

The CSS Tools of the library are separate from the CSS files required by some of the controls in order to be displayed correctly; some of the controls contain a folder within their unpacked directories called assets, and in this folder there may be images, a stylesheet, or sometimes both depending on the control. The CSS files discussed in this chapter are separate, autonomous components of the library, and are on a level with both the utilities and controls.

In this chapter we're going to examine these tools in detail and learn exactly what they can do for your web pages and applications, if used in conjunction with other components of the library, or completely on their own.

We will look at the following:

- What each of the four tools does
- Rules contained within each CSS file
- Why and how you should use the tools
- How and why elements are normalized
- The solid foundation provided by the Base CSS Tool
- How fonts are styled with the Fonts CSS Tool
- Some of the different templates found within the Grids CSS Tool

Tools of the trade

There are some similarities between the CSS Tools and the other components of the library and there are of course some differences. Like each of the other components, there is also a full version of each file with comments and whitespace preserved for readability, and a minified production version.

If you wish, you can also have Yahoo! serve the CSS files used by the tools to you across the Internet by linking to the files held on their servers, just as you can with the other library components.

Several different configurations of the CSS Tools have also been put together, which combine some of the different tools into single files, making them easier and more efficient to use together. `reset.css` and `fonts.css` have been aggregated into one file for your convenience, which is probably because the YUI team recommend the use of these two tools in all YUI implementations. A `reset-fonts-grids.css` file has also been created due to the high likelihood that the huge range of page templates available in `grids.css` will also be used very frequently.

There is also a cheat sheet that combines information on all four of the CSS Tools. Reset, Fonts, and Base just need to be linked to the page to do its magic. Only the Grids Tool needs more coding from us.

Element normalization with reset.css

Often, one of the most painful exercises in web development is simply getting everything to look consistent across the major browser platforms. No standard states how a particular HTML element should look. The intent of a markup might be self-evident; we would expect an `<h1>` to look larger or bolder than an `<h2>`, and both larger than plain text but there is no standard saying by how much. Developers will often design and test an implementation in one particular browser, and then when everything is working and rendering correctly in their browser of choice, they will have to refine it and tweak it until it works and renders similarly in all of the other major browsers.

Due to the differences between the default stylesheet in use in the various browsers, getting pages to render in the same way can be a challenge. Something that lines up perfectly in IE will undoubtedly be misaligned in other browsers. And of course, when you correct the differences so that it renders in the way you want it to, say in Safari, you'll find that when you go back to IE, it's out of alignment there once again.

For a quick example of CSS inconsistencies at work, take a look at the following screenshot; the subtle differences in font size, padding, and margins make the text fit into one line in one browser but fail to do so in another. There is no right and wrong here as there is no standard to comply with, but our layout ends up broken anyway:

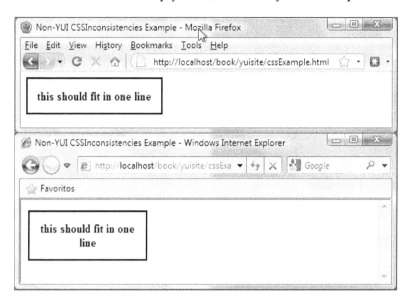

Until now, the quickest way around these issues has been to use a modern browser to design in and resort to separate stylesheets, hacks, or filters so as to make the various versions of old, though still popular browsers, play along. Still, there is no guarantee that future browsers will not choke on any hacks or filters that you may be using in your stylesheet, so it is best to try to avoid them whenever it is possible for you to do so.

Using a range of different stylesheets for different browsers and browser versions can also be problematic in terms of maintenance, as you will find that when you want to make a change to the way in which your site is displayed, there are many more files that need to be updated.

The CSS Tools can provide a firmer guarantee that future browsers will still display everything correctly and can cut down on the number of files that you need to actively maintain (as Yahoo! will kindly maintain these for you).

The `reset.css` file provided by the YUI Library avoids the need to use most hacks or workarounds by standardizing the default rendering of all of the most common HTML elements across the different browsers, saving you the tricky troubleshooting that sometimes needs to be done to get everything lined up and looking right in all browsers.

Most styles have been removed, set to zero, or otherwise neutralized, so you can worry about presenting your content, without trying to remember whether additional padding in a particular browser is going to put everything out of place.

Element rules

`reset.css` consists mostly of element selectors that match nearly all content containing HTML elements and reset them to a non-styled state. This enables the designer to apply consistent styling that works across all browsers.

The font size of all text is set alike and all italics or bold typefaces are cancelled. Margins, padding, and borders are set to zero; space in between table cells is collapsed. Lists have no indentation and no bullets or numbers. All text is left-justified.

As an example of what `reset.css` does to elements, the following screenshot shows a collection of all of the elements targeted by this CSS Tool, before `reset.css` has been applied. Most of the elements have visible styling applied to them by the browser, and this varies slightly between different browsers.

I've chosen Firefox on Windows to highlight this example because the `<fieldset>` element is one of the few examples of this browser styling an element badly. Note that no `<br>` elements or positional CSS have been used in this example at all; all of the styling has been applied automatically by the browser.

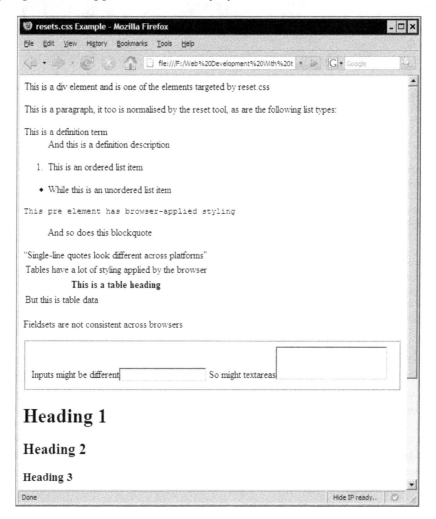

Next, we can see what a difference `reset.css` makes to this page by including a reference to the file in the `<head>` of the page. With `reset.css` linked, all elements are reset.

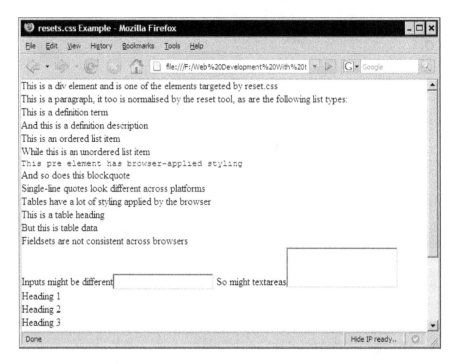

Hence, the Reset CSS Tool can be an invaluable asset when either used as part of a YUI implementation, or completely isolated from the rest of the library, and linked to by pages entirely of your own design. This tool is completely compatible across the A-grade browser spectrum. (Refer to *Chapter 1* for details.)

It's also very easy to change the default rendering provided by this file. You may wish to have certain images that do have a border, so all you need to do is add your own class attribute to the `<image>` and define a new CSS class in a separate CSS file of your own making.

If you only ever use one file from the library, this one alone could provide the most benefit in the long term (but of course you won't want to exclude the rest of the fantastic functionality provided by the YUI!).

First base

Where the `reset.css` tool breaks down the default stylesheets of the different browsers, the `base.css` tool then builds upon this level foundation to provide basic styling across a range of commonly used elements.

There are certain elements on your page that just should be styled differently from other elements. Heading text for example, simply should stand out from body text; that's the whole point of heading text in the first place.

So the Base CSS Tool reintroduces some of the presentational styles of the common elements that the Reset CSS Tool neutralizes, but it does so in a way that is consistent across browsers. Italics and boldface are restored to those elements where you would expect them.

Headings are all made bold and given increasing sizes that can be rendered reliably in all browsers. Those sizes are expressed in relative (percentage) units so the headings will scale correctly if the user zooms in. Space is provided both above and below each heading and also after paragraphs and other block elements.

Ordered, unordered, and definition lists are given a left margin to indent by the same amount. Ordered lists are given a decimal marker, while unordered lists are given a disc marker, both placed on the outside of the list item's box.

Table cells are given a solid, black, 1-pixel border and an overall padding of half an `em`. This helps to space things out and make tables a little more readable. `<th>` elements are also given a bolder typeface.

Why then does `reset.css` cancel all styles if we then restore them with `base.css`? The separation is done so we are not forced to use `base.css`, but can use our very own style. In fact, there is no aggregate that includes `base.css` as we are not expected to use it as supplied. In such cases, we would still use `reset.css` to start from a reliable, known state, and from there we can build. We can use `base.css` as a template for this customization.

As `base.css` builds upon `reset.css`, and also upon `fonts.css`, which we'll see in a moment, if included, it must come after them. We will probably use the aggregate `reset-fonts-grids.css` so `base.css` should come after that aggregate file. Reversing the order would have `reset.css` destroying the styles set by `base.css`.

If we include a reference to the base.css stylesheet in our test page, some of the elements that were normalized by the Reset CSS Tool will have styling applied, as demonstrated by the following screenshot:

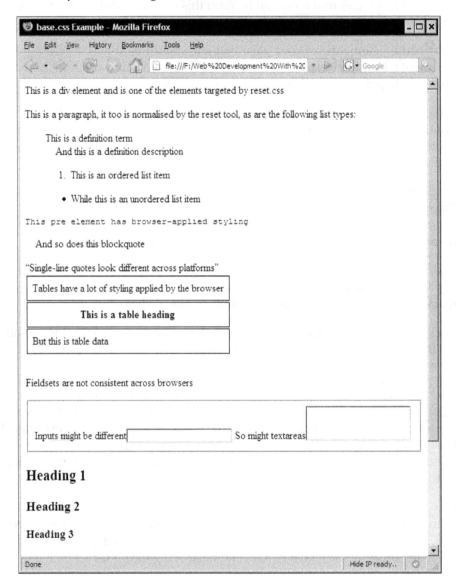

Tidying up text with fonts.css

The next CSS Tool, fonts.css, is provided so that you can easily standardize all of your text to a single font-face, font-size, and line-height. In terms of the amount of actual code, this file is tiny; in fact much smaller than the Reset CSS Tool we looked at earlier, providing just five rules in total.

It standardizes all rendered text on the page to the Arial font, except for text within <pre> and <code> tags, which instead use the monospace typeface.

The first rule targets the <body> tag and sets the font-family attribute to arial, helvetica, clean, or sans-serif. This provides a clear font degradation path; if browsers or operating systems don't have Arial installed or for some reason can't display it, the platform tries Helvetica next, and so on, right down to sans-serif if necessary (although it's unlikely that the browser would need to travel all the way down to the end of the degradation path).

This is also important for Unicode support; if the font in use cannot map a Unicode character to a font-glyph in the current font set, it can use the font degradation path to map a Unicode character from another defined font set. This helps to avoid those unsightly little squares that sometimes appear in e-mails or on web pages when they try to show characters outside of the most basic Latin character set.

Some of the rules start with a star, such as *font-size:small and *font:x-small. This is a hack that allows to targeting the rule for IE, which ignores the star. Other browsers will not, and that will cause a lot of error messages in their console, a source of concern to many a developer. These can be safely ignored.

Like the Reset CSS Tool, fonts.css is extremely easy to use and requires no further participation from you once you have linked to the stylesheet. You don't need to use any particular class names or give elements specific id attributes in order to make use of the normalization services provided by these two tools, and the Fonts CSS Tool is compatible with all A-grade browsers. Moreover, it still works with many browsers that once were A-grade but have been dropped since because those were, in fact, the worst offenders. So very little has been added to support newer browsers as they are mostly well-behaved.

An important resource available both in the tool guide and the cheat sheet is the table of font sizes measured in percentage to the base font. It is safer to give sizes in relative units (% or em) because in browsers that do text-only zoom, text whose font-size is given in absolute units such as pt or px will not zoom. The following table provides the equivalent relative sizes of a few font sizes in pixels. A larger table is available along with the YUI documentation and the cheat sheets:

Font size in pixels	Font size in %
10	77
11	85
12	93
13	100
14	108
15	116
16	123.1
20	153.9
24	182

The downloadable example has checkboxes to activate each of the three CSS Tools individually to see their effect on any browser.

Layout pages with ease using grids.css

Experience has shown that certain layouts tend to work better than others. The **Interactive Advertising Bureau (IAB)**, that tries to standardize ads displayed on the Web, regularly publishes guidelines for their size. As screen resolutions increase, we can make use of more screen real estate, but we still have to support older, narrower displays so it is better if we stick to narrower, more conservative sizes. `grids.css` allows us to easily arrange the components in a page in several of the most common layouts or combine them to build our own.

In comparison to the other three CSS Tools, the `grids.css` file is a lot bigger, containing a much wider range of selectors and rules. This tool is used in a different way than the other two; instead of just linking to the file and forgetting about it, you will need to make use of specific class names, give element-specific IDs, and use the correct nesting structures in order to have your pages laid out in the format that you want.

One of the features of the Grids CSS Tool is that it automatically centers your content in the viewport keeping your content within a fixed width, avoiding the distortion that often happens when adjusting to various screen widths. Another of its features is the fact that the footer, if you wish to use it, is self-clearing and stays at the bottom of the page, whichever layout template you're using.

Setting up your page structure

Yahoo! recommends a particular basic structure to use when building web pages; your document should be broken up into three different content sections: a header <div>, a body <div>, and a footer <div>. All three of these different sections should also be wrapped in an outer containing <div>. The following code shows how pages should initially be structured:

```
<!DOCTYPE HTML PUBLIC "-//W3C//DTD HTML 4.01//EN"
                      "http://www.w3.org/TR/html4/strict.dtd">
<html lang="en">
  <head>
    <meta http-equiv="content-type" content="text/html;
         charset=utf-8">
    <title>Mark-up Example</title>
      <link rel="stylesheet" type="text/css"
           href="reset-fonts-grids.css">
  </head>
  <body>
    <div>
      <div id="hd">This is your Header</div>
      <div id="bd">This is the body</div>
      <div id="ft">This is your footer</div>
    </div>
  </body>
</html>
```

You can use one of the four preset page widths when constructing pages linked to the Grids CSS Tool by giving the outer containing <div> element one of the following values for its ids attribute:

- doc for a 750 pixel wide page geared towards resolutions of 800x600
- doc2 for a 950 pixel wide page that is aimed at 1024x768 resolutions
- doc3 for a full 100% fluid page width suitable for all monitor resolutions
- doc4 for a 974 pixel page width, an increasingly popular and robust width

All four of these page width specifications have auto margins and have their content aligned to the left. The width is specified in em units, as these units of measurement scale better across platforms during text size changes driven by the visitor. Using a combination of templates and different class attributes in your mark-up you can specify a wide range of different page layouts.

The third layout, for 100% page widths, includes a 10 pixel margin on both sides of the page so as just to prevent any bleed between the page contents and the browser's user interface color.

The basic building blocks of your pages

Going back to the recommended layouts of pages, the developers at Yahoo! recognize that the main content, the body `<div id="bd">`, of your page will probably be split into different blocks itself, featuring perhaps a navigation menu on one side of the page as well as a main block of content.

These blocks of content can be represented in your HTML code by `<div>` elements with a class attribute of `yui-b` to denote a basic block. The main block should then be wrapped in a container `<div>` with a class attribute of `yui-main`. The main block is where your primary page content should reside. Although the basic `yui-b` block that is not nested within a `yui-main` block is known as the secondary block, it can still appear before the main block in your code and can appear either on the left or right-hand side of the page. From now on, we won't be showing the HTML outside of our `<body>` as it doesn't change:

```
<body>
  <div id="doc3">
    <div id="hd">This is your Header</div>
    <div id="bd">This is the body
      <div class="yui-b">This is the secondary block</div>
      <div class="yui-main">
        <div class="yui-b">This is the main block</div>
      </div>
    </div>
    <div id="ft">This is your footer</div>
  </div>
</body>
```

In order to use these content-organizing blocks, you'll also need to specify one of six preset templates. These block templates specify the width of the two blocks in much the same way as the three page templates specify page width. The following block templates are available:

- `.yui-t1` for a 160 pixel secondary block on the left
- `.yui-t2` for a 180 pixel secondary block on the left
- `.yui-t3` for a 300 pixel secondary block on the left
- `.yui-t4` for a 160 pixel secondary block on the right
- `.yui-t5` for a 180 pixel secondary block on the right
- `.yui-t6` for a 300 pixel secondary block on the right

In all of these templates, the main content block will take up the remaining space on the page (which is dependent on the page template in use). To use these templates, you just need to add one of them as a class attribute of the outer containing `<div>` element, whichever template you wish to use.

```
<body>
  <div id="doc3" class="yui-t1">
    <div id="hd">This is your Header</div>
    <div id="bd">
      <div class="yui-main">
        <div class="yui-b">This is the main block</div>
      </div>
      <div class="yui-b">This is a block</div>
    </div>
    <div id="ft">This is your footer</div>
  </div>
</body>
```

We have also changed the order of the main and secondary blocks. You might wish your visitors to see the information they've asked for first and then the secondary panel, be it comments, info-boxes or banners. Even though the secondary panel appears later in the code, it will still be shown on the left-hand side of the screen. The way it is ordered on the screen is independent of the order in which it is pumped to the page. If at a later stage, we change the `.yui-t1` template into its mirror `.yui-t4` we don't need to change the order of the content sent to the page.

The addition of the blocks and additional template will produce a page with a layout as shown in the following screenshot. Again styling has been used for clarity:

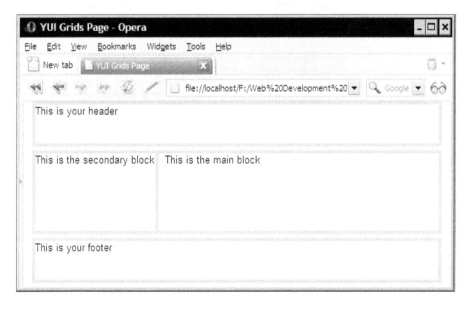

These templates, combined with the three different document widths and the two types of class attributes, added to the different block configurations give you a total of up to 42 different visual presentation models. But that's not all; your main content block can be further subdivided with grids and units.

Grid nesting

If you would like to split your main block of content into two or more different columns, you can nest some more <div> elements within your main block. You need to add a container <div> to the main block. This is known as a grid. The two new columns that are formed in the grid are known as units and are made up of two nested <div> elements within the grid <div>.

To make a grid, the container <div> within the main block <div> should be given a class attribute of yui-g and each unit <div> should have a class attribute of either yui-u first for the first unit or yui-u for the second unit, as illustrated by the following code sample:

```
<body>
  <div id="doc" class="yui-t1">
    <div id="hd">This is your header</div>
    <div id="bd">
     <div class="yui-b">This is the secondary block</div>
     <div id="yui-main">
       <div class="yui-b">This is the main block
         <div class="yui-g">
           <div class="yui-u first">This is a unit</div>
           <div class="yui-u">This is another unit</div>
         </div>
       </div>
     </div>
    </div>
    <div id="ft">This is your footer</div>
  </div>
</body>
```

The following screenshot shows how the grid units will appear on the page:

Due to the lack of support of the `:first-child` pseudo-selector in some A-grade browsers, when nesting grids within grids (to make four columns within the main content block for example), the first grid should have a `class` attribute of `yui-g first`.

By default, the two unit columns that make up a grid are of equal width, but you can easily deviate from this by using one of five "special grids", which specify more than two columns or a range of different column proportions. The five special grids have class selectors of:

- `.yui-gb` for three columns of equal width
- `.yui-gc` for two columns where the first has double the width of the second
- `.yui-gd` for two columns where the second has double the width of the first
- `.yui-ge` for two columns where the first has three times the width of the second
- `.yui-gf` for two columns where the second has three times the width of the first

We can see one of these special grids in action by simply changing the class name of our grid in the previous example:

```
<body>
  <div id="doc" class="yui-t1">
    <div id="hd">This is your header</div>
    <div id="bd">
      <div class="yui-b">This is the secondary block</div>
      <div id="yui-main">
        <div class="yui-b">This is the main block
        <div class="yui-gb">
          <div class="yui-u first">This is a unit</div>
          <div class="yui-u">This is another unit</div>
          A third unit created with the yui-gb special grid
        </div>
        </div>
      </div>
    </div>
      <div id="ft">This is your footer</div>
    </div>
</body>
```

This change in class name will result in our grid appearing as shown in the following screenshot:

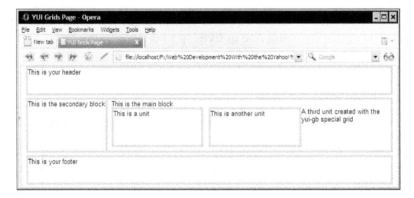

There is a large number of different variations of page layouts that the Grids CSS Tool allows you to implement. All you need to do is define your pages in the correct structure, and give the right elements the right class attributes and IDs. It may seem a little daunting at first, trying to remember all those different class names and nesting rules, but with a little bit of practice, it all becomes second nature.

In addition to the online documentation and cheat sheets, the CSS Grids page on the YUI developer site also points to a very nifty little tool that allows you to generate page templates for use with `grids.css`, the **Grid Builder** tool. Simply choose your desired layout, add in any header or footer text and the tool will then generate the basic template code for you to copy and paste into your own files:

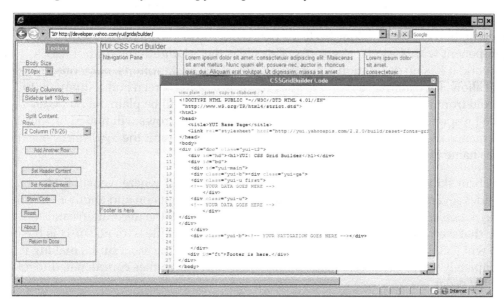

A word on Sam

Completely separate from the CSS Tools, but still composed entirely of CSS, the Sam skin provides a default theme for each of the library's controls. Each control contains a skin CSS file in its `assets` folder and should be linked to using the standard `<link>` tag in the `<head>` of any pages on which the controls are displayed.

In order to use the skin files, as well as linking to the stylesheet used by the skin, you will also need to give the containing element (whether that is the `<body>` or a `<div>`) a special class name:

```
<body class="yui-skin-sam">
```

Or, for finer control:

```
<div class="yui-skin-sam">
  <div id="someControl"></div>
</div>
```

This makes using the skin extremely easy. The Sam skin takes its name from its creator Sam Lind. At its launch, it was expected that developers would contribute further skins but that has not yet happened as each site develops the skins for the components it uses instead of a whole set for all existing controls.

When exploring the `assets` folder of a component we might wish to customize; however, we often find ourselves somewhat confused at the number of CSS files present. In the `assets` folder itself we will always find a file named after the component with a `-code.css` suffix. This file is the minimum the control needs to work; it has no decoration whatsoever, no colors, backgrounds, nor icons. It will allow, for example, a menu to stick to the top of the screen and a submenu to unfold from it covering the main contents, but all text will be plain, menu items won't respond to the cursor hovering on them, and no arrows will hint at further submenus. We can easily see how this would look if we omit the `.yui-skin-sam` class name in our pages.

The Sam skin is further down under `assets/skins/sam/` where we will find, besides several image files, at least a file with a `.css` extension and another with the `-skin.css` suffix. The `-skin` file is the one containing all the decorations and it is the one that we would use as the basis for our own skin. The file with no suffix is the one we will usually load. It is minified, even though it lacks the `-min` suffix, making it completely unreadable. It is made of the `-core` and `-skin` files concatenated together in that order.

If we wanted to create our own skin we would create our own folder under `assets/skins` and copy the `-skin.css` file from the `sam` folder. We would then modify this file, starting with a global search and replace of `.yui-skin-sam` into `.yui-skin-xxxx` or whatever we wanted to call our style.

We can then change any style attributes we want such as fonts, colors, backgrounds, icons, or any other decoration while being careful not to disturb the layout or positioning of the elements on the page. We would then concatenate the `-core` and `-skin` files together (in that order) and minify them with the YUI Compressor. That is the one we would include in our pages.

The `assets` folder might contain other `.css` files; they are old versions kept for backward compatibility.

Summary

The CSS Tools are the smallest and without doubt the easiest component of the library to use, but their contribution in the form of time-saving and functionality provided is no less than that of the utilities and controls.

First the Reset CSS Tool provides normalization services to the most common HTML elements so that borders, margins, and padding, among other things, are set to zero across all of the most common browsers.

The Base CSS Tool then builds upon the level foundation provided by Resets to give certain elements back some of the styling that marks them out from other elements. This tool is the only one that isn't part of the minified aggregated `resets-fonts-grids.css` file.

Next, all of your page text is standardized to the `Arial` font and is given a fixed line height. Sizes are also fixed to a consistent size across the document with the Fonts CSS Tool.

Finally, the precise layout of your page can be declared through the use of a range of CSS classes, IDs, and templates defined for you in the Grids CSS Tool.

3
DOM Manipulation and Event Handling

Every time you view a web page in your browser, a tree-like structure representing the page and all of its elements is created. This is the **Document Object Model (DOM)**, and it provides an API that you can use to obtain, add, modify, or remove almost any part of the web page, and without which modern web design as we know it would not exist. The YUI makes accessing and working with the DOM much easier, and allows you to perform a variety of common DOM scripting tasks with ease.

An integral part of any web application is the ability to react to different events that occur upon the different elements found on your pages. Browsers have had their own event models for some time now, allowing you to easily add code that handles something being clicked on for example, or something being hovered over. The YUI takes this one step further, replacing the existing browser event model with its own, which is more powerful, yet easier to use.

In this chapter, we're going to cover these topics:

- Some of the issues surrounding the use of the native DOM API and how the YUI helps us overcome some problems and extend it
- How the Selector Utility extends our ability to select DOM elements in the page by using standard CSS selectors
- The different ways in which browsers respond to and report events and how the YUI standardizes it into a single mechanism
- The Element Utility that simplifies the creation of complex UI controls by abstracting the functionality of a DOM element

We're also going to get stuck into some more coding examples where you'll get to work with these fundamentally useful library components directly.

Working with the DOM

You may have worked with the DOM and not even realized it; for example if you've ever used `getElementById` or `getElementsByTagName` (two common methods), then you have worked with the DOM.

The first of the above two methods returns the element that has a matching `id` attribute from the document. The second method returns an array of elements of a specific type such as an `<img>`.

In a nutshell, the DOM gives you access to the structure and content of a web page (or XML document), and allows you to make modifications to either using almost any common scripting or web programming language around.

Most of you, I'm sure, would have at least come across these two basic DOM methods and understood the concepts behind their use. I would be surprised if a high percentage of you have not used them frequently.

DOM concepts

Each of the DOM level recommendations defined by the W3C have been designed to promote interoperability between different platforms and to be language independent, so the DOM can be accessed and manipulated not just by JavaScript, but by other popular programming languages such as Java or Python.

The different levels are also designed to be backwards compatible and to function on any browser that implements them. However, since Level 2, the DOM has not been one single specification, but a range of specifications where each supplies one or more interfaces that tackle a particular aspect of DOM manipulation.

The methods and properties that you make use of in order to work with the DOM are exposed through these interfaces, but except for each level's Core Specification, the specifications do not have to be implemented in full.

So different browsers, after implementing the Core Specification, may pick and choose which, if any, of the other specifications they wish to implement.

This often leads to inconsistencies between browsers, and when working with the DOM you'll often find that certain features you wish to make use of are not universally implemented.

The `setAttribute` method for example, often fails to have the desired effect in IE depending on the attribute that you wish to set. Using it to set an element's class attribute will not work in IE, although Firefox is happy enough to let you use it.

Firefox has pretty much always had a built-in DOM viewer, IE8 finally has one built-in, though an add-on has been long available, and both Safari and Chrome, based on the same WebKit platform, have good developer tools, and any of these can be an invaluable tool when putting pages together.

Using any of these tools, you can easily see how the DOM breaks documents down into a series of nodes in a tree-like structure. The following screenshot shows the 1 top-level DOM representation of the Google homepage in the Firefox DOM inspector:

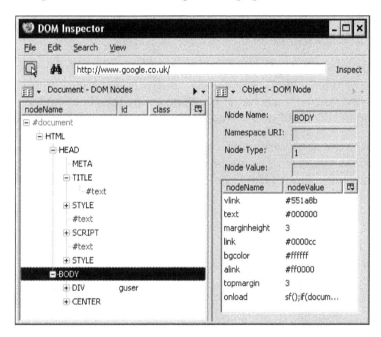

As you can see, the left-hand pane shows a logical tree representation of the page's structure and makes it easy for you to see which elements are parents, which are siblings, and which are child elements. The right-hand pane gives information about a selected node and its attributes and properties. This can be a very useful tool for checking that any DOM scripting (such as adding or removing elements) is going according to plan.

Common DOM scripting techniques

The DOM is best known among web developers for its ability to dynamically alter the structure and content of web pages using easily implemented scripting techniques. JavaScript contains a useful (although somewhat restricted) set of built-in methods for accessing, manipulating, and even replacing DOM nodes.

Nodes are a fundamental part of the DOM; each object in the DOM is represented as a node. Each node may be a branch node, which has child nodes and possibly parent nodes and sibling nodes, or it may be a leaf node, which may have siblings and parents but not children of its own.

In the previous screenshot, you can clearly see that the page is made up of a series of objects, where each individual object is a node. The nodes shown in that example are branch nodes because each one has at least one child. The **HTML** node, for example, has **HEAD** and **BODY** child nodes, and both of these have their own child nodes.

A special node is the document node, commonly referred to as the document object. It is the root of the whole tree, as can be seen in the previous screenshot, where it is shown as **#document**. Due to this privileged status, it has some extra properties and methods that are only available to it. Other methods may be called on any type of node.

Common DOM methods

We've already seen the two main ways of obtaining elements from the DOM — `.getElementById()` and `.getElementsByTagName()`. Once an element has been obtained, it's very easy to navigate your way through the tree using properties such as: `firstChild`, `parentNode`, or `previousSibling` for example.

So you can grab an element from the page and then move up, down, or sideways across the tree, navigating parents, siblings, or child elements alike. Each branch node also has an accessible `childNodes[]` collection that exposes information about each of the child nodes.

The DOM gives you methods that allow you to create different objects such as `.createElement()` or `.createTextNode()`. Both of these methods are only available under the document node.

Once you've created your new element or text node, you can insert it into the DOM (and therefore the document) using `.appendChild()`, `.insertBefore()`, or `.replaceChild()`. You can also copy nodes using `.cloneNode()`, or remove elements using the `.removeChild()` method.

Alternatively, you can fill a node with new content by setting its `.innerHTML` property with a string containing HTML code. Writing into the `.innerHTML` property of the document is what happens when a new HTML document is read and is thus highly optimized. We used this technique when assembling the results of our DateMath example.

Each node in the document has a series of properties that allow you to determine various bits of information about it, such as the `data` it holds, its `id`, `nodeName`, `nodeType`, `tagName`, or even its `title`. You can also use the `.hasChildNodes()` method to determine whether the node is a branch node or a leaf node.

Any attributes of each node are available to you under the `attributes` collection. The methods `.getAttribute()`, `.setAttribute()`, and `.removeAttribute()` are also available for use by the discerning web programmer to make working with element attributes easier, although this is one area in which browser support can vary wildly between platforms.

Further reading

The DOM, together with events (which will see in this same chapter) are the cornerstones of modern web development and web application design, and some fascinating documentation exists to further your understanding of these two important concepts. The W3C site for example, provides detailed descriptions of all of the standardized DOM levels.

DOM—the old way

To better understand the benefits that using the YUI Dom utility introduces, it may be useful to see a brief example of how the DOM can be used with just plain old JavaScript. We can then recreate the same example but this time using the YUI so that you can instantly see the difference in the two approaches.

Those of you who are familiar with the workings of the traditional DOM (by this I mean non-YUI techniques) can safely skip this section, but any of you who have not had much exposure to it may find this example beneficial.

We'll create a very simple `form` with just a single text `<input>` field on it and a `submit` button. If the `submit` button is clicked while the text `input` field is empty, we'll then use the DOM to add a simple warning message to the `form`. In your text editor add the following HTML:

```
<!DOCTYPE HTML PUBLIC "-//W3C//DTD HTML 4.01//EN"
                      "http://www.w3.org/TR/html4/strict.dtd">
<html lang="en">
```

```
<head>
  <meta http-equiv="content-type" content="text/html;
                              charset=utf-8">
  <title>Traditional DOM Example</title>
</head>
<body>
  <form id="form" action="">
    <div id="container">
      <label for="input1">Enter some text</label>
      <input type="text" id="input1">
      <button id="submit" type="submit">Submit</button>
    </div>
  </form>
</body>
</html>
```

This all we need for the HTML code; we won't worry about any presentational or positional CSS. Now for some JavaScript; all we have to really concern ourselves with is getting the contents of the text field and checking that it is not empty. If it is empty, we can then create the error message and add it to the page.

We'll also need a way of calling the function into action once the **Submit** button is clicked. We can do all of this using the following set of functions, which can be added to the <head> section of the HTML code in a single <script> block:

```
<script type="text/javascript">
  //define the checkInput function
  function checkInput() {

    //get the value of the input
    var input = document.getElementById("input1").value;

    //if the value is an empty string…
    if (input == "") {

      //create a new element and a new text node
      var newspan = document.createElement("span");
      var newtext = document.createTextNode("You didn't enter
                                          anything!");

      //get the container element
      var newparent = document.getElementById("container");

      //add the new text node to the new element
      newspan.appendChild(newtext);

      //add the new element to the container
      newparent.appendChild(newspan);
```

```
        return false;
      }
  }

  //the init function adds a listener for the submit event
  function init() {
    document.getElementById("form").attachEvent("onsubmit",
                                                  checkInput);
  }

  //execute the init function when the window loads
  window.onload = init;
</script>
```

I would like to point out that the above example is absolutely how things should *not* be done. This is very common, but very bad coding practice, and is something that we can thankfully leave behind when working with the YUI.

Save the file and view it in IE; if you click the button without entering anything into the text field, our message is added to the page.

The way it works is very simple. We've used a mixed bag of DOM methods to achieve this basic functionality, such as getting the value of the data entered into the text field and obtaining the container element using .document.getElementBy(), and creating our new content with the .createElement() and .createTextNode() methods.

We've also made use of the .appendChild() method to first add the new textNode to the new <span> element, then to add the <span> element to the container element. The final DOM maneuver involves using the .attachEvent() method to attach the onsubmit listener to the form and calls the .checkInput() function when the event occurs.

You'll notice that the form does not work when viewed in Firefox, which highlights a classic problem of working with the DOM. The .attachEvent() method is a Microsoft-only event and so is not understood by Firefox. To get this example to work in Firefox, we must detect which browser is in use and provide the .addEventListener() method to Firefox instead:

```
  function init() {
    if (document.addEventListener) {
      document.getElementById("form").addEventListener
                                ("submit",checkInput, false);
    } else {
      document.getElementById("form").attachEvent
                                ("onsubmit",checkInput);
    }
  }
}
```

Additional code routines like this are commonplace when using the traditional DOM methods because of the inconsistencies between different browsers. There are other ways of avoiding the above problem, for example, we could use the following statement in the `init()` function instead:

```
document.getElementById("form").onsubmit = checkInput;
```

But I thought it would be more interesting to show one of the common pitfalls of traditional DOM manipulation.

Still, the example does not fully work. In some browsers, though the error message will be shown, the form is still submitted. You might also be wondering what that third argument in the call to `addEventListener` is as `attachEvent` has none. We could go on enumerating inconsistencies and pitfalls, but I think the point is already made; this is too complicated and fragile. The browser, after clicking **Submit** with an empty text, should look like this:

DOM—the YUI way

We will be referring a lot to **DOM** and **Dom**. We will use DOM, all uppercase, to refer to the Document Object Model and its implementation in a browser, thus we will have a DOM node or DOM element (the same thing) or the DOM, meaning all of it, the full page. We will use Dom to refer to the YUI Dom utility.

Now let's change our basic `form` from the previous example so that it makes use of the YUI Dom utility instead of relying on standard JavaScript methods. The HTML markup can stay the same, but remove the entire `<script>` block from the `<head>` of the page.

You'll need to link to the Dom utility; with this file saved in your `yuisite` folder, the `build` directory will be accessible. Link to the Dom utility using the following `<script>` block:

```
<script type="text/javascript"
src="yui/build/yahoo-dom-event/yahoo-dom-event.js">
</script>
```

We're linking to the `yahoo-dom-event.js` file because the YAHOO object is required, and we can make good use of some of the Event utility's methods (we'll be looking at the Event Utility in detail later in this chapter).

In the `<body>` of the page, just after the closing `</form>` tag, add the following code:

```
<script type="text/javascript">
    YAHOO.util.Event.onDOMReady(function () {
        var Dom = YAHOO.util.Dom, Event = YAHOO.util.Event;;

        Event.on("form1", "submit", function(ev) {

            //work out whether the input field is empty
            if (Dom.get("input1").value === "") {

                //create a new element
                var newspan = document.createElement("span");

                //fill it with the message
                newspan.innerHTML = "You didn't enter anything!";

                //insert the new element after the submit button
                Dom.insertAfter(newspan, "submit1");

                //prevent the form from submitting
                Event.preventDefault(ev);
            }
        });
    });
</script>
```

The first few lines should come as no surprise. We set to listen to make sure the DOM is ready and, when it is, our anonymous function will be called so that we have our sandbox and, within it, we create our traditional shortcuts for both the Dom and Event utilities.

In *Chapter 1* we have already seen how we can respond to an event. Then it was the click of the icon that would pop up the calendar; here we listen to another event, the `submit` event of the form `form1`.

We have defined the function that will respond to the form submission in-line, much as we have done for our anonymous sandbox function all along.

This time we don't need to worry about catering for different browsers, the YUI will do that for us; whether it is `attachEvent` or `addEventListener` or the event is called `submit` or `onsubmit` it is now irrelevant.

Inserting the error message has also been simplified. Using the DOM we had to refer to the `<div>` with an `id` of `container` and append it there. The YUI allows us to insert the new text directly after the submit button, and allows us to refer to it by its ID, we don't need to get it first and then use it. This is something quite standard over all the YUI: if a method needs a reference to a DOM node, it can also take a string with its `id` attribute and it will find it for you.

Run this code in any browser. It will look exactly the same as the page in the previous screenshot, but under the hood, things are working much better. We use less code this way and although there's only one `input` field to validate (and only very basic validation at that), imagine the benefits of using the YUI for form validation on an entire form with many input elements.

DOM manipulation in YUI

The YUI Dom utility enhances your DOM toolkit in several important ways, giving you more power and more control. First of all, it adds a whole range of new methods for obtaining DOM nodes such as:

- `.getAncestorByTagName()`
- `.getAncestorByClassName()`
- `.getChildren()`
- `.getElementsByClassName()`

These give you much more flexibility than the standard DOM node retrieval methods. As if these additions weren't enough in themselves, the YUI Dom utility also gives you a range of methods for defining your own parameters with which to obtain elements. These include:

- `.getAncestorBy()`
- `.getChildrenBy()`
- `.getElementsBy()`
- `.getFirstChildBy()`
- `.getLastChildBy()`
- `.getNextSiblingBy()`
- `.getPreviousSiblingBy()`

In some of these methods that would return an array of elements, as you are likely to loop through that array, you can provide instead a function that will be executed on each of them. These methods, then, not only locate the nodes but do the looping for you. The function that actually does the looping is also available to you: `batch()`.

If you ever tried positioning elements in your code you probably had to figure out what would work with each browser and in what conditions, whether to use, for example, the CSS `top` attribute or the DOM's `scrollTop`, `offsetTop`, or `clientTop`. The YUI provides `.getRegion()`, `.getX()`, `.getY()`, and `.getXY()`. You can also change these positional properties as well using `.setX()`, `.setY()`, and `.setXY()` and they all simply work as expected.

Another important point is that you don't need to worry about whether these methods should be called on the special document node or on standard nodes. All of the methods defined by the classes making up the Dom utility are used in conjunction with the library namespace `YAHOO.util.Dom` prefixed to the method name.

If you look through the W3C Level 1 Core Specification, which defines most of the basic DOM manipulation and traversal methods, you'll notice that an `insertAfter` method does not exist. The YUI Dom utility kindly adds this method to our toolset, giving you more flexibility when adding new content to your pages, as we saw in our first YUI Dom example.

Although a specification exists for working with stylesheets using the traditional DOM, support for class names is limited and is sometimes not implemented by browsers. The YUI rectifies this lack of support by providing several methods that allow you to work closely with class names, which we'll see later.

Many DOMs make light work

Traditionally, the DOM is sometimes regarded as a bit of a pain to work with, but all of that ends when using the Dom utility. A lot of the other utilities and controls make use of the functionality that it provides, so it is usually part of any library implementation you create.

The Dom utility has a few classes and is relatively small compared to some of the other utility files. Except for the Region class and Point, which is a subclass of it, they are static, that is, you don't need to create instances of them. They provide browser normalization functions that help to iron out the differences between DOM implementations among some of the more common browsers, and are made up mostly of convenience methods. Let's look at them in more detail.

The Dom class

The first class is YAHOO.util.Dom. All of its members are static methods, you don't need to create an instance to use them and there are no properties at all. The methods available deal mainly with element positioning, setting CSS classes and styles, and getting elements by a range of different means, although there are also a couple of useful methods used to obtain the viewport width and height, and other information like that.

The Dom utility allows you to use the shorthand .get() method to get an element using a reference to it, such as its id, but you can also get elements based on class name, or by using the .getElementsBy() method to create a custom test, such as by attribute. This method takes three arguments: the first is a reference to a function that will receive a reference to each object and returns true if it is part of the set you are looking for, the second is optional and is used to pre-select some elements by tag name, and the third (also optional) is where to start the search.

```
Dom.getElementsBy(  // we are assuming our habitual shortcut
    function(el) {
        return el.type == "text";
    },
    "input",
    "container",
    function(el) {
        Dom.setStyle(el,"background-color","red");
    }
);
```

In this code segment, which could easily be inserted into the sandbox of the previous example, we are using `.getElementsBy()` to look for input elements of type `text` starting from the element with an `id` of `container`. Instead of storing the resulting array for further use, we add a function that will do what we want on those elements that match the previous conditions: we set their background to red.

If you're ever using a utility that assigns default `id` attributes to elements dynamically, and you wonder where these `id` attributes come from, the answer is the `.generateId()` method found here in the Dom class. It generates either a single `id` or array of `id` attributes for cither an element or array of elements passed into it as an argument. It can also generate a prefix for the `id` if this is passed as a second, optional parameter.

Using the Dom class

Let's put some of the available methods from the Dom class to work in a basic page. In your text editor, begin with our standard template and make sure to include `yahoo-dom-events.js`, and then create our sandbox with the usual shortcuts. Instead of showing the whole code at once, I'll show a little bit of HTML and the code that manipulates it so, we'll start with checking the view port dimensions:

```html
<div class="box" id="info">
   <h2 class="header">Page Information</h2>
   <p><span id="portWidth">
      The current viewport width in pixels is: </span></p>
   <p><span id="portHeight">
      The current viewport height in pixels is: </span></p>
   <p><span id="childClass">
      The first child of this div has a class of: </span></p>
   <p><span id="children">
       This div has </span><span> child elements</span></p>
</div>
```

You can see from the `<span>` elements the kind of information we are going to obtain in this example. In the sandbox, we add:

```javascript
//add the information after the given label
var addInfoText = function (where, what) {
   var newSpan = document.createElement("span");
   newSpan.innerHTML = what;
   Dom.addClass(newSpan, "infoText");
   Dom.insertAfter(newSpan, where);
};

//show some assorted information
addInfoText("portWidth",  Dom.getViewportWidth());
addInfoText("portHeight", Dom.getViewportHeight());
addInfoText("childClass", Dom.getFirstChild("info").className);
addInfoText("children",   Dom.getChildren("info").length);
```

The first function, addInfoText(), helps us add any information (what), anywhere (where) by referring to the ID of the accompanying text. It creates a <span> to hold it, fills it with the corresponding piece of information, adds a class name to the span to highlight the result (I have omitted the definition of that class; any suitable decoration would do) and finally inserts it after the given element.

We use that function to show information we can obtain using the Dom utility. We can easily find the viewport dimensions, as well as class names and the number of children of a certain element we locate by its id.

This allows us to see how .addClass() and .insertAfter() can be used but it really makes little sense to enclose the label in a <span> instead of using it as a placeholder for the variable part of the text, which is what we will discuss next.

The Region class

The other class is YAHOO.util.Region, which in turn has the subclass YAHOO.util. Point. A region defines a rectangular area of an imaginary grid covering the page. You hardly ever create an instance of Region directly, it is most often returned by calling Dom.getRegion().

Region has top, bottom, left, right, height, and width properties, plus values at indices 0 and 1, which correspond to the left and top properties for symmetry with the .getXY() and .setXY() methods. It also has methods to detect whether a region is contained in another region, to calculate its surface area, and the intersection and union with another region.

We will measure the dimensions of this region:

```
<div class="box" id="region">
    <h2 class="header">Region Information</h2>
<p>The region of this div is:
    <span id="area" class="infoText"></span></p>
</div>
```

Using this code:

```
//get the Region of the element called region
var elemRegion = Dom.getRegion("region");

//use YAHOO.lang.substitute to format that information
Dom.get("area").innerHTML = Lang.substitute(
    "Top: {top}, right: {right}, bottom: {bottom}, left: {left}",
    elemRegion
);
```

We first get the `Region` for the element we are interested in. We are going to put it into the `<span>` with an `id` of `area` so we can use `.get()` to locate it and set its `innerHTML`. So far nothing new. Now, we will use one of those functions that would be nice to have in native JavaScript and which the `YAHOO.lang` class provides (which we alias to `Lang` to make shorter). Method `.substitute()` is like a primitive `printf` for JavaScript. It takes a formatter string with placeholders for the data. Each placeholder is a name enclosed in curly brackets. Those placeholders will be filled by properties of that name from the object provided as the second argument. The `Region` object already has properties with those names so we use them for the placeholders.

For our next example we will use the following HTML segment:

```
<div class="box" id="positions">
   <h2 class="header">Positional Methods</h2>
   <p>The X position of this div is:
       <span id="elemX" class="infoText"></span></p>
   <p>The Y position of this div is:
       <span id="elemY" class="infoText"></span></p>
   <button id="btnMove">Move this div!</button>
</div>
```

In this segment we have two placeholders to fill with the coordinates of the box, but we have also added a button to play with it. We first fill in the initial information:

```
//we write a function to show the position of the box
var showPositions = function () {
   Dom.get("elemX").innerHTML = Dom.getX("positions");
   Dom.get("elemY").innerHTML = Dom.getY("positions");
};
//we call it a first time
showPositions();
```

As we are going to show the positional information more than once, we create a function to do it. In it, we just fill in the `innerHTML` of each placeholder with the result of checking, via `.getX()` and `.getY()`, the coordinates of element positions. Now, we do something about the button:

```
// when the move button is clicked
Event.on("btnMove", "click",  function() {
   //the X and Y coordinates of the info box are swapped
   Dom.setXY("positions",Dom.getXY("positions").reverse());

   //show those coordinates again
   showPositions();

   //hide the move button
   //Dom.setStyle("btnMove","display","none");
});
```

We listen for a click on button `btnMove` and when it happens, we read the XY coordinates with `.getXY()`, which returns an array with two items corresponding respectively to the left (x) and top (y) coordinates, then we use method `.reverse()` of `Array` to swap them and set the element to those values via `.setXY()`.

We show the new coordinates again, which should have been reversed from their previous values and, if we wished to allow only one swapping, we could further hide the move button, though it is funnier to keep flipping it from one place to another.

Some of the methods can loop through a set of results. Let's say that, for whatever reason you might want to imagine, we want all the table cells within a particular area that have a specific class name, to have the same width. We could do it like this:

```
var makeSameWidth = function () {
    var maxWidth = 0;
    Dom.getElementsByClassName("infoText", "td", "region2",
        function(el) {
            maxWidth = Math.max(Dom.getRegion(el).width, maxWidth);
        }
    );
    Dom.getElementsByClassName("infoText", "td", "region2",
        function(el) {
            Dom.setStyle(el, 'width', maxWidth + 'px');
        }
    );
};
```

We use method `.getElementsByClassName()` that allows us to search in a way not envisioned in the traditional DOM model. We ask it to give us all the elements with the class name of `infoText`, ignoring those elements that are not `td` and starting at element `region2`.

As the method can produce an array of elements, it can also accept a function to operate on those same elements. That function will receive a reference to each of the elements found, which we name `el`. In the first call to `.getElementsByClassName()` we read the `.width` property of the region each cell occupies and compare it to the widest we have found so far. In the second call, we set the width of them all to the widest we've found in the first loop.

Note that a `Region` returns all its sizes as integer pixel values. When we use `.setStyle()` to set the width, we have to add the `'px'` units to the end to make it a valid CSS size setting. Another important point is why we haven't used `.getStyle()` to read the width of all elements. The problem is that the width CSS property can have values such as `auto` and `inherit` and some browsers will report those values as strings; instead of a number you'll get `"auto"`. `Region` will report the actual width as it results from auto-adjusting or inheriting.

The page with all the segments put together looks like this:

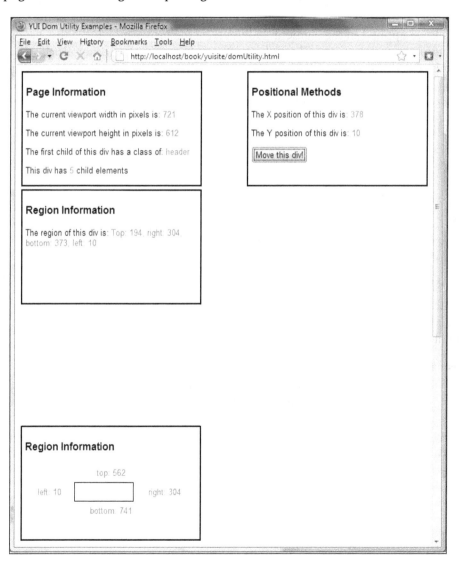

The image shows the third info box already moved to its alternate position, leaving the empty space behind. Should the button be clicked again, the box would return to that gap.

Additional useful Dom methods

There are also some useful tools for working with CSS. The DOM standard simply states that the `class` attribute or `className` property (`class` is a reserved word in most languages—even in JavaScript, though it is not used—so they had to come up with a less conflicting name) is a string containing the name or names of the CSS classes to be applied to the element. However, some browsers handle this property as something special, so not all regular methods to manipulate other attributes work with this one. Also, as a single element can have more than one class name at once, dealing with manipulating those classes is a little tricky, usually involving regular expressions or other string manipulation tricks.

The YUI provides us with several methods instead:

- `.addClass()`: Adds a single class name to an element, without affecting others that might already have it.
- `.removeClass()`: Removes the given class name leaving the others intact.
- `.replaceClass()`: Removes the first class name given, if found, and adds the second, regardless of whether it found the first, and leaving all the rest alone.
- `.hasClass()`: Checks whether the given class is within those in the element.

All of these also operate on an array of elements; their first argument can either be a single DOM node or a nodelist and they will perform the same action on each element (`.hasClass()` will return a Boolean or an array of Booleans).

If, instead of changing the CSS style of an element by changing the class name we want to get or set a style directly, we can use methods `.getStyle()` and `.setStyle()`. These methods are smart enough to know that when you are looking for `float`, it should translate it to `styleFloat` for IE and `cssFloat` for other browsers and that as IE does not handle `opacity`, it should apply a proprietary hack to do it.

Methods .getAttribute() and .setAttribute() let you read and write from any attribute, those that the DOM actually defines and also custom ones. Some browsers do not respond well to attributes that are not part of the definition of the DOM. These methods take care of that.

Methods .isAncestor() and .inDocument() allow you to ask whether a DOM node is an ancestor of another, that is, the second is contained in the first, or if an element is part of a particular document, as the same application might be manipulating several documents in different iframes.

Finally, given the following fragment:

```
<h1>header</h1>
<p>content</p>
```

it would seem obvious that DOM's .nextSibling property for the <h1> element should point to the <p> element but, depending on the browser, it might not be so. For some browsers, the next sibling is a text element containing a new-line character, for others, it is discarded as a whitespace character. Anyway, besides this inconsistency, you might really want to know which is the next DOM element, even if there was any significant text in between. The Dom utility provides .getNextSibling(), .getPreviousSibling(), .getFirstChild(), .getLastChild(), and .getChildren() that do what their similarly named DOM properties do but counting only DOM elements.

Other classes

The YAHOO.util.Point class extends the Region class and is used to define a special region that represents a single point on a grid. As expected, properties top and bottom would coincide, as would left and right, while width and height would be zero as is the area. A point cannot contain an area but the inverse might be true, an intersection would return the point itself while a union would operate normally.

The YAHOO.util.Dom.Color has a short table of standard color names such as YAHOO.util.Dom.Color.KEYWORDS.aqua and their values in hexadecimal. It also has utility functions .toHex() and .toRGB() to help converting color strings to these formats.

The Selector Utility

If all the getXXX methods available in the Dom utility are not enough to for us, the Selector Utility lets us locate nodes using CSS3 selectors. This is becoming increasingly popular as it doesn't require us to learn one more syntax such as that of XPath. We can use the same selectors used when declaring styles in a CSS stylesheet.

Just as for the Dom utility, you don't need to create an instance of Selector to use its methods, which either return an array of elements or a Boolean. Its methods are:

- .query(): Returns an array of elements based on a given selector. You can also specify a location to start the search, to reduce the time it takes to complete, and tell it that you want just the first one it finds.

- .filter(): Returns a selection of an array of nodes based on a further selection criteria.

- .test(): Returns true if the given node matches the selection criteria.

A single property is likely to be used in regular situations; document lets you state the default document where the search is to be performed, handy if you have multiple frames or iframes.

A selector can be, for example: #region span.info, requesting all tags of type <span> with a class name of info (besides other possible class names) contained in a node with an ID of region. The standard at http://www.w3.org/TR/css3-selectors/ is quite extensive in the options it offers. For example, these two statements would return the same array of elements:

```
var infoTexts = Dom.getElementsByClassName("infoText", "td",
                                            "region2");
var infoTexts = YAHOO.util.Selector.query("#region2 td.infoText");
```

While in this particular example the complexity of both statements is very much the same, .getElementsByClassName() cannot go any further or do any other search (we will need to use any of the other .getElementsBy() methods), but the query expressions used by .query() can be of any complexity and handle every sort of condition.

The Selector Utility is not part of the Dom utility, you need to explicitly include selector-min.js to use it.

Listening for Events the easy (YUI) way

The Event Utility makes listening for any event extremely easy. The events you may wish to listen for could be traditional events that are available under the browser's own event model, such as the `click` event, or they may be custom events that you define yourself. This is where the real power of this utility resides. You should avoid working with events in the traditional way and give in completely to the ways of the Event Utility.

The Event Utility provides a framework that makes it easier to create event-driven applications, where you can listen for and react accordingly to interesting moments defined by the utilities, as well as in your own application. It has many features to help you create rich and interactive web applications including:

- **Automatic handler deferral**: If the HTML element to which the event listener is to be attached, is not found by the script immediately, it is deferred for up to 15 seconds after the page has loaded to give the element time to appear. This only works when using the element `id` directly in the listener function, not when using a reference to the element.

- **Automatic scope correction**: The Event Utility automatically adjusts the scope of your event handler so that the `this` variable always refers to the DOM object that the event is attached to, rather than the window object. This frequently happens in IE or other non-standards based browsers when handling events.

- **Automatic browser abstraction**: Obtaining properties of the event object is another area of current web design where huge incompatibilities between IE and other browsers exist. The Event Utility doesn't care which browser is in use, it overcomes the differences by always passing the actual event object to the callback function as a parameter. A series of utility methods exist that allow you to easily access the properties of this event object, which we'll look at in just a minute.

- **Easy event handler attachment**: Any event handler for any DOM events or any custom events can be attached to any DOM element or series of elements using either a string variable (which could also be an array) representing the DOM element(s) or a literal reference to the DOM element itself.

- **Automatic listener cleanup**: When the `onUnload` event is detected, the event utility will automatically try to remove listeners it has registered. It does this using the `_simpleRemove()` and `_unload()` methods, which are private members of the `YAHOO.util.Event` class. You can also remove listeners manually when they are no longer required using the `.removeListener()` or `.purgeElement()` methods.

Event models

Browser event support started way back in second generation browsers when the individual browsers of the time began exposing certain events to JavaScript through their respective object models.

This was the real turning point for the interactive Web and laid the foundations for the event-driven web applications that proliferate on the Internet and the language of JavaScript as it stands at the present time. As I mentioned earlier in the chapter, the event model is very closely related to the Document Object Model and events are made possible by the DOM.

Old-styled events

Early events such as `onclick`, `onmouseover`, and `onmouseout` allowed developers to add event-handling code that reacted to user-initiated actions do not respond predictably in all circumstances.

Like different event models, different browsers deal with the `event` object in different ways. The `event` object contains information about the most recent event that has occurred, so if a visitor clicks a link for example, the `event` object's type property will be set to `click`, and other information will also be made available, such as the `EventTarget` property, which indicates the target element that the event was originally dispatched to.

One of the main differences in how the event object is used in different browsers centers on how the object is accessed. In IE the event object is accessed through the `window` object, whereas in Firefox, the event object is automatically passed to your event handler as an argument.

YUI event capturing

The YUI provides a unified event model that works across all A-grade browsers. It also introduces an interface that allows you to create your own custom events. These are important enhancements in several ways.

Firstly, you can save yourself a lot of code as the event handlers can be attached to almost any element in a consistent way, regardless of peculiarities in their inner workings. Handlers can even be attached to multiple elements with ease or multiple handlers can be attached to a single element. A word of caution: if a browser does not signal a particular event, or the Event Utility cannot guess it from other clues, the event will simply not be fired. It is a good idea to check PPK's Quirksmode site, mentioned previously; if the Event Utility does not fire an event you expect, it might simply be because the browser itself doesn't.

The `event` object and how it is accessed has also been refined so that it can be obtained in the same way regardless of the browser to a certain extent. You don't need to add separate code routines that look for the object under `window.event` as well as an argument of your handler because the YUI always passes the event object to your event handler, making it available whenever you need to access it.

Evolving event handlers

In the early event models event handlers were attached directly to their HTML elements as attributes. For example, a click handler would go into the HTML for the link as an `onclick` attribute:

```
<a href="someurl" onclick="someFunction(); return false">
```

Once the W3C provided the standardized event model, handlers could be implemented directly in the accompanying script without cluttering the HTML mark-up that defined the page:

```
document.getElementById('someElement').onclick = someFunction;
```

The YUI Event Utility takes the direct implementation method one step further, giving you a standard method of attaching certain listeners to selected elements:

```
YAHOO.util.Event.addListener(someElement, "someEvent",
                             myHandler);
```

The Event Utility provides an extensive range of methods, all of them equally as useful in their own way as the `.addListener()` or its shorter alias `.on()` method and all designed to make coding an event-driven application quicker and easier.

Reacting when appropriate

Traditionally, the easiest way to execute some code without any event being initiated by the visitor to the page was to use the `window` object's `onload` event. We even made use of this when we looked at the traditional DOM example earlier in this chapter.

This method can cause unpredictable behavior in some browsers if the code that is executed by the `onload` event targets elements of the page that do not yet exist and therefore should not be used.

The Event Utility brings with it several methods that help to avoid this problem including: `.onDOMReady()`, `.onAvailable()`, and `.onContentReady()`. They are all similar, but have their subtle differences.

The `.onDOMReady()` method allows you to execute arbitrary code as soon as the DOM is structurally complete. It is a much more effective method than reacting to the old-school `onLoad` event of the `window` object. The event fires as soon as the DOM is complete.

You can also target specific elements with ease using either `.onAvailable()` or `.onContentReady()`. These two methods allow you to execute some code as soon as an element is detected in the DOM. The syntax and use of these two methods are very similar, except that `.onContentReady()` does not fire until the target element, as well as its next sibling are detected in the DOM.

Unless we need to react fast to some particular content being available, the easiest is what we have been doing all along, use `.onDOMReady()`:

```
YAHOO.util.Event.onDOMReady(function () {
});
```

All our code should be contained in the anonymous function that is the listener to this event and we call the sandbox.

If we know the page to be very long and we want to trigger some functionality for our visitor we can, instead, do:

```
YAHOO.util.Event.onAvailable("div1", function () {
});
```

A look at the Event Utility

There are five classes defined within the Event Utility. The first, `YAHOO.util.Event` provides the mechanism to interact with the events built into the browser, which is supplemented by `YAHOO.util.KeyListener`, which deals solely with listening for keyboard events.

The other classes provide means for your own applications to declare, fire, and listen to events in a similar way to how the browser does. We'll see this later.

Listeners

The .addListener() (alias .on()) method is the one we'll use most often, as this is the method that adds the listener, which executes the callback function whenever the event in question occurs. It takes up to five arguments:

1. The HTML element or array of elements to bind the event listener to, either by their IDs or actual references to DOM elements

2. The type of event to listen for

3. A reference to the callback function to execute on detection of the event

4. (Optional) an arbitrary object to pass as an argument to the callback

5. (Optional) a Boolean that, when true, signals that the object in the previous argument should be the execution scope

If this last argument is true, the object passed in the preceding argument becomes the execution scope instead of the element that the event occurred on. The fourth argument will then be referred to as this within the listener, replacing the reference to the element that triggered the event.

The callback function can either be first defined as a regular function and then referred to in this argument, or it can be defined in-line, like this:

```
var clickListener = function() {
    alert("I was clicked");
};
YAHOO.util.Event.on("clickMe","click",clickListener);

// or:

YAHOO.util.Event.on("clickMe","click", function() {
    alert("I was clicked");
});
```

The first three arguments are known as the event signature.

Removing listeners is just as easy as adding them. The .removeListener() method unbinds bound events and takes three arguments, the element the listener is defined for, the type of event, and optionally, a third argument specifying the callback function originally used to register the event. The .purgeElement() method may also be used to remove any listeners defined on an element for any event registered with the .addListener() method. Purging event listeners is vital in some browsers (IE) because event listeners are not removed automatically along the elements they are attached to. Removing elements without purging their event listeners causes memory leaks.

The .stopEvent() method combines the functionality of the .stopPropagation() and .preventDefault() methods for your convenience so you can achieve the effect of two useful methods with minimal code. So .stopPropagation() stops the event from bubbling up to the document level, while .preventDefault() prevents the default action of the event from being carried out by the browser automatically. The latter is what is traditionally achieved by returning false from the event listener.

The listener also has a series of methods to simplify finding information about the event. It is often quite confusing to find in the event object properties with very similar names, such as keyCode and charCode; target, currentTarget, relatedTarget, and plenty of varieties of X and Y coordinates, which behave in peculiar ways in different browsers. The Event Utility provides .getTarget(), .getRelatedTarget(), .getXY(), .getPageX(), .getPageY(), and .getCharCode() all of which take as their argument the event object received by the listener and provide the expected information in a consistent manner in all supported browsers.

Event delegation

Events consume plenty of resources; if you have a series of nodes such as list items within a list, or cells within a table and you have to detect an event on any, or all of the individual nodes, setting an individual listener on each node takes too much memory. Most browser events bubble. If you click a button that resides in a <div> within a <form>, the browser will first fire an event on the button, then on the <div>, then on the form and it will keep going up to the document body. It is better then to delegate the detection of the event to a container common to all of them. Take the following HTML:

```
<table id="tableContainer">
    <tr><td id="cell11">cell 11</td><td id="cell21">cell 21</td></tr>
    <tr><td id="cell12">cell 12</td><td id="cell22">cell 22</td></tr>
    <!--and so on until -->
    <tr><td id="cell19">cell 19</td><td id="cell29">cell 29</td></tr>
</table>
```

If we wanted to listen on a click on each of those cells, we would need to set 18 listeners. Instead, we only set one:

```
Event.on("tableContainer","click", function(ev) {
    var cell = Event.getTarget(ev);
    alert("The cell clicked was: " + cell.id);
});
```

Method .getTarget() tells us what node was actually clicked on, so there is no need to set individual listeners at all; after all, there is nothing but cells in the table. We must be careful, if we had:

```
<div id="checkboxContainer">
   <input type="checkbox" id="chk1" /> checkbox 1<br/>
   <!--and so on until -->
   <input type="checkbox" id="chk9" /> checkbox 9
</div>
```

The same container has both the checkboxes and their labels. We may or may not want to respond to clicks in the labels, so we have to check what was clicked:

```
Event.on("checkboxContainer","click", function(ev) {
   var checkbox = Event.getTarget(ev);
   if (checkbox.tagName.toUpperCase() === "INPUT") {
      alert("The checkbox clicked was: " + checkbox.id);
   }
});
```

Though tag names should be uppercase, some browsers in certain modes might report tags as they are in the source, so it is always safer to make them uppercase when comparing them. By this simple means we respond only to clicks on the checkboxes. If we had the Selector Utility loaded, we could have done:

```
If (YAHOO.util.Selector.test(checkbox,"input[type=checkbox]")) {
```

Additionally, version 2.8 has received an extra plug-in: event-delegate.js ported from YUI 3. Just by adding it to the list of dependencies after the Event Utility has been loaded, plus the Selector Utility (see the Dependency Configurator), it will add an additional method to it, delegate that simplifies the above even more:

```
Event.delegate("checkboxContainer","click", function(ev, checkbox) {
   alert("The checkbox clicked was: " + checkbox.id);
},"input[type=checkbox]");
```

Instead of using .on(), we call .delegate(). We have to add a further argument, a CSS3 selector for the elements we want to actually respond to. Once the event bubbles up to the container, its source element will be matched against this CSS3 selector and our listener will be called only if it matches. It further simplifies our job by providing the clicked node as an extra argument.

Other plugins

The DOM events focus and blur do not bubble, thus, they cannot be detected via event delegation because they don't reach the containers for those elements. The Event Utility adds two pseudo-events, focusin and focusout, which we can listen to as if they were native to the browser. We can use those two event types like any other event; the Event Utility will figure out what elements within the container received or lost the focus. These event types are only needed for delegation; if we are listening to a single node, focus and blur will work. This feature is included in the Event Utility by default.

Not all browsers have methods to signal the mouse cursor entering or leaving an area. A further plugin, event-mouseenter-min.js, spreads this feature to all A-grade browsers. Just by adding the plugin, we can use the event types mouseenter and mouseleave across all browsers, regardless of whether those events are built into them.

Custom events

Events are a very effective way to respond to a rich user interface; any action our visitors do on a window fires an event we can respond to. If we are about to make a new type of control, such as a better button, a calendar, or an editor—a better mousetrap, we would like to have the same ability to signal when something interesting happens. Most YUI components have an extensive number of events.

The extra functionality provided by the library brings with it a whole host of fresh events that allow us to intercept interactions made between our visitors and the components of the library.

The Animation Utility features three custom events that define important moments during an animation such as when the animation begins (onStart), when it ends (onComplete), and during every frame of the animation (onTween).

The DataSource Utility provides a series of both interaction and execution events that mark the occurrence of things like a request being made of the live data source, or a response being returned from the data source.

Some of the components of the library simply define too many events to list. The DataTable control, for example, had 59 different events defined when this book first went to press, and the list has grown since then but I hesitate to count them as there are enhancement requests filed to add some more.

All these events also provide more meaningful information. If a user clicks an item in a TreeView control, it is of little use to pass on the raw event information object as received from the browser. The control itself resolves the target information from the browser into something that makes sense to the developer: the tree node that has been clicked.

The evolution of Custom Events

The YUI Library has a couple of flavors of Custom Events. The original mechanism, which the older components still support, was improved and new components use the newer one. Backward compatibility for old components is always a big consideration in the library; once a component is released on **General Availability (GA)** its published interfaces are frozen, so the older components could not be updated to follow the new schema.

This affects how to listen to an event; different components might do it in different ways and many have aliases so you have to check the documentation for that particular component to find out which way it uses. Any of the following ways might be the valid way to subscribe to a `click` event in a component called `myComponent`, where `myListener` is a reference to a function:

```
myComponent.clickEvent.subscribe(myListener);
myComponent.subscribe("clickEvent", myListener);
myComponent.addListener("clickEvent", myListener);
myComponent.on("clickEvent", myListener);
```

The event might also be named `clickEvent`, as shown, or simply `click`. Out of these eight possible ways, a component might offer one, two, or even three of the above. We simply need to check which ones.

At this point it is fair to note that most readers might not be interested in developing their own controls, after all, that is what the YUI library is there for. For those readers, what follows might not be of any interest and may be skipped without harm; the rest of this book does not rely on any information presented here. You may jump to the next chapter. If, at any time, you are interested in some more in-depth information on how those events you are listening to were created or fired, you may come back and find out.

EventProvider

The `YAHOO.util.EventProvider` class is the easiest way for us to create and respond to custom events. It is part of the Event Utility and provides the following methods, which I'll simply enumerate as their names are already descriptive enough. EventProvider has no public properties, events, or attributes.

- `.createEvent()`
- `.fireEvent()`
- `.hasEvent()`
- `.subscribe()`
- `.unsubscribe()` and `unsubscribeAll()`

The first two are used by the object that will signal the event, the rest by the object that will listen to it. Events are identified by a name, a simple string, which must be supplied as the first argument to all the above, except `.unsubscribeAll()` where it is optional. Though in many components these names end with `Event` (`clickEvent`, `dataReturnEvent`) it is a carry over from an earlier utility (CustomEvent) to avoid name collisions but that cannot happen with EventProvider so the `Event` suffix is now discouraged.

There is no need to create an event before firing it. There is no point in wasting memory in keeping track of an event that nobody will listen to. Events are automatically created when an object subscribes to them. The only reason for calling `.createEvent()` is if you want to use any of the configuration options it offers. As usual, these options are specified as an object literal in the second argument, with one or more of the following properties:

- `.scope`: Event listeners will run in the scope of the object that fires them unless a different scope is specified when subscribing to them or by using this option.

- `.silent`: If this is `true`, it will not log messages even in the `-debug.js` version.

- `.fireOnce`: Listeners will only be signaled once, regardless of the actual times this event is fired.

- `.onSubscribeCallback`: Allows the object firing the event to know when another object subscribes to it. If firing the event requires some costly setup, it can be deferred until (if ever) the event is subscribed to by providing a function that will be called for each subscription.

The .fireEvent() method takes an arbitrary object as the second argument after the event name. It is always a good idea to make it easy on the listener by providing meaningful information. If we were to signal a click on a node of a tree, a cell in a table or on a radio button, it makes sense that we resolve the basic event as fired from the browser into something more meaningful to the listener, a reference to the node or cell clicked or the value of the radio button checked instead of leaving the burden of finding it out to the listener. On the other hand, it is also good to provide the raw DOM event as received from the browser itself, just in case someone needs to extract any extra information such as modifier keys (*Shift*, *Ctrl*, or *Alt*) or which mouse button produced the click. Thus, the second argument to .fireEvent() is usually an object with all this information assembled as its properties.

Two objects that communicate with one another can be tightly or loosely coupled. When an object has a reference to another object and calls its methods, it is said to be tightly coupled: the caller has a direct reference to the *callee* and knows exactly what method to call and what arguments to pass in that call. For example, a menu is tightly coupled with its menu items and so is a tree with each of its nodes, and each non-terminal node with its children. However, it is not a good idea to make such tight coupling go both ways. A node on a tree might not know whether it is attached to the root of the tree or to another node, nor might a menu item know if it is hanging out of the main menu bar or from a sub-menu and, in fact, it should neither know or care.

This is when events come in handy. Instead of calling a specific method on a particular object when something happens, an event is like a letter addressed "to whomsoever it may concern". An object might simply signal "I've been clicked" and let the other objects, if any cares, deal with it. That is called loosely coupled.

Any object we create can be augmented with EventProvider:

```
YAHOO.lang.augment(myEventfulObject, YAHOO.util.EventProvider);
```

This would enrich our object with the ability to fire events and allow listeners to subscribe to them.

Custom event basics

We will use an example to show how to use events. In the section about event delegation we have already seen how to respond to a series of related events with a single event listener. We will assume that we will use radio buttons quite often and so, we want to make it easy to draw and respond to them. We could do it this way: we will have our standard page with only the basic `yahoo-dom-events.js` dependency and, in the body, a single empty element:

```
<div id="radios"></div>
```

Now, within our standard sandbox, we will add the following code:

```
//function to create a set of radio buttons
var createRadioButtons = function(container, config) {
    // markup will collect the HTML we produce
    var markup = "",
        // we create a common name to give the radios
        name = Dom.generateId(), c;

    // loop through the array of options for the radio buttons
    for (var i = 0; i < config.length; i++) {
        c = config[i];
        // if it is not yet an object (usually a string or number)
        if (!Lang.isObject(c)) {
            // we make it one
            c = {value:c};
        }

        //adding the markup for each successive radio button
        markup += '<p><input type="radio" name="' + name +
                '" value="' + c.value + '" ' +
                (c.checked?'checked':'') + '\/> ' +
                (c.label || c.value) + '<\/p>';
    }
    // insert it into the container
    Dom.get(container).innerHTML = markup;
};
```

A function `createRadioButtons` will create the radio buttons for us. Showing how it would be called will make it easier to explain the code above:

```
createRadioButtons("radios", [
        {value:1, label:"one"},
        {value:2, label:"two",checked:true},
        {value:3, label:"three"}
]);
```

We call `createRadioButtons` with the ID of the container we've set in the page and an array of options, each option made of an object with `value`, `label`, and `checked` properties.

We will create the HTML for the set of radio buttons and pile it up in `markup`. As the radio buttons have to share a single name so they are exclusive of one another, we generate one using the Dom method `.generateId()`. We then loop through the array of options concatenating the HTML markup for each option into `markup`. When we read each item of the array into `c` we check whether it is an object, and if not, we make it one. Thus, if the label and value are to be the same, we can simply provide a series of strings.

The HTML should be self-explanatory, the only segment of code that might seem strange is the use of the OR (||) operand. In JavaScript, if the left-hand side expression of an OR is truish, OR will return that value. JavaScript is quite flexible in what it considers true or false, which is why we want to differentiate `true` from truish, `false` from falsy. Besides the actual Boolean constants, `null`, `undefined` (non-existent), `0`, and an empty string are all falsy; all the rest are truish. So, if the first operand of OR is `123`, OR will immediately return `123` as it considers it truish and there is no need to check the right-hand side operand as it won't affect the result. If the left-hand side operand is falsy, then it returns whatever is in the right-hand side. Once again, it does not return a Boolean value, it simply returns the value of the right-hand side, which might also be truish or falsy so if there are further OR operands the result will be the first value not falsy or the very last one if all the others are falsy.

When we do `(c.label || c.value)`, we ask for the value of the property `label` but, if that one is empty or non-existent, then we use the value of the property `value`. The OR operand is sometimes called default, because if the left-hand side is falsy, usually non-existing, it defaults to the right-hand side operand.

Finally, we insert our entire `markup` into the container. To set a listener for our radio buttons, we could add a function such as this:

```
//function to set the event listener
var onRadioButtonsClick = function(container, fn) {
    // The contents is the same as in the Event Delegation example
    Event.on(container, "click", function(ev) {
        var radio = Event.getTarget(ev);
        if (radio.tagName.toUpperCase() === "INPUT") {
            // instead of popping an alert box,
            // we call the listener function
            fn(radio.value);
        }
    });
};
```

Our onRadioButtonsClick() function receives the container for the button group and a function that will be called when a button is clicked. The content of this function is almost the same as we have used in the event delegation example, except that instead of showing an alert box we call the event listener. Once we have those two functions, to create a set of radio buttons and then set a function to listen for a click on them, we can do this:

```
createRadioButtons("radios", [1, 2, 3, 4]);
onRadioButtonsClick("radios", function(value) {
    alert("The radio clicked was: " + value);
});
```

The first statement sets the radio buttons and we have used the short option providing just the values that will also be used for labels. Then we set the listener by referring to the container for those buttons and providing a function that will receive the value of the option clicked and simply show it.

The Element Utility

Of course the example we just saw is not really practical, but it gives a good idea of what we want and it will help us appreciate the way the YUI library allows us to handle it. The onRadioButtonsClick() function is a primitive event subscriber, and we could simply improve on that by using EventProvider. However, as soon as we wanted to add some extra functionality we would surely find that such a solution is very limited.

The reasonable solution is to define a class representing the set of radio buttons. Instead of creating the class from scratch, we will use YAHOO.util.Element as its basis. All the most recent YUI controls inherit from Element, and so will we.

Element is a wrapper around a DOM node. It is what an idealized DOM object should be, consistent in its methods and properties. For those used to object-oriented programming it is the logical way to do it. Instead of having the DOM API, with all its quirks and issues and the YUI Dom and Events collection of utilities to work around them, the natural thing in OOP programming is to wrap each DOM node in a class that will represent our ideal DOM object. Element is exactly that ideal object, with another advantage: Element can also be the wrapper for our custom controls; at this time Element is the base class for 17 of YUI's controls. Element provides a common interface for HTML built-in controls as well as for the enhanced controls we might develop.

In practice, though, Element is rarely used to wrap DOM nodes because it does take some memory and processing time and, overall, using the YUI Dom utilities is a decent and much cheaper alternative; however, in YUI3, the Node class, which is the much improved equivalent to Element, is the best and only way to work.

The Element Utility is made of several parts. Beyond the base DOM wrapping functionality, it is already augmented by YAHOO.util.EventProvider and YAHOO.util.AttributeProvider, which comes as part of the Element Utility itself, which we will briefly see later.

Subclassing from Element

When defining a class, we don't need to wait for the DOM to be ready as our class will not interact with the DOM until it is instantiated; moreover, our classes will probably be in a separate file with all the rest of our classes and utility functions, to be included in all our pages. This means that our usual way to enclose our code in a sandbox will be a little different, as we can see here:

```
(function () {
    var Dom = YAHOO.util.Dom, Event = YAHOO.util.Event,
        Lang = YAHOO.lang;

})();
```

An anonymous function is defined containing our usual shortcuts and it is enclosed in parentheses and followed by parentheses. The last set of empty parenthesis tells the interpreter to execute the freshly defined function right away, instead of waiting for an event to execute it. The set of parentheses enclosing the function itself is due to some ambiguity on how interpreters might understand this segment of code. The parentheses make sure the function is first defined and then executed.

Within the sandbox, we create the constructor of our class. JavaScript actually has no classes; a class is defined by its constructor, which is nothing more than a function. Methods and properties can be added later to add functionality. If any difference can be made between a regular function and a constructor it is that, following the usual coding conventions, we name the constructor with uppercase initials, as follows:

```
var RB = function(container, config, options) {
};

YAHOO.namespace("yuibook.forms");
YAHOO.yuibook.forms.RadioButtons = RB;

Lang.extend(RB, YAHOO.util.Element);
```

We will initially concentrate on how to define a class that inherits from another in YUI. First, we define the constructor of our class, in this case, RB. We'll discuss its contents later. RB is a local variable to the anonymous function, the sandbox, so it is completely invisible to anything outside, thus completely useless as a library component. Making it global might contaminate the Global Namespace, something we've been trying to avoid all along. YUI offers us a solution; make a branch under the YAHOO namespace in which to put our own stuff. We do so by using the .namespace() method naming our branch, in this case yuibook.forms. The name will usually be the name of your organization and the collection of common objects this class belongs to. As the RadioButtons are likely to be used along with other form-related controls, we call ours forms, which, usually, is also the name of the file it will be stored in. We can go any number of levels deep, each separated from the previous with a dot.

Now we make it public; our internal shortcut for the constructor is made public under the recently created namespace as YAHOO.yuibook.forms.RadioButtons. This name is not hidden within the sandbox; YAHOO is already public, so properties added to it will be publicly accessible as well. Our class or the whole YAHOO.yuibook.forms library can now be used from anywhere.

Finally, the call to YAHOO.lang.extend says that our RB class will extend YAHOO. util.Element. This copies over all the methods and properties of Element (and its components such as EventProvider) into our new RB class and also adds a superclass property to it that will point directly to Element's own original methods, which we can use as shown here:

```
var RB = function(container, config, options) {
    //call the constructor of the base class
    RB.superclass.constructor.call(this, container,options);

    //from here on the same code as previously
    var markup = "", c, name=Dom.generateId();
    for (var i = 0; i < config.length; i++) {
        c = config[i];
        if (!Lang.isObject(c)) {
            c = {value:c};
        }

        markup += '<p><input type="radio" name="' + name +
                '" value="' +  c.value + '" ' +
                (c.checked?'checked':'') + '\/> ' +
                (c.label || c.value) + '<\/p>';
    }
    // set the property via Element wrapper
```

```
    this.set("innerHTML", markup);

    this.on("click", function(ev) {
        var target = Event.getTarget(ev);
        if (target.tagName.toUpperCase() === "INPUT") {
            // save it
            this._value = target.value;
            //fire event from element
            this.fireEvent("selectionChanged", {
                value: target.value,
                event: ev
            });
        }
    });
};
```

Now we can see the contents of the constructor. First, we call the constructor of our base class or superclass that .extend() copied for us, so we can maintain the chain of initialization for all our classes. The constructor of Element takes two arguments, the DOM node it will wrap and a series of initialization options. We take both from the first and third arguments of RB's constructor.

We have to use method .call() when calling the constructor of our superclass to adjust the scope of the function being called to that of the caller, represented by the this JavaScript variable. This is plain JavaScript and it won't be discussed here.

Half the code that follows is taken verbatim from the previous example. The difference comes in this line:

```
    this.set("innerHTML", markup);
```

Element, as a wrapper for the DOM object, allows us to get or set all its properties. Instead of assigning the markup directly to the innerHTML property of the container, now we have the container wrapped by Element so we can set it through it, as we could with any other property.

Being a wrapper, Element also wraps the events produced by the DOM node it wraps, thus, when we say:

```
    this.on("click", function(ev) {
```

What it means is that we listen to the click event on the DOM node Element is wrapping, in this case the container for the radio buttons. We could have written this line as:

```
    Event.on(container, "click", function(ev) {
```

As this Element instance is wrapping `container`, both are almost the same, except that the first calls the listener in the context of this Element instance, which allows us to use `this` inside our listener knowing it points to Element.

Once again, the code that follows is almost the same as we've been using for the last few examples. We listen for a click on a button and we signal the event. In this case we don't pop up an alert box or call a given function — besides saving the value which we'll use later on — we call the `.fireEvent()` method, which we inherit from Element:

```
this.fireEvent("selectionChanged", {
    value: target.value,
    event: ev
});
```

The call to `.fireEvent()` takes the name we want to give the event and an argument we want passed on to the listener, in this case, the value of the option clicked and, as mentioned before, the raw event object from the browser, for any additional information the listener might want.

Right after the sandbox where we created the `RadioButtons` class we can add the code that will make use of it:

```
YAHOO.util.Event.onDOMReady(function () {

    var radios = new YAHOO.yuibook.forms.RadioButtons("radios",
        [1,2,3,4]);
    radios.on("selectionChanged", function(oArgs) {
        alert("The radio clicked was: " + oArgs.value);
    });
});
```

We now create our regular sandbox as a listener to the onDOMReady function because we will be accessing the DOM now; we are not just defining a library but actually interacting with elements in the page so we need to wait for it to be ready. We don't define any shortcuts as we won't need any.

We create a set of `RadioButtons` by creating a new instance of the class we have just defined, giving the `id` of the container to store the radio buttons in and the options for the radios: both the `label` and `value` for them will be the plain digits 1 to 4 and none will be selected.

Then we set a listener. Using the `.on()` method that our `RadioButtons` class inherits from Element, we subscribe to the `selectionChanged` event and set a function as a listener that does nothing more than pop up an alert box.

Though EventProvider forces no restrictions on the name of the events, Element does. Element already echoes any event fired by the DOM node it wraps so click cannot be used as it already exists.

Our firing a selectionChanged event instead of the native click does not seem to be a big gain, but the example is very simple and there is little extra information the event might provide. In more complex objects simply resolving the raw event into a more meaningful one is immensely valuable. But there is a further advantage. We might call our object MutuallyExclusiveSelection or something like that and have an option to either render it as a set of radio buttons or as a dropdown box. Creating it via such an object and listening to the custom event decouples us from the actual HTML used to represent it. That is also a good reason to give the event a name further detached from the actual HTML elements used to represent it; we've made no reference to whether they are radio buttons or something else.

We might have tried to respond to the change event but that one is, unfortunately, quite buggy in a few browsers. Listening to the click event is safer but not enough. First, we should check that the button clicked is not already checked, to signal real changes and not any repeated clicks, which should be simple enough as we store the value of the last button checked, so we can check if the click is on a different one. Second, we should take care of selection by keyboard, which means setting another event listener and doing some complex logic, which we won't show. Anyway, this points to another advantage of doing these advanced controls or of using the YUI library: it lets us compensate for shortcomings in the browsers.

All this would have added to the code in our constructor, which is unwise. In practice, our constructor would be really brief; it would simply chain back to the constructor of the superclass and then call several methods to break up the initialization into more manageable pieces. A typical constructor would look more like this:

```
var RB = function(container, config, options) {
    RB.superclass.constructor.call(this, container, options);
    this._createRadioButtons(config);
    this._bindEvents();
};
```

Adding custom methods and properties

Our `RadioButtons` class only has a constructor and all the methods are those it inherits from Element with none of its own. Adding extra properties is quite easy, in fact, we have done it already. When listening for a click and before firing the `click` event, we saved the value of the option clicked in a property:

```
this._value = target.value;
```

As JavaScript is a dynamic language, variables and properties come into existence by using them. In this case, `._value` will exist once we have assigned it the `value` of `target`, but we could have it defined explicitly, which is always preferable. Methods, however, need to be defined. It is easily done with the `.extend()` method:

```
Lang.extend(RB, YAHOO.util.Element,
  {
    _value: null,
    getValue: function() {
        return this._value;
    }
  }
);
```

We have added a third argument, an object, made up of the name of the properties and methods we want to add and their initial values. We define `._value` to be `null`, instead of the `undefined` that JavaScript would otherwise report and we define a `.getValue()` method that simply returns the value of this property.

We put a leading underscore in `._value` because we mean it to be private. We cannot actually make it really private, JavaScript doesn't know about private members, but at least we can signal our intent. We do so because, though reading from that variable will render a valid value, setting it would do nothing much. A developer using our library might expect that by setting that variable, the corresponding UI element would change to reflect this setting. We have not provided for that; moreover, such a property would be left out of sync with the UI element it is supposed to report on. Instead we provide a `.getValue()` method and no matching `.setValue()` so, it is clear that the value is read-only.

We would define the `._createRadioButtons()` and `._bindEvents()` methods we mentioned earlier just as we did with `.getValue()`. The downloadable samples show this.

Using AttributeProvider

We could also mimic the behavior of the those attributes of the DOM nodes Element wraps by adding a read-only `value` attribute. Instead of adding a `.getValue()` method, we could do as follows:

```
Lang.extend(RB, YAHOO.util.Element, {
    _value: null,
    initAttributes: function(oConfig) {
        RB.superclass.initAttributes.call(this, oConfig);
        this.setAttributeConfig('value', {
            getter: function() {
                return this._value;
            },
            readOnly: true
        });
    }
});
```

We define a method called `initAttributes`. This is an override; Element already has an `.initAttributes()` method; here we are defining our own version that will replace the original one. When `.extend()` copies over the methods and properties of the base class to our new class, it also copies them to the `superclass` property, so the original one is not lost. The very first thing we do in our `.initAttributes()` is to call the original one, thus, we add our attributes to those already set by Element.

We then call method `.setAttributeConfig()`, which lets us add properties to Element; in YUI parlance they are called **Configuration Attributes** and as such are listed in the API docs and elsewhere. The ability to handle such configuration attributes is provided by `YAHOO.util.AttributeProvider`, which comes packed into the same `element-min.js` file.

Here we define attribute `value` and we give its properties. We say it is going to be read-only and that to retrieve its value, we provide a `getter` method, which is a function returning the value. Then, instead of calling `.getValue()` which no longer exists, we can do:

```
alert("The current value of the radio set is: " + this.get('value'));
```

From a programming point of view, our custom configuration attribute behaves like one more of all the native DOM attributes that Element wraps. We have already used `innerHTML`, which comes from the DOM element itself, then gets wrapped by Element and, as we subclass Element, our `RadioButton` inherits. Our group of radio buttons, the whole of it, behaves as if it really was a single object instead of the bits and pieces it is really made of.

We could keep adding other configuration attributes in this fashion to control the behavior of our control. We can actually store the value inside the attribute itself instead of in ._value, we can make it read-only as we did, write-once or leave it open for read-write (the default). We can have a validator to reject invalid values. If the attribute should have a side effect besides just storing the value, we can have a method function to take care of doing that. We could have our value attribute made read-write and write a method function so that the correct radio button gets selected when the value is set.

We have already mentioned that we made the ._value property private because we don't want other developers to assume that setting that property might have any effect. JavaScript objects provide only methods and properties and the latter are completely passive ones (at least up to version 3) and can't trigger any action. AttributeProvider lets us have a better property, if you wish. Configuration attributes, in contrast to plain properties, can reject erroneous values (via a validator) or convert them to a suitable one (via a setter), they can produce side effects (via a method) and fetch the value from elsewhere (via a getter).

Using configuration attributes has two further advantages. The first is that the third argument we declared in our constructor for RadioButtons is passed directly to its superclass constructor, that is, Element. That argument will normally be an object literal with the names of any configuration attributes we want to set and their initial values. Element will take care to set them, even those of the configuration attributes we have added.

The other benefit of configuration attributes is that two events are created automatically for each attribute defined. For our value attribute we would have beforeValueChange and valueChange events. There is nothing we need to do to have them created or fired. Whenever the value attribute is about to be set, the beforeValueChange event will be fired. The listener to this event will receive the new value to be assigned and may reject it by returning false. The second will be fired after the value has actually changed and its side effects, if any, have occurred.

Likewise, for any xxxx configuration attribute, there will be beforeXxxxChange and xxxxChange events. This points to a final restriction on our selection of names for events. Remember that AttributeProvider will always create events for each attribute following this naming pattern so, though EventProvider imposes no restrictions on the name of events, Element does both because it echoes the native events fired by the DOM node it wraps, as we've mentioned before, and because AttributeProvider also creates events.

Summary

The YUI Dom utility isn't meant to replace the DOM specifications from the W3C. It uses them as a foundation to develop the tools available to you when working with the DOM. It enhances the existing DOM specifications, giving you more power in the fight for cleaner code.

It may seem a little complicated at first, but the Dom utility is actually one of the easiest utilities to use. You don't need to create any objects using constructors or factory methods; you just include the utility reference in your code and make use of the methods you need. If you've already got some experience in manipulating the DOM using traditional methods, picking up the new methods defined by the YUI Dom utility won't take long at all.

The Selector Utility enhances the ability to locate any elements in a page, replacing the several native DOM `.getXxxx()` methods and those added by the Dom utility with the flexible syntax of CSS3 selectors.

The DOM and events go hand-in-hand and the latter would certainly not exist as we know them without the former. Like manipulating the DOM, intercepting and reacting to common events that are initiated as a result of user interaction, forms the basis of modern web design. Any web solution is going to rely on events to a certain degree and they are something that you should already be very familiar with.

The YUI harmonizes the different event models at work in different browsers allowing you to do the same things but with less code and less browser detection. It also extends the capabilities of each browser's event model, adding new event tools to the already well defined set and even introduces new tools that allow you to define and react to your own custom events.

The Element Utility puts together features of both so that we can wrap a native HTML element in it and use Element's own methods to manipulate it, and it also lets us create our own enhanced controls as a subclass of Element so we can add to its own methods and properties, those of our particular control.

Incidentally, we have learned how to create a new class inheriting from an existing one.

4
Calling Back Home

As far as web interface design techniques are concerned, AJAX is definitely the way to go. So, what JavaScript library worth its salt these days wouldn't want to include a component dedicated to this extremely useful and versatile method of client/server communication?

The term AJAX has been part of the mainstream development community's vocabulary since early 2005 (with the advent of Google Mail). However, some of the key components that AJAX consists of, such as the `XMLHttpRequest` object, have been around for much longer (almost a decade in fact). The goal of asynchronously loading additional data after a web page has rendered is also not a new concept or requirement.

Yet AJAX reinvented existing technologies as something new and exciting, and paved the way to a better, more attractive, and interactive Web (sometimes referred to loosely as Web 2.0) where web applications feel much more like desktop applications.

AJAX can also perhaps be viewed as the godfather of many modern JavaScript libraries. Maybe it wasn't the sole motivating factor behind the growing plethora of available libraries, but it was certainly highly influential and orchestral in their creation and was at least partly responsible for the first wave of modern, class-based JavaScript libraries.

Like many other cornerstone web techniques developed over the years, AJAX was (and still is) implemented in entirely different ways by different browsers. I don't know if developers just finally had enough of dealing with these issues.

The very first JavaScript libraries sprang into existence as a means of abstracting away the differences in AJAX implementation between platforms, thereby allowing developers to focus on the important things in web design instead of worrying about compatibility issues.

The result in many cases is a quick and easy way for developers to cut down on the amount of code they are required to produce, and a better more interactive experience for end users and website visitors.

The term AJAX has lost part of its original meaning—Asynchronous JavaScript and XML. A lot of the data is not formatted using XML at all, but nobody has come up with anything better to replace that last X in AJAX. There are also other ways to communicate besides the original library. Though YUI supports several alternatives, we will only cover those that are out of beta. In this chapter, we will see:

- The Connection Manager, which encapsulates all the various ways in which different browsers handle communications with a server
- The JSON utility, which lets us encode and safely parse JSON data
- The Get utility to overcome the same-origin-policy restriction

Introduction to Connection Manager

Connection Manager provides a fast and reliable means of accessing server-side resources, such as PHP or ASP scripts, and handling the response. A series of supporting objects, mostly invisible to us, manage the different stages of any transaction, while providing additional functionality where necessary.

Connection Manager handles only asynchronous communications, that is, the client sends a request and immediately carries on without waiting for a reply. When the reply does arrive, your code will be notified somehow, as we'll see shortly. This is in contrast to the old, synchronous model where the client sends a request and it can't do anything until the response comes. The asynchronous model is the one that allows a user to type in a search box while choices matching what has already been typed keep showing up. Also, it is used for tiles in a map to be rendered as they come while the user can keep zooming and panning, or starting a different search. The Connection Manager does not handle synchronous communication, where everything is frozen until the reply comes, which makes no sense in makes no sense in a modern environment.

Connection Manager's single class `YAHOO.util.Connect`, just like the Dom utility, has all its members static; you don't need to create an instance of it to use. Don't worry though, this doesn't restrict you to only making one request at a time; Connection will manage as many separate requests as you need, and will queue the ones that exceed the browser's limit.

As all its members are static, advanced coders may want to take note that Connect cannot be subclassed because it doesn't have any instance members.

It wraps up the cross-browser creation of the XMLHttpRequest (XHR) object, as well as a simple to use object-based method of accessing the server response and any associated data, into a simple package that handles the request from start to finish. This requires minimal input from you, the developer, saving time as well as effort.

Another object created by Connect is the response object, which is created once the transaction has completed. The response object gives you access via its members to a rich set of data including the id of the transaction, the HTTP status code and status message, and either the responseText or the responseXML members depending on the format of the data returned.

The XMLHttpRequest object interface

When working with the Connection Manager utility you'll never be required to manually create or access an XHR object directly. Instead, you talk to the utility and this works with the XHR object for you using whichever code is appropriate for the browser in use. This means that you don't need separate methods of creating an XHR object in order to keep each browser happy.

A transaction describes the complete process of making a request to the server and receiving and processing the response. Connection Manager handles transactions from beginning to end, providing different services at different points during a request.

Transactions are initiated using the .asyncRequest() method. As it is a static method we don't need to create an object instance to use it, we simply call it YAHOO. util.Connect.asyncRequest(). The method takes several arguments:

- The HTTP method that the transaction should use, usually the strings GET or POST
- The URL of your server-side script that should handle this request, including the URL-arguments
- A configuration object that, among others, will contain references to the functions to be called when the communication completes
- If the method was a POST, the data to be posted; this is optional

Connection Manager takes these arguments and uses them to set up the XHR object that will be used for the transaction on your behalf. Once this has been done, and Connection has made the request, it will call one of the functions you provided depending on the result of the operation. These functions are usually referred to as *callbacks*.

We have been using callbacks all along. Whenever we set an event listener, the function we provide is a callback, that is, when the event actually fires, the event utility calls back. Just as with a user clicking a button, we never know when and if it is going to happen. We just draw the button, set the event listener (the callback), and if the user decides to click, we are ready for that.

With an AJAX request it is the same; we trigger the communication and the server may hopefully reply fast, but that might not be so. If it does, we are ready for that. And as with a button, there are only two choices—either it is clicked or not, a communication might complete successfully or not. That is why we provide two functions, one to handle successful replies, the other for unsuccessful ones. Those are provided in the third argument—the configuration object—as we'll see later.

A question often asked is if there is any means to do a synchronous request instead of an asynchronous one. The answer is no, as such a request would block the browser and prevent the user from interacting with it. This would degrade the user experience. In those cases, the old Web 1.0 way is preferable, as the user can see that a new page is being fetched, which is more acceptable than seeing a frozen browser.

A common pitfall is expecting the data to be ready after the `.asyncRequest()` call. This method simply sends the request and immediately returns. The reply won't have arrived by this time and this is what callbacks are for.

A closer look at the response object

When the callback functions are called they will receive a response object as an argument. The response object has the following properties:

- `tId`: A unique reference to this transaction
- `status`: The HTTP status code
- `statusText`: The HTTP status text
- `responseText`: The reply in text format
- `responseXML`: The reply in XML format
- `argument`: Any arguments passed in the request

If the transaction fails, the response properties will be empty. The `tId` is mostly for internal use and we hardly care about it. The `status` and `statusText` are the usual HTTP codes, like the infamous **404 Not Found**, or hopefully, **200 OK**. If the communication was successful we will get either of the response properties. For XML data, `responseXML` will provide us with an XML DOM object representing that reply; for all other replies (even for badly formatted XML) we get it in `responseText`.

One of the properties we can set in the configuration object when calling
`.asyncRequest()` is `argument`. Sometimes we have a series of transactions going on
at the same time and we might want to funnel them all to the same callback. To tell
them apart, we can provide an `argument` when we call `.asyncRequest()` and that
same argument will come back in the `argument` property of the response object.

If we need to obtain the HTTP response headers sent by the server as part of the
response, these can be obtained using either the `getResponseHeader` collection, or
the `getAllResponseHeaders` member.

In the case of file uploads, some of these members will not be available via the
response object. File uploads are the one type of transaction that do not make use of
the XHR object at all, so the HTTP code and status message members cannot be used.

The Callback object

The third argument to `.asyncRequest()` is usually referred to as the Callback
object, since its main purpose is to provide the references to the callback functions.
Connection Manager was one of the first library components and the vocabulary
used in the YUI has evolved. Nowadays, we would call this a "configuration object",
but the old name stuck and since all the documentation uses the traditional name, we
will do likewise. The configuration options available to us are:

- `success`: A callback function to be called on successful completion of
  the request
- `failure`: A callback function to be called on a communication failure
- `upload`: A callback function to be called on a successful file upload
- `argument`: Any value that we want to associate to this transaction
- `timeout`: The number of milliseconds to wait for a reply
- `scope`: The scope we want our callback to execute in
- `cache`: Whether we want to use the browser's cache

The most common members you would use in your callback object would usually
be the `success` and `failure` functions to handle these basic response types, with
each member calling its associated function when a particular HTTP response code is
received by the response object. When doing a file upload, we use `upload` as well as
`success` because uploads receive a different response object and they may happen at
a different time.

We have already mentioned the `argument` property, which can contain a value, an object, or an array. This value will be returned to the callback in the response object as a reference to this particular transaction. For example, our visitor might be marking checkboxes in a list of messages and we want those checkboxes to be sent to the server. We initiate an async request for each click, but we don't wait for the answer, we allow the user to go on clicking. As the replies come back, possibly in a different order from that in which they were sent, some successful others not, the `argument` property allows us to identify which checkbox originated this transaction and confirm or revert the mark.

If we want to limit the time for a response to arrive, we can set the `timeout` in milliseconds. Otherwise, it will wait until the underlying communication object returns a fail, whatever that might be. We can actually abort the transaction at any time. `.asyncRequest()` does return a value—the connection object—which can be used in `.abort()` to cancel the transmission at any time before it is completed.

If the callback functions provided are methods within an object, we will want them to execute in the context of their instances. If we don't say otherwise, they would execute in the global context. We can set `scope` to adjust it to what we want.

Finally, to avoid the extreme caching in some browsers, we may fool it by setting `cache` to false, which will make `.asyncRequest()` append a random argument to the URL to fool the cache. This is not to be done indiscriminately; each request will, in fact, be cached, but one per URL (since they are all different), though never used again. This will flood the cache with replies that will never be retrieved again; it is better to prevent caching by using the proper headers in the response from the server.

The Connection Manager fires a few events, which, more or less, correspond to the different callback functions. They can be safely ignored in favor of the callbacks.

Basic communication

In our first example we will send a number to our server, which will reply with that number squared. This is all the code we will use on our server:

```php
<?php
    $val = floatval($_REQUEST["value"]);
    echo ($val * $val);
?>
```

If we type in our browser `http://localhost/yuisite/squared.php?value=5`
we will get back **25**. This simple server script shows us something very important.
Although the AJAX transactions are transparent to our users, they are very simple
HTTP requests, which we can initiate from our browsers, so a good way to test if our
server is responding appropriately is to simply type a request and see what comes
back. Also, as we see in this example, there doesn't need to be any XML involved at all.

Using our usual template for our test pages, we add:

```
<form id="form" method="get" action="squarer.php">
    <input type="text" name="value" id="value" />
    <input type="submit" name="submit"/>
</form>
<div id="result"></div>
```

In the headers, besides the usual `yahoo-dom-events.js`, we will also add a reference
to `connection-min.js`. As usual, the Dependency Configurator can provide us with
the proper URLs to use.

In a `<script>` tag right before the closing `</body>` tag, we add:

```
YAHOO.util.Event.onDOMReady(function () {
    var Dom = YAHOO.util.Dom, Event = YAHOO.util.Event;

    //define the AJAX success handler
    var successHandler = function(o) {

        //insert the answer in the results box
        Dom.get("result").innerHTML = o.responseText;
    };

    //define the AJAX failure handler
    var failureHandler = function(o) {

        //alert the status code and error text
        alert(o.status + " : " + o.statusText);
    };

    Event.on("form","submit",function(ev) {
        //we don't want the form submitting on its own
        Event.stopEvent(ev);

        //initiate the transaction
        YAHOO.util.Connect.asyncRequest("GET", "squarer.php?value=" +
            encodeURIComponent(Dom.get("value").value),
            {
                    success:successHandler,
                    failure:failureHandler
            }
        );
    });
});
```

As usual, when the DOM is ready, we create the sandbox and define our shortcuts. We define two functions, successHandler() and failureHandler(); these are our callbacks. Both receive a single argument, which we simply call o. I don't know where this comes from, but everyone's been using o for the response object since time immemorial (proof that we have short memories). So, we'll just stick with the tradition. In the success callback we will use o.responseText, where our reply, not being XML, should come. We simply insert it into the <div> with an id of result.

Our failure callback shows an alert message with the HTTP response. If we mistype the URL of our server, we might get an alert stating **404 : Not Found**.

We set a listener to intercept the form submission and the first thing we do is to prevent it. We will be sending the data via AJAX so we don't want the normal submission to go ahead. We then trigger the AJAX request. We specify that it is going to be a GET request, and assemble the URL using a string for the fixed part, which gets the value concatenated to the end. Then, we read the value from the element with an id of value and encode it. This is a very important step often forgotten. A single unencoded space signals the end of a URL, other characters accidentally entered by the user might also spoil our URL, so even when filtered by other means, no value should ever go into the URL unencoded.

Finally we set the callback object, which simply contains references to our two callback functions.

Remember in *Chapter 1, Getting Started with YUI* when we mentioned Progressive Enhancement? This little application is a good example. If our user doesn't have JavaScript enabled, the application still work; the only difference is that the result will be shown alone in a new page. We only had to take care to put a valid action attribute on the form and use the same name for the arguments whether they are sent via AJAX or in the traditional way.

On the server, we could differentiate one case from the other. Our AJAX request does not send the value of the submit button, the regular form does, so our PHP script could look like this:

```php
<?php
    $val = floatval($_GET['value']);
    if ($_GET['submit'] != "") {
        echo "The square of $val is ";
    }
    echo ($val * $val);
?>
```

In this way, we can still cater to users without JavaScript enabled. This expands our reach not just to that 95% of visitors with A-grade browsers but to every possible visitor.

Sending forms

If we have a form with far more fields than the single one that we've used in the previous example, assembling the URL is a little harder. In our next example, we'll send a larger form. We will use the following HTML:

```
<form id="register" method="post" action="login.php">
  <fieldset>
    <legend>Please sign up!</legend>
    <div class="formfield">
        <label for="rfname">First name:</label>
        <input id="rfname" type="text" name="fname" /></div>
    <div class="formfield">
        <label for="rlname">Last name:</label>
        <input id="rlname" type="text" name="lname" /></div>
    <div class="formfield">
        <label for="runame">Username:</label>
        <input id="runame" type="text" name="uname" /></div>
    <div class="formfield">
        <label for="rpword">Password:</label>
        <input id="rpword" type="password" name="pword" /></div>
    <div class="formfield">
        <input type="submit" name="register" value="Join!" />
        <input type="reset" value="Clear" /></div>
  </fieldset>
</form>
```

It represents the second half of a "login or register" form. We use the following code to send it:

```
YAHOO.util.Event.onDOMReady(function () {
    var Dom = YAHOO.util.Dom, Event = YAHOO.util.Event,
        Connect = YAHOO.util.Connect;

    var validateNotEmpty = function(fields) {
        var ok = true;
        Dom.batch(fields, function(el) {
            ok = ok && el.value.length;
        });
        return ok;
    };
```

```
        //define registerForm function
    Event.on("register", "submit",function(ev) {
        Event.stopEvent(ev);
        if (validateNotEmpty(
            ["rfname","rlname","runame","rpword"]
        )) {

            //define success handler
            var successHandler = function(o) {
                //show success message
                alert(o.responseText);
            };

            //define failure handler
            var failureHandler = function(o) {
                alert("Error " + o.status + " : " +
                    o.statusText);
            };

            Connect.setForm("register");

            //define transaction to send stuff to server
            Connect.asyncRequest("POST", "login.php?source=ajax", {
                success:successHandler,
                failure:failureHandler
            });
        } else {
            alert("Please fill all fields");
        }
    });
});
</script>
```

Within our sandbox we have defined our usual shortcuts plus an extra one for
YAHOO.util.Connect. We then define a validation function, validateNotEmpty(),
which uses the .batch() method of the Dom utility to loop through any number of
elements checking that their length is greater than zero. This function takes either a
reference to a single element, an array of elements, a single string with the ID of an
element, or an array of strings with IDs. The YUI allows us not only to write brief
code, but also very flexible code.

We set a listener for the form submission event, and within it, the first thing is to prevent the form from submitting in the normal manner. We then call the validation function passing it an array with the IDs of the fields to check and if they do validate OK, we set both `success` and `failure` callbacks and right before calling `.asyncRequest()`, we call method `.setForm()`. This method will read all the fields in the given form and will assemble them either to the document part of the HTTP message if it is a POST request or concatenate it to the base URL if it is a GET request.

We then call `.asyncRequest()` to do a POST request, providing the base URL, in this case `login.php?source=ajax`. The reason to add the `source=ajax` argument is so that in a progressive enhancement scenario, our server can differentiate the request sent via AJAX from a regular request. Method `.setForm()` will gather all the fields that have a `name` property, even the submit button, so we can no longer count on that trick.

Method `.setForm()` returns the URL arguments properly escaped, but usually there is no need to save it, it will keep it for the very first `.asyncRequest()` call that comes. You must make sure there is no other `.setForm()` call in that execution thread since the most recent one called is the one that counts.

If the form had fields of the `<input type="file" ..` type, `.asyncRequest()` will handle the file upload. It will fire separate callbacks for the file upload—upload callback—and for the rest of the data. In this case, a second argument is needed, a Boolean set to true so that `.setForm()` is aware that you meant to do the upload. If using HTTPS servers, a third argument needs to be set to true as well.

The PHP script to handle that would have to insert that record into a database and return the appropriate response. We made a much simpler script:

```php
<?php
    $fname = trim($_POST["fname"]);
    $lname = trim($_POST["lname"]);
    if ($fname =="Groucho" && $lname =="Marx") {
        echo "You wouldn't want to join a club that accepts you";
    } else {
        echo "Welcome $fname";
    }
}
?>
```

So, we simply read the first and last names and accept everyone except Groucho Marx.

The full example can be downloaded as indicated in the Preface. It has a more complete example and the server has sample MySQL instructions that could be used both to login and to register.

The files with the code for the Connection Manager component have been recently divided into two, the `connection-core.js` that has the basic XHR handling and the full version, which is the one we have been using. `connection-core.js` is somewhat smaller and does not contain method `.setForm()` nor file upload or cross-domain requests using SWF, which is beta and won't be covered here. Be sure to select the right one in the Dependency Configurator.

Posting

`.asyncRequest()` can handle both GET and POST requests and, for that matter, any string you provide as the first argument will do just as well, though it won't work with `.setForm()`. We can handle POST transactions without the assistance of `.setForm()`, we simply need to provide the document to be posted as the fourth argument to `.asyncRequest()`.

```
Connect.setDefaultPostHeader(false);
Connect.initHeader("Content-Type","application/json; charset=utf-8");
Connect.asyncRequest(
    'POST',
    'JSONsend.php?data=true',
    {
        success: successHander,
        failure: failureHandler
    }
    YAHOO.lang.JSON.stringify(javaScriptObject)
}
```

Connection Manager assumes that data sent is always www-url-encoded. If you plan to send data in any other format, you have to set the headers accordingly. Here we are sending a native JavaScript object, which we convert into a JSON string and set in the fourth argument to `.asyncRequest()`. Previously, we have told Connection Manager to forget about the standard headers and set the Content-Type to application/json, or whatever other format the payload might be in. Sending data as POST is not incompatible with sending other bits of information within the URL as if it was a GET request. The server, if PHP, will pick part from $_GET and the document from $_POST.

Yahoo Query Language (YQL)

For the rest of our examples, we will use a new resource also provided by Yahoo! though not related with the YUI Library. Yahoo! has opened most of its databases to the public via a simple interface. It is an SQL-like language that allows you many of the standard SQL query operations. You can see it in operation at the YQL console at:

`http://developer.yahoo.com/yql/console/`

You can send an HTTP request to: `http://query.yahooapis.com/v1/public/yql` appending any of several arguments, among them the `q` argument containing the YQL request, such as:

```
select title, abstract, url, source from search.news
       where query="dakar"
```

The YQL service will retrieve a listing of records from the `search.news` table related to the Dakar car rally returning the `title`, `abstract`, `source`, and URL pointing to the original article. Yahoo! provides an ever increasing number of tables such as news, weather, geo-location, maps, Flickr!, and social sites all through a simple interface and in different formats.

We will use YQL in the following examples because it can return the data in XML, JSON, and JSONP so we will show how to handle each kind of response and it will help us show how to overcome the cross-domain scripting (XDS) restriction.

Overcoming the XDS restriction

As a security measure, the XHR object does not allow cross-domain requests. That means all the data we fetch has to come from the same domain as the page that requests it. If my page came from `http://myCompany.com` the XHR object will not let me do an HTTP request to `http://query.yahooapis.com`.

We'll need an intermediary PHP file that will actually retrieve the XML file from the remote server and pass it back to us. This script will act as a proxy and we have to locate it in the same domain as our own pages.

In order to complete this example we'll need to use a full web server setup, with PHP installed and configured. Our proxy PHP file will also make use of the cURL library, so this will also need to be installed on your server.

The installation of cURL varies depending on the platform in use, so full instructions for installing it are beyond the scope of this book, but don't worry because there are some excellent guides available online that explain this quick and simple procedure.

Let's see this proxy:

```php
<?php
    if (extension_loaded("curl")) {
      $session = curl_init();

      $url = 'http://query.yahooapis.com/v1/public/yql?' .
                              $_REQUEST['urlArgs'];
      curl_setopt($session, CURLOPT_URL, $url);
      curl_setopt($session, CURLOPT_RETURNTRANSFER, true);
      $xml = curl_exec($session);
      curl_close($session);

      if (empty($xml)) {
        header("HTTP/1.0 404 Not Found");
      } else {
        header("Content-Type: text/xml");
        echo $xml;
      }
    } else {
        header("HTTP/1.0 501 cURL not available");
    }
?>
```

We won't comment on the use of cURL but what this code does is, firstly ensure that the PHP interpreter has the cURL extension loaded and produce an error if not; then it appends to the YQL service URL the urlArgs argument that came in from our client and does a cURL request using that same URL. When the reply comes back it checks if it is empty, which signals an error, and we ask PHP to return a **404 – Not Found** error. If a reply comes we make sure to send the proper Content-Type header and the reply.

We could have made the proxy generic by omitting the base URL of the YQL service, which would have turned this proxy into an open proxy. This is not a good idea; eventually such a proxy will be found and used for purposes you don't even want to know about. Always make your proxies very specific and useless for anything but your application. The more rigid and less flexible they are the safer.

A further warning, don't use any arbitrary number for a reply code, there are specific behaviors expected from browsers upon receiving some of these codes, and they will happen before you can do anything to prevent them. Check the standard at http://www.w3.org/Protocols/rfc2616/rfc2616-sec10.html.

We will use this same proxy for JSON requests so the `text/xml` header looks somewhat inappropriate. However, the XHR client doesn't really mind. It does care about XML because if it doesn't have the right header and the proper format, it won't return it in the `responseXML` property. All other replies, even badly formatted XML, will go into `responseText`, which is what we want anyway.

Working with XML

In this example we're going to look at a common response type you may want to use, and the one that became tied to the AJAX acronym — XML. We will request news items from Yahoo! using YQL and display them on the page.

This is the HTML segment specific to our news reader:

```html
<body id="doc" class="yui-t1">
    <div id="hd">
       <h1>XML News Reader</h1>
    </div>
    <div id="bd">
        <div id="yui-main">
            <div id="newsitems" class="yui-b"></div>
        </div>

        <div class="yui-b">
            <form id="form" method="get" action="#">
                <input id="query" type="text" value="election" />
                <input type="submit" value="submit"/>
            </form>
        </div>
    </div>
</body>
```

We will use the `reset-fonts-grids.css` and `base.css` CSS tools and we'll lay out the page using one of the standard grids, the page made of a header, body, and footer (not shown) section with the `bd` section containing a main panel that will hold the news and a secondary panel that will allow us to submit different queries.

We will also include `yahoo-dom-events.js` and `connection-min.js` as in the previous example (we could do this with `connection-core-min.js`). Right after the previous code and before the closing `</body>` tag, we add:

```html
<script type="text/javascript">
    YAHOO.util.Event.onDOMReady(function () {
        var Dom = YAHOO.util.Dom, Event = YAHOO.util.Event,
            Lang = YAHOO.lang, Connect = YAHOO.util.Connect;
```

```
    var YQL_QUERY = 'select title,abstract,url,source from ' +
                    'search.news where query="{query}"',
        YQL_URL_ARGS = "format=xml&diagnostics=false&q=",
        MY_PROXY = "myproxy.php?url=",
        FORMAT = '<h2>{title}<\/h2><p>{abstract}<\/p><address>' +
                 '<a href="{url}">{source}<\/a><\/address>';


//define the AJAX success handler
var successHandler = function(o) {

    //get the root of the XML doc
    var root = o.responseXML.documentElement;

    //locate the news items
    var allNews = root.getElementsByTagName("result");

    //output
    var output = [];

    Dom.batch(allNews,function(news) {
        var newsItem = {};
        Dom.batch(news.childNodes, function(el) {
            newsItem[el.tagName] = el.textContent;
        });

        output.push(Lang.substitute(FORMAT, newsItem));
    });
    Dom.get("newsitems").innerHTML = output.join("\n");
};

//define the AJAX failure handler
var failureHandler = function(o) {

    //alert the status code and error text
    alert(o.status + " : " + o.statusText);
};

var query = function() {
    var yqlQuery = Lang.substitute(YQL_QUERY,
        {query: Lang.trim(Dom.get("query").value)});
    var yqlUrl = YQL_URL_ARGS +
                        encodeURIComponent(yqlQuery);
```

```
                var url = MY_PROXY + encodeURIComponent(yqlUrl);

                //initiate the transaction
                Connect.asyncRequest("GET", url, {
                    success: successHandler,
                    failure: failureHandler
                });
                return false;
            };
            query();

            Event.on("form","submit",query);

        });
    </script>
```

After creating the sandbox in response to the DOM becoming ready, we create the usual shortcuts plus one for `YAHOO.util.Connect`. Then we go on to create three constants. We know that JavaScript has no concept of constants, they are all regular variables, but we use uppercase letters so our intention is clear.

The first, `YQL_QUERY` is the template for our YQL query. The actual search term will go into the placeholder marked `{query}`. Then we define `YQL_URL_ARGS`, which contains a couple of options as URL arguments to be sent to the YQL service; here we want the reply in XML and we don't care to receive any extra diagnostics information.

We go on to define `MY_PROXY`, which is the URL for the PHP proxy we've seen a couple of pages back. The last one, `FORMAT`, is the template for the HTML markup we will produce for each news item. The placeholders in this string, such as `{title}` and `{abstract}`, match the fields requested in the YQL query.

In these few lines we have given a lot of flexibility to our application. We can change the `YQL_QUERY` and `FORMAT` strings in such a way that we can show more or less fields, and completely change their presentation aided by some CSS, which we have not shown, and the rest of our code will still work. We can even query a different table. There are no references to the tables or fields read from YQL elsewhere.

Our `successHandler` callback function first locates the root of the reply and then we pick all the nodes tagged `<result>`, which returns a nodelist, that is, an array. We will assemble our reply in the array output, which we initialize to an empty array. Method `.batch()` from the Dom utilities is then called to operate on the results list. We will compose a `newsItem` object in a format more amenable to JavaScript. We initialize `newsItem` and then use another call to `.batch()` to loop trough all the tags that might have come in the reply thus converting an XML segment into a JavaScript hash.

We use `.substitute()` to fill in our `FORMAT` template with the data from that hash. This is what allows us to change `YQL_QUERY` and `FORMAT` at will; we didn't assume any particular field names. Whatever elements come in each `newsItem` will be copied to the hash, and `.substitute()` will just fill in the blanks with whatever it finds.

The filled-in template is then pushed into `output`. String manipulation is often slow; appending a new item to an array is faster. We will later use `.join("\n")` to turn this array into a string, which might offset the gain elsewhere. For a large number of long strings, this is a faster alternative than concatenating a little bit at a time; for few or short strings, it might not be worth it. Anyway, that is just for you to know.

After looping through all the `newsItems`, we `.join()` all the output and insert it into the `innerHTML` of the `newsItems` node.

There is nothing new about the `failureHandler()` callback, except that now we know how we can cause it to be called by sending appropriate status codes from our proxy.

Then, we define function `query()`. First, we use `.substitute()` to fill the `YQL_QUERY` with the value of the `query` input box, after trimming extra spaces. We then concatenate this `yqlQuery` after the `YQL_URL_ARGS` URL options but, since it will contain objectionable characters, such as spaces, we first apply `encodeURIComponent()` to it.

This will be the full URL request we would send the YQL server if we didn't have the cross-domain scripting restrictions and were not forced to use a proxy, so we need one more step. We concatenate the URL `MY_PROXY` with the previous URL, but as this also becomes an argument, we run it once again through `encodeURIComponent()`. Finally we do the actual async request.

We immediately call the `query()` function so our page will show our initial set of news, and we also set `query()` as the listener to a form submit, so it will refresh the news panel with the new query.

This is how it looks after we have requested news about the Dakar rally:

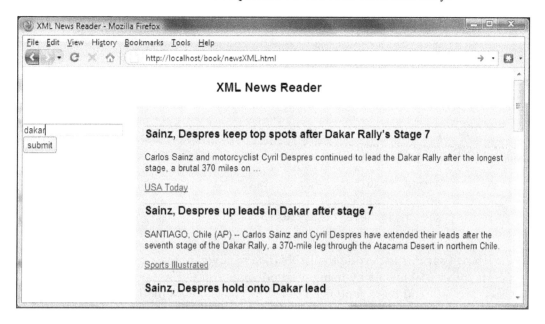

Processing a JSON reply

JSON is becoming a very popular data format for web applications because it is shorter and easier to work with than XML. JSON can be easily converted to true JavaScript objects so you are relieved from using DOM XML methods; this makes it much easier on the client side. JSON encoders/decoders are already part of some JavaScript implementations in preparation for the upcoming spec for ECMAScript, in which it is included. The YUI JSON utility calls the built-in JSON parser if the browser has one.

JSON is easy to implement in the server. It is already compiled into PHP since version 5.2 and in those languages where it is not already built-in, there are plenty of libraries to choose from. For a listing, see: `http://www.json.org`.

The code for this version is quite similar to the one we used previously. Besides the YAHOO, Dom, and Event trio and the Connection Manager, we need to include `json-min.js`. We need to tell the server to provide us with the data in JSON format instead of XML by changing the following string:

```
var YQL_URL_ARGS = "format=json&diagnostics=false&q=";
```

The next change is in the `successHandler` function, which it is now far simpler:

```
//define the AJAX success handler
var successHandler = function(o) {

    // read and parse the data
    var data = YAHOO.lang.JSON.parse(o.responseText);
    var allNews = data.query.results.result;

    //output
    var output = [];
    for (var i = 0; i < allNews.length; i++) {
        output.push(Lang.substitute(FORMAT, allNews[i]));
    }
    Dom.get("newsitems").innerHTML = output.join("\n");
};
```

We see how easy it is to decode the JSON data received in the `.responseText` property into variable data by using method `.parse()`. Now `data` contains a native JavaScript object and there is no need to use any XML DOM methods to locate the information — the news resides in `data.query.results.result`. Since `allNews` is a native JavaScript array it is easy to loop through it and use `.substitute()` on its items. And that's it, the rest is the same.

Using JSONP with the Get utility

Although browsers don't allow XHR requests to go across domains, there is a way around this limitation. One is to use the Flash object; the Connection Manager supports this, though it is still beta. The other is to insert a `<script>` tag into the document with an appropriate `href` attribute, which can load anything from anywhere on the net.

However, this alternative requires a little help from the server. If you simply load a JSON-encoded object into a `<script>` tag, it will be executed and immediately lost, since it wasn't assigned to anything nor processed in any way. Let's explain that. Imagine you add this segment of code to any page:

```
<script>{a:2}</script>
```

The object literal containing a property `a` with a value of 2 will be evaluated and lost. Now, if instead, we had:

```
<script>callbackFunction({a:2})</script>
```

The interpreter will then look for and execute a function called `callbackFunction()` and pass it the same literal as an argument. That function can then process that object literal in any way it wants. Additionally, the function `callbackFunction()` acts as a success callback since it will be executed when the code is successfully loaded.

The YQL service can create JSONP replies provided that you add a callback URL argument specifying the name you want to give that callback function. The service will then enclose the data in a call for that function.

We can try it by using any of the previous two examples and deleting the references to `connection-min.js`, and if present, `json-min.js`, and add `get-min.js` instead of those two. The first change we need to do is in the constants at the top. There will be no `MY_PROXY` constant since now the request can go directly to the YQL service. The second is the `YQL_URL_ARGS` that is now called `YQL_URL` because it now holds the whole URL:

```
var YQL_URL = 'http://query.yahooapis.com/v1/public/yql?' +
        'format=json&diagnostics=false' +
        '&callback=YAHOO.yuibook.connection.callback&q=';
```

This string now contains the base URL, which so far was in our proxy to prevent it from being an open one and, thus, insecure. The second line is the same as in the previous example; we still want the data to be in JSON format. The big difference is in the last URL argument: `callback`. This is the name of the function that the JSONP server will use to enclose the returned data. Why such a long name? So far, most of our functions were for internal use within the sandbox: none of them were visible outside, which was good to avoid polluting the global namespace, and we were free to name them as we wished. In contrast to this, the `callback` function has to be globally accessible but we know it is better to avoid global variables so we place it in a branch of our own under the `YAHOO` namespace.

It is important to notice that there is no longer a `successHandler()` function, our callback function is now the one that will get called when the reply comes; so, instead of the former `successHandler()`, we have:

```
YAHOO.namespace("yuibook.connection");

//define the AJAX success handler
YAHOO.yuibook.connection.callback = function(response) {

    //reach straight for the data, there is no JSON decoding!
    var allNews = response.query.results.result;

    //output
    var output = [];
    for (var i = 0; i < allNews.length; i++) {
```

```
        output.push(Lang.substitute(FORMAT,allNews[i]));
    }
    Dom.get("newsitems").innerHTML = output.join("\n");
};
```

We use `YAHOO.namespace()` to define our branch for the `yuibook` book and for the `connection` chapter. We then use the whole name to define the function, the same one we passed as the `callback` URL argument in `YQL_URL`. The callback function receives the data as its single argument. There is no further need to decode the reply; we can just reach for the data into `response`. The rest of the function is the same as we've used for JSON data.

We have a further difference in this example in the `query()` function. First, there are fewer arguments to concatenate into a long URL — there is no proxy so there is one less step. Second, we no longer call `.asyncRequest()` but the Get utility `.script()` method:

```
var query = function() {
    var yqlQuery = Lang.substitute(YQL_QUERY,
        {query: Lang.trim(Dom.get("query").value)});
    var yqlUrl = YQL_URL + encodeURIComponent(yqlQuery);

    //initiate the transaction
    YAHOO.util.Get.script(yqlUrl, {
        onFailure:failureHandler
    });
    return false;
};
```

We define only an `onFailure` handler in our call to `.script()`. The name of the property has changed with an `on` prefix, to conform to the evolved naming conventions of the library. The configuration object for `.script()` also has several options, very much like those of `.asyncRequest()` except for the `on` prefix on methods. An `onSuccess` callback can be of interest to developers who might want to purge each callback function as it is no longer needed, to keep memory consumption down. A `.purge()` method in its response object will delete the `<script>` node just loaded. Anyway, the Get utility automatically deletes those scripts when they reach 20, a value we can change via thee `.PURGE_THRESH` property.

For a global application avoiding the use of a proxy means a great advantage, a visitor on the other side of the world from you will have a nearby entry point to Yahoo!'s network, but unless you have the resources to deploy your proxy globally, that user would have had to come to your servers to be rerouted back to Yahoo!, while using JSONP, the communication is direct in between that visitor's browser and Yahoo! servers.

Loading library components via Get

The Get utility can also be used to load library code and CSS files; it is what the YUI Loader utility uses. The Get utility will not purge CSS files automatically, but be careful with library files to set the .autopurge configuration attribute to `false` so they don't get erased automatically after several calls.

Summary

The YUI Connection Manager utility provides an almost unequalled interface to AJAX scripting methods used today among the many JavaScript libraries available. It handles the creation of a cross-platform XHR object and provides an easy mechanism for reacting to success and failure responses among others. It handles common HTTP methods such as GET and POST with equal ease, and can be put to good use in connection (no pun intended) with a PHP (or other forms of) proxy for negotiating cross-domain requests.

If JSON is used, an increasingly attractive alternative, the JSON utility can be used to encode and decode native JavaScript objects into strings that can be easily transmitted.

Finally, the Get utility allows us to go across domains without the need of a proxy, as long as the server supports JSONP. It also dynamically inserts code or CSS Styles in our application.

5
Animation, the Browser History Manager, and Cookies

The Animation Utility is used to add a variety of effects to your pages that can really bring your web application to life. It's a very easy component of the library to use, but delivers a powerful and robust mechanism by which elements can be made to grow, move, and even change color.

When using web-based applications that are based on DOM-scripted or AJAX-driven dynamic page changes, it is usually impossible to return to a previous page state using the back button of the browser. The **Browser History Manager** (**BHM**) Utility provided in the YUI is the first step towards a web of online applications where the functionality of the back and forward browser buttons has been restored.

The Cookies Utility allows us to improve the user experience by preserving a minimum set of settings on the client side. While we can keep full tables of user preferences on the server side by using database tables, we cannot do that for a user who has not registered. Cookies allows us to keep track of some information on a per-browser basis.

In this chapter we will look at:

- Enhancing our pages with attractive animations
- Why the BHM is needed and how it can be implemented
- The different components of the BHM
- Recording state changes
- Retrieving bookmarked state
- Storing and reading cookies

Introducing the Animation Utility

The Animation Utility provides a quick and easy solution to add a variety of animations to elements on your pages. You can specify that elements should grow, shrink, or even scroll across the page, and you have complete control over how and when these animations should occur. Almost any property of an element with a numerical value, such as `width` or `height` for example, can be animated.

The class structure of the Animation Utility

`YAHOO.util.Anim` is the base class that provides most of the basic properties and methods that are used to create animations. It features a constructor which is used to create an instance of the animation object, a series of methods which allow you to control the animation, and a set of custom events which are fired at different moments during the animation.

The Animation constructor

Animating an object is as simple as creating a new instance of an Animation object and applying it to an element on your page. The constructor used to create this object takes four arguments.

1. A reference to the element to animate. As usual in the YUI, it can either be an actual DOM reference or the value of the `id` attribute for the element.

2. A configuration object that defines how the element should be animated.

3. (optional) A number representing the approximate duration of the animation. If this is not specified the animation will default to 1 second.

4. (optional) A reference to one of the members of the `YAHOO.util.Easing` class. If this argument is not supplied `YAHOO.util.Easing.easeNone` is used.

None of the arguments is really mandatory, but no animation will take place if the first two are not supplied. We can use `.setEl()` to assign the element to be animated and properties `.attributes`, `.duration`, and `.method` correspond to the other three arguments, respectively.

`Anim` will complete the animation in the time given. In a slower or heavily loaded machine, the animation will look jumpy; in a faster machine it will be smoother.

Easing, a feature we will be looking at in just a little while, allows the animation to depart from a simple linear movement, making it bouncy at each or both ends, overshoot them or slow down. This is an easy way to add interest to a basic animation.

Animation's attributes

One of the most important properties provided by the Anim class is .attributes. It contains an object which allows you to specify which property of the specified element is animated, and how it will change. This is exactly the same as the second argument of the constructor.

The animation .attributes is normally an object literal specifying, first, the CSS property that is to be animated. Almost any CSS style attribute that accepts a numeric value can be animated: width, height, top, left, margin, border, opacity, and so on. Any number of these properties can be animated at the same time. For each, we can specify:

- by: The element should change by a specified amount from the current value.
- to: The element should go to the specified value from the current value. It will override the by property if both are present.
- from: The element should begin from the specified value instead of the current value.
- unit: This specifies the units, such as pixels (px) or ems that the other properties should be measured in.

To stretch an element with an ID of box 100 pixels towards the right and bottom over 3 seconds, slowing down when it reaches the end, we could do:

```
var sampleAnim = new YAHOO.util.Anim("box", {
  height: {by: 100},
  width: {by: 100}
}, 3, YAHOO.util.Easing.EaseOut);
sampleAnim.animate();
```

The from attribute will default to the current value of the property if not specified. Providing a from different from the current value might make an initial jump; however, from is required when the value of the attribute, as reported by the browser might be in other units from those specified. For example, let's assume we had a box, one line in height, that is, 1em, the following setting:

```
{height: { by: 4, unit: "em"}}
```

will probably make a big jump as the browser will report the height in pixels which, depending on the font-size setting, can be 9 to 13 px. So this animation will try to animate it from, say, 10 back to 4 assuming they were all in em units, which is not true.

Custom Animation events

The custom events defined in the base animation class are:

- onStart
- onTween
- onComplete

It should be plainly obvious to all when each of them fire, but for the record onStart is fired when the animation begins, onTween occurs during every frame of the animation, and onComplete is fired when the animation ends, which is particularly useful as it allows for chaining animations or other actions once an animation is completed.

The onTween event has the potential to bring your application down if it is not used in the correct way. As this event fires on every single frame of the animation, the code that it executes needs to be highly efficient, otherwise the animation, and potentially your entire application, will grind to a halt. Generally, you won't need to use this event for this exact reason and it will only become useful in highly specific situations. If using it can be avoided, it should be.

The subclasses

The animation class has three subclasses: YAHOO.util.ColorAnim, YAHOO.util. Motion, and YAHOO.util.Scroll. Each of these provides an additional constructor with which you can create a different type of animation. None of them have their own properties, and only the ColorAnim class has its own method, but all three of them inherit the methods and properties they need from the base class.

YAHOO.util.ColorAnim extends the base animation class by allowing you to animate the color of an element. Unlike the base class, the ColorAnim class does allow you to work with element properties that are specified using HEX or RGB rather than just numerical values.

The attributes object used by colorAnim is extremely flexible and can accept any style property that has a numerical value as its first member. To change the color of text within an element from black to red you could use the following object:

```
var attsObj = {
  color: {from: "#000000", to: "#ff0000"}
};
```

`ColorAnim` breaks up the color value into its separate RGB components so that, in the example above, the next color value would be #010000 and not #000001

The `YAHOO.util.Motion` subclass allows us to handle two-dimensional values such as x-y coordinates and to specify a path of points that an object can follow across the page to reflect movement. The path is specified using the `points` attribute where the second member of the `value` object is an array with X and Y coordinates. Though in principle this could be done by animating the `top` and `left` attributes in the same animation, `Anim` might not keep them changing at the same pace, resulting in a jagged path.

The `points` attribute is used in the same way as the plain numerical attributes looked at earlier on. To move an element 100 pixels along both the X and Y axis, for example, you could use the following attributes object:

```
var attsObj = {
  points: { to: [100, 100] }
};
```

Motion can also take an array of control points, which will be used to draw a Bezier curve for the element to follow.

```
var attsObj = {
    points: {
        to: [100, 100],
        control: [[40, 120], [-40, 240]]
    }
};
```

`YAHOO.util.Scroll` extends the base animation class (via `ColorAnim`) by allowing you to scroll overflowing elements. The amount of scroll is specified using the `scroll` attribute in the `attributes` object, where once again the second member of the value object is an array containing the number of units to scroll the element across or down the page.

The following object could be used to `scroll` the hidden contents of an element into view vertically:

```
var attsObj = {
  scroll: { by: [0, 200] }
};
```

To `scroll` an element horizontally you simply specify a positive value for the first array item.

Additional classes

Along with the aforementioned subclasses a few other classes are also defined within the Animation utility. The YAHOO.util.Bezier class is used in conjunction with the Motion class and allows for motion that follows a curved path.

The YAHOO.util.AnimMgr class defines the Animation Manager. It's unlikely that you'll need to use this class directly, but it is present in any animation implementation and controls the animation queue. Animations are executed one at a time and when several animations are registered it is the Animation Manager that organizes them into a controlled queue.

The members of the YAHOO.util.Easing class provide a series of animation enhancements used to add visual interest and appeal to your animations. They are based on easing equations created by Robert Penner in 2001.

Easing effects will often turn a flat animation into something much more visually appealing. An element that moves across the screen, for example, will often appear to move more smoothly and finish more tidily when easing is used whereas bouncing can make it funnier.

For a full list of all of the different types of easing available, be sure to check the API documentation for the Animation Utility.

Using Animation to create an Accordion Widget

We can put the Animation Utility to good use to create a simple, yet visually appealing, Accordion-style content area. Using our standard template for the examples, we'll make sure to include the inevitable yahoo-dom-events.js and, for this example, animation-min.js and, in the <body>, the following HTML:

```
<div id="accordion">
  <h1>Section 1</h1>
  <div>
    <p>Lorem ipsum dolor  … Sed dictum.</p>
  </div>
  <h1>Section 2</h1>
  <div>
```

```
        <p>Lorem ipsum dolor … Sed dictum.</p>
        <p>Lorem ipsum dolor … Sed dictum.</p>
    </div>
    <h1>Section 3</h1>
    <div>
        <p>Lorem ipsum dolor … Sed dictum.</p>
        <p>Lorem ipsum dolor … Sed dictum.</p>
        <p>Lorem ipsum dolor … Sed dictum.</p>
    </div>
</div>
```

The content of each paragraph is that long fake Latin typesetting placeholder text, here abbreviated, but the idea is that it really should cover several lines. There may be any number of sets of <h1> and <div> elements and each may vary in the size of the contents, but only one <div> per <h1>.

First we will take a look at the CSS styles required for this example:

```
#accordion  {
    width:400px;
    border-bottom: thin solid black;
}
#accordion h1, #accordion div {
    border-style:solid;
    border-color:black;
}
#accordion h1 {
    background-color:#99ccff;
    color:white;
    text-align:center;
    margin:0;
    border-width:thin;
}
#accordion div {
    border-width: 0 thin;
}
```

We are setting styles specifically for this segment of HTML by prefixing all the styles with the #accordion selector, which corresponds to the id of the segment we want to affect. In this way, other <h1> or <div> elements elsewhere in the page will not be changed.

We are setting the overall width and drawing thin black borders around the headings and text in such a way that there are no duplicated borders. We are further coloring the background of <h1> elements making the text white and centered. This should make it look like this:

All the text is visible fully expanded. The heading above is also an <h1> to show that outside headings are not affected. For users without JavaScript enabled, this is what the page would look like; all the text is visible by scrolling down and no other interaction is possible.

We want to transform the above HTML into an Accordion Widget where, by clicking on the heading bar, the content can be toggled from expanded to collapsed, and as we are going to use this pattern in many places, we want to make it a regular component in our library. We would like to be able to make it work by using the following code, which we can begin adding before the closing </body> tag:

```
<script type="text/javascript">
    // accordionize!
    YAHOO.util.Event.onDOMReady(function () {
        var accordion = new YAHOO.yuibook.Accordion("accordion");
    });
</script>
```

When the DOM becomes ready, we simply create a new instance of our `Accordion` control telling it which segment of the page to turn into an Accordion. The result of such action would produce a page like this:

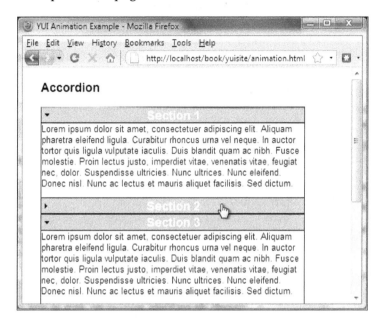

Section 2 is now collapsed after being clicked upon and, fitting to the content of this chapter, the collapsing happened smoothly. The cursor now shows a different shape, signaling that the headers are now active and small arrows towards the left margin further signal the collapsed or expanded state.

To make it reusable, we would normally store this code in a separate `.js` file, but we'll keep it in the same example file to make it simpler to look at it all in context. We add another `<script>` segment with our Accordion control right before the previous:

```
<script type="text/javascript">
    (function () {
        var Dom = YAHOO.util.Dom, Event = YAHOO.util.Event;

        //constants to be used elsewhere
        var PANEL_HEIGHT = "yuibookOriginalHeight",
            COLLAPSED ="yuibookCollapsed",
            EXPANDED = "yuibookExpanded",
            ACCORDION = "yuibookAccordion";

        YAHOO.namespace("yuibook");
```

```
//Our Accordion class
YAHOO.yuibook.Accordion = function (container, config) {
    //Make sure container is an object reference
    container = Dom.get(container);
    //if config is undefined, make it an empty object
    config = config || {};
    this._h1 = (config.header || "H1").toUpperCase();

    //add yuibookAccordion className so our CSS becomes valid
    Dom.addClass(container, ACCORDION);
    //add arrow indicator to header
    Dom.addClass(container.getElementsByTagName(this._h1),
              EXPANDED);

    //get the animation instance ready
    this._anim = new YAHOO.util.Anim();
    //take Anim configuration from config or use defaults
    this._anim.duration = config.duration || 0.5;
    this._anim.method = config.easing ||
                      YAHOO.util.Easing.easeBoth;

    //Pick the click bubbling to the container
    Event.on(container,"click",function(ev) {
        var heading = Event.getTarget(ev);

        //If the target of the click was, indeed,
        //the H1 element:
        if (heading.tagName.toUpperCase() == this._h1) {
            // pick the panel that is after it
            var panel = Dom.getNextSibling(heading);
            //make it the object of our animation
            this._anim.setEl(panel);
            //read current height
            var panelHeight = parseInt(
                    Dom.getStyle(panel,"height"),10);
            //if zero, it means it is already collapsed
            if (panelHeight !== 0) {
                //save the original height of this panel
                //as an attribute in the panel itself
                panel[PANEL_HEIGHT] = panelHeight;
                // collapse it
                this._anim.attributes = {height: {to:0}};
            } else {
```

```
                //expand it to the original height
                this._anim.attributes = {height:
                                    {to: panel[PANEL_HEIGHT]}};
            }
            // do animate it
            this._anim.animate();
        }
        // execute the event listener in the scope
        // of this object
      }, this, true);
    };
  })();
</script>
```

We've seen two kinds of sandboxes, the one we usually create in response to the DOM becoming ready and the one we use for creating library components, which do not depend on the state of the page, as we used back in *Chapter 3*. The latter is what we are using here, as this is going to be part of our toolbox.

Within it, after the usual shortcuts, we create a series of constants which are so just in name (all uppercase) because they are nothing more than regular variables. Writing these constants has several advantages:

- Should any of these strings need to be changed, it is done in only one place.
- If, in repeating the literal string, there is a typo, there is no tool that can help us find out while if we mistype the name of the constant, a tool such as JSLint, will signal it.
- A tool such as the YUI Compressor will be able to do a better job as non-global variable names can be compressed to one or two letter names while string literals cannot be compressed at all.

These tools are covered in the last chapter.

To make the component accessible from outside its own sandbox, a must for a library component, we use method .namespace() to create our branch under YAHOO. What happens if this component is included in a file along the other we built in *Chapter 3*? They both create the same yuibook branch under YAHOO, is there any conflict? In fact, .namespace() creates the given namespace if it doesn't already exist, it won't delete any existing branch.

Our library component will only have a single class, YAHOO.yuibook.Accordion so we don't need to create a whole subbranch to locate several classes in. This constructor will receive a reference to the container to be turned into an Accordion and an optional configuration object which may container any of the following options:

- header: The actual tag to be used to identify the heading of each Accordion fold. It defaults to h1

- duration: The time, in seconds, the folding should take, it defaults to half a second.

- easing: A reference to any of the methods in YAHOO.util.Easing, it defaults to .easeNone()

Within the constructor we normalize the arguments. Using DOM's .get() allows container to be either an actual DOM reference or a string with the id of an existing element. The expression config = config || {} ensures that config defaults to an empty object if no value was passed as an argument. We do this because later on we will assume config is always an object, even if it might be an empty one.

We set the value for our ._h1 property that will identify the tag name used for a header. We take either the value of config.header, if not undefined, or the default h1 and we make sure it is uppercase. If config was not an object, even an empty one, the expression config.header would fail, that is why we normalized it first.

We then add a couple of class names to the existing elements and for both we use the constants defined previously. The ACCORDION class name (actually, the value of that constant) is given to the overall container, which serves as the key to the CSS styles which we'll see later. The other, EXPANDED, is applied to all the headers because, naturally, they are expected to be expanded, as there was nothing there to collapse them. Method .addClass() is capable of applying the same style to an array of elements, as the one .getElementsByTagName() is bound to return.

Next, we create the instance of the Anim object that will do the animations and set its duration and method (easing) properties using either the values of the config object or our defaults.

Now we set the listener for the click on the header. As it is a library component, we don't even know how many headers there might be so we do it in the most generic way, by Event Delegation (see *Chapter 3*). We capture the `click` event when the browser bubbles it up to the container of all those headers. We then read the target of the click, assuming it might have been a header and then actually check that it was so. As we will use the `this` keyword within the listener to refer to this very object, we need to adjust the scope of the listener thus, after we define the listener function, we add `this`, `true` as the fourth and fifth arguments to do the scope correction. We could have used Event's `.delegate()` method, but that would have required us to load a couple of extra dependencies, a cost hardly justified in this case.

The `panel` to be folded is whatever follows that heading. We use method `.getNextSibling()` because regular property `.nextSibling` is unreliable. In this example, it would return the line break in between the header and the `panel` that is going to be the element to be animated and we set by using `.setEl()`.

We read the `panelHeight` of that panel to learn if it is collapsed or not. We use `parseInt()`, to discard the `px` suffix. An often forgotten argument of `parseInt()` is the second, `base`, argument. If not explicitly told, `parseInt()` guesses and if the string to be parsed starts with `0` it assumes it is octal, something that is not amusing when parsing, for example, month numbers because `08` for August will return 0 as 8 is not a valid octal character and `parseInt()` will stop at the first non-digit in whichever base it assumes the number might be, if not explicitly told.

If `panelHeight` is anything but zero, the panel is expanded. We need to save its current height to restore it whenever it needs to be expanded again. We store it in the `panel` DOM element itself as we are free to add extra attributes to it. To do so, we simply do `panel[PANEL_HEIGHT]` = `panelHeight`. We then set the animation attributes to animate the `height` attribute down to `0`.

To expand the `panel`, we set the animation attributes to animate the `height` attribute to whatever value was stored in the `PANEL_HEIGHT` attribute of `panel`. In either case, we finally call the `.animate()` method to make it happen.

Basically, this is all that is required to fold and unfold the different Accordion panels when their corresponding heading is clicked.

Listening to the end of the Animation

When adding the arrows, it didn't look good that the arrows toggled in between expanded and collapsed immediately while the folding took half a second. It really looks more natural if the toggling happens when the animation is finished. Thus, we set a listener for the `onComplete` event of the `Anim` object. We should place this code immediately after the previous event listener.

```
// when the animation completes
this._anim.onComplete.subscribe(function () {
    //this now points to the animation object instance
    var panel = this.getEl();
    var heading = Dom.getPreviousSibling(panel);
    //toggle the expanded/collapsed className
    if (Dom.hasClass(heading, COLLAPSED)) {
        Dom.replaceClass(heading, COLLAPSED, EXPANDED);
    } else {
        Dom.replaceClass(heading, EXPANDED, COLLAPSED);
    }
});
```

The animation object, stored in `this._anim` signals the `onComplete` event by calling the given function. Within it, `this` will refer to the animation object, not to our Accordion object which, fortunately, is all we'll need. We always need to be careful on what `this` might be pointing to; it is easy to make wrong assumptions. Unless overridden via the optional extra arguments in the `.subscribe()` method, `this` always points to the object firing the event, in this case the Animation instance, not the Accordion object that contains it.

Within the listener we read the `panel`, which was the element that had just been animated and from it we pick the heading, which should be the element right before it. If that heading has class `COLLAPSED` we replace it with `EXPANDED` and vice versa.

The CSS for Accordion

One of the differences between the first image corresponding to a non-JavaScript enabled page and the second one was the change in the cursor when floating above the heading and the arrows on the left. The cursor gives our visitor a hint that the element below will respond if clicked. It would be misleading to show such cursor when nothing would happen.

This is done with this segment of CSS, which should be included in our example along the previous though in an actual deployment, it would be contained in a `.css` file with the same name as the component it belongs to. Just as there is a `calendar.css` for `calendar-min.js`, as we used in *Chapter 1*, we would have an `accordion.css` to our `accordion.js`. In this example we will also include it right in the same page along previous CSS:

```css
.yuibookAccordion h1 {
    cursor:pointer;
}
.yuibookAccordion div {
    overflow:hidden;
```

```
}
.yuibookAccordion h1.yuibookExpanded {
    background:
        url(yui/build/assets/skins/sam/menu-button-arrow.png)
        5px center no-repeat;
}
.yuibookAccordion h1.yuibookCollapsed {
    background:
        url(yui/build/assets/skins/sam/menuitem_submenuindicator.png)
        5px center no-repeat;
}
```

In contrast to JavaScript files, CSS files become active whenever they are loaded, the browser cannot tell that `accordion.js` (which it will ignore if JavaScript is not active) is associated with `accordion.css` that will always be processed.

We have to make sure the effects of the CSS file kick in only if JavaScript is active. We do that by adding the `ACCORDION` class name to the container for it and we use it as the first selector to the styles above. If the page had not been "accordionized", these styles would have never been applied.

In them we change the cursor over the header, we add `overflow:hidden` so the contents of the panel are cropped as it is being collapsed and we add the two arrow icons. We use two icons from the YUI library, which we set as a non-repeating background image, which spares us from creating and handling an `<img>` element along the header.

Just as nothing in the code was tied to the HTML code, the CSS related to the Accordion is unrelated to the overall presentation of the page; the look of the page, whether enhanced with JavaScript or not is the same and is no business for our library code. If we wanted to provide some coherent style for all our accordions, we would do that in a separate skin file, in fact, the two styles setting the small arrows should be part of the skin, not of the core, as they are not essential—though they are supported—by our code.

Using Element

The Accordion control, as presented, is very basic and, for the purpose of this chapter, we wanted to concentrate on using the `Anim` object. Should we want to add more functionality, it would soon become obvious that this is not the way to go. If we wanted to add events or even more attributes, it would soon become unwieldy and we would regret not having used `YAHOO.util.Element` all along.

It is easy to get by without `Element` for something as simple as this, only one constructor is defined and there are no public properties or methods, but in a real case, do use `Element` and, as an exercise, I would like to encourage you to convert this to a subclass of `Element`.

Dealing with motion

We'll have a little fun this time. Using our standard template with `yahoo-dom-events.js` and `animation-min.js`, we'll just add a single HTML element:

```
<div id="box"></div>
```

We will make a square of it by adding some CSS styles in the `<head>`:

```
<style type="text/css">
   #box {
     width: 100px;
     height: 100px;
     background-color: pink;
     border: thin solid gray;
   }
</style>
```

We'll make it a pink square a hundred pixels on each side and with a thin gray border. Before the final `</body>` tag, we will add:

```
<script type="text/javascript">
    YAHOO.util.Event.onDOMReady(function() {
        YAHOO.util.Event.on("box", "mouseover", function() {

            //define and run the animation
            var anim = new YAHOO.util.Motion(this, {
                points: {
                    by: [10, 10],
                    control:[[600, 150],[300,300]]
                }
            });
            anim.animate();
        });
    });
</script>
```

As usual, in response to the DOM becoming ready, we create the sandbox where we set an event listener on the pink box to check when the mouse is over it. When that happens, we create an animation to animate this, which within the event listener for the element "box" will point to it, and providing the animation attributes as the second argument and we then run that animation.

The box will respond to our placing the cursor on the box. As we created an instance of Motion, it will move from the original position 10px down and to the right, but not in a straight line. For that I could have used a more formal blue box. Besides the by property, the animation attributes also have some control points. Motion will draw a Bezier curve from the current location, using those two control points and ending 10 points down and to the right of the starting location, and make the box follow it. Whenever we place the cursor over it, even while moving, it will escape going around a curved path.

We will not discuss what the control points are because that would force us to explain what a Bezier curve is, which is done better elsewhere, including Wikipedia which has some good animations of the process or drawing such a curve.

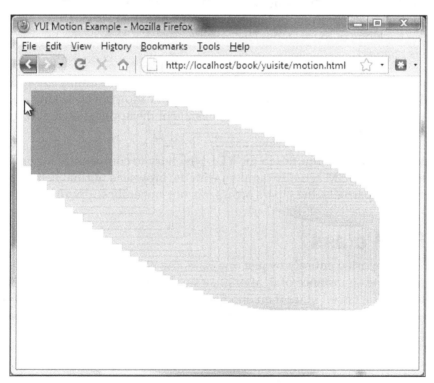

The previous image corresponds to this program with a shadow added by listening to the onTween event. It clearly shows the curved path taken by the box. The initial position was that of the top-left shadow, the final position 10px offset from it. The downloadable set of examples contains this version, which, as it added nothing to the subject of this chapter, won't be commented here

Restoring the browser's expected functionality

The BHM Utility allows you to register different steps in the interactions that mark changes in your application's state. Viewing different months of the Calendar control, for example, marks a change in state, and you may have noticed when we looked at this control earlier in the book that the back button of the browser remained grayed out and unavailable to us no matter how many different months were viewed.

Once a step has occurred that is defined within the BHM as a change in state, the back button of the browser becomes available and when clicked, takes the application back one of these steps. The expected functionality of the browser's interface is restored.

As well as defining different changes in state that may occur within your application, the BHM utility also tackles the problem of web application bookmarking. A simple method can be called that retrieves the initial state of the application according to the state that it was bookmarked in.

In contrast with the other utilities in the YUI, which try to compensate for browser's inconsistencies, the BHM actually tampers with the browser's normal behavior and succeeds so only partially, the Opera browser is not currently supported by the BHM.

The BHM class

The BHM is supported entirely by just one class, the YAHOO.util.History class. You cannot create an instance of it, after all, a single page cannot have more than one history so you don't need more than one BHM to manage it. The members of this class number surprisingly few and consist of eight methods, all static, and a single custom event. The methods available include:

- .getBookmarkedState() — used to get the state of the application as stored in the bookmark URL fragment identifier
- .getCurrentState() — gets the current state of your application

- `.getQueryStringParameter()` — returns the specified parameter from the query string
- `.initialize()` — initializes the BHM
- `.navigate()` — used to store application states
- `.onReady()` — the preferred method of detecting when the BHM is ready to be used
- `.register()` — registers an application with the BHM

The custom event defined by the `History` class is the `onLoadEvent` that fires when the BHM has finished loading, however you must subscribe to this event before calling the `.initialize()` method so Yahoo! recommends that the `.onReady()` method be used instead.

Using BHM

Let's build a page that makes use of the BHM Utility to record state information about one of the controls that we looked at earlier in the book — the Calendar control. We will keep track of the calendar pages (month/year) the user visits.

Begin with the following initial HTML:

```
<!DOCTYPE HTML PUBLIC "-//W3C//DTD HTML 4.01//EN"
                      "http://www.w3.org/TR/html4/strict.dtd">
<html lang="en">
  <head>
    <meta http-equiv="content-type"
                              content="text/html; charset=utf-8">
    <title>YUI Browser History Manager Utility Example</title>
    <script type="text/javascript"
        src="yui/build/yahoo-dom-event/yahoo-dom-event.js"></script>
    <script type="text/javascript"
                src="yui/build/calendar/calendar-min.js"></script>
    <script type="text/javascript"
                 src="yui/build/history/history-min.js"></script>
    <link rel="stylesheet" type="text/css"
          href="yui/build/calendar/assets/skins/sam/calendar.css">
    <style type="text/css">
        #yui-history-iframe {
            position:absolute;
            top:0;
            left:0;
            width:1px;
```

```
          height:1px;
          visibility:hidden;
        }
    </style>
  </head>
  <body class="yui-skin-sam">
    <iframe id="yui-history-iframe" src="yahoo.gif"></iframe>
    <input id="yui-history-field" type="hidden">
    <div id="mycal"></div>
  </body>
</html>
```

Save this file as `bhmCalendar.html` in the appropriate folder. There are several important changes to this code compared with the original Calendar example. We link to the `yahoo-dom-event.js` and `calendar-min.js` files as we did before and of course need the BHM source file `history-min.js`. The Calendar container element is still the `<div>` element with an `id` of `mycal`.

The other major change is the addition of an `<iframe>` and a hidden `<input>` field. The `<iframe>` is required for the sole purpose of making the BHM compatible with Internet Explorer. The hidden `<input>` element is used to record the initial state of the Calendar, as well as the current state. The `<iframe>` must be linked to a pre-existing file on your web server—an empty HTML file will do, or an image, as in this example, that is already being used in your site.

We don't have any text `<input>` or the calendar icon to worry about this time, but we still need to make sure the `<iframe>` doesn't interfere with the rest of the page content. That is the purpose of the brief segment of CSS style in the page.

The BHM script

We can now move on to add the initial JavaScript for this example. Directly after the Calendar container in the HTML file add the following `<script>` block:

```
<script type="text/javascript">
    YAHOO.util.Event.onDOMReady(function() {
        var BHM = YAHOO.util.History;
        var TITLE = "YUI Browser History Manager Utility Example - ";

        //get present date and define initial page for calendar
        var today = new Date();
        var defaultPage = (today.getMonth() + 1) + "/" +
                                            today.getFullYear();
        var bookmarkPage = BHM.getBookmarkedState("myCal");
        var initialPage = bookmarkPage || defaultPage;
```

```
var myCal;

//define the pageChanger callback
var pageChange = function(page) {

  //set calendar page and render calendar
  myCal.cfg.setProperty("pagedate", page);
  myCal.render();
  document.title = TITLE + page;
};

//register the calendar with BHM
BHM.register("myCal", initialPage, pageChange);

//define the beforeRender function
var beforeRender = function() {

    //get the current calendar date
    var calDate = myCal.cfg.getProperty("pagedate");
    var newPage = (calDate.getMonth() + 1) + "/" +
                                      calDate.getFullYear();

    //get the current page according to BHM
    var currentPage = BHM.getCurrentState("myCal");

    //is calendar date different from BHM date?
    if (newPage != currentPage) {

        //add a new page to BHM
        BHM.navigate("myCal", newPage);
    }
};

//create calendar when BHM is ready
BHM.onReady(function() {

    //create the calendar object
    myCal = new YAHOO.widget.Calendar("myCal", "mycal", {
        navigator:true,
        pagedate: initialPage
    });

    //configure the calendar to begin on Monday
    myCal.cfg.setProperty("start_weekday", "1");
```

```
        //subscribe to the beforeRenderEvent
        myCal.beforeRenderEvent.subscribe(beforeRender,
                                          myCal, true);
        myCal.render();
        document.title = TITLE + initialPage;
    });


    //initialise BHM
    BHM.initialize("yui-history-field", "yui-history-iframe");

  });
</script>
```

We will try to preserve the different months of the calendar the user visits. The state the BHM is to preserve what in the Calendar is called the page-date.

As before, the code is in a sandbox that is created when Event signals that the DOM is ready. We create a single shortcut, BHM, and a constant for the page title.

The first we do is retrieve the current date and process it so that it appears in the format MM/YYYY. This is then stored in the `defaultPage` variable and is used, as I'm sure you can guess, as the default page-date of the Calendar control. However, we might have arrived at this page navigating via the BHM thus, the page we are meant to show might not be this but the one BHM tells us to.

We read the bookmarked state from the BHM into `bookmarkPage`. This is the one BHM has preserved in the history. If we arrive at this page for the first time, it will be `null`. We then calculate `initialPage` that will be `bookmarkPage`, if not null, or `defaultPage`.

The Calendar object variable is also declared here so that it can be passed between functions (although the Calendar control is not actually initialized at this stage).

Next we define the `pageChange` callback function, which is called every time the BHM detects that our Calendar has changed page. This may happen when we interact with the Calendar by navigating through month panels, or it may occur when the back or forward button of the browser is used. Programmatically, there is no difference between the two.

As we are responsible for updating the Calendar following a change in state, the `pageChange()` function sets the page date according to the new page that it receives as an argument and re-renders the Calendar and also updates the title of the document so that it will be shown in the **History** dropdown in the browser's toolbar.

We register our Calendar with the BHM using the `.register()` method; this involves supplying a unique identifier as the first argument (we'll use the same as the `id` of the calendar), the default state of the object, in this case, the `initialPage` of the Calendar as the second argument, and lastly the `pageChange` callback function as the third argument. The default state is one of the items stored in the hidden `<input>` field.

Next we define the `beforeRender()` function. This function is executed prior to every render of the Calendar, which occurs on the initial page load, or on any change of page so it is a good place to detect the change of state. First the `beforeRender()` function gets the current date from the calendar and processes it so that it appears in the `MM/YYYY` format. The result is then saved in the `newPage` variable.

The current page according to the BHM is then obtained using the `.getCurrentState()` method and stored in the `currentPage` variable. The `newPage` and `currentPage` variables are then compared. If they are found to be different, the BHM knows that the state of the Calendar has changed and can add the `newPage` variable as the next step in the BHM using the `.navigate()` method. Perhaps, the name of this method should be `.bookmark()` because that is what it does. It doesn't do any navigating, it is the complement to `.getBookmarkedState()`, when you get to a new state, you `.bookmark()` it, when you want to retrieve where you are, you get your previously bookmarked state.

If the `.navigate()` method is called, the `pageChange()` function will be executed once more, which will in turn trigger the `beforeRender()` function again. The `if` statement here is really important as it prevents this perpetual loop of our functions.

We finally listen to the BHM's `.onReady()` method to actually create the Calendar control, which enables us to ensure that the Calendar is not created before the BHM is ready to work. The BHM runs asynchronously and needs a little time to start up before we start calling its methods related to recording the history. The `initialPage` variable is used to display the present date, and the `beforeRenderMethod` is subscribed to.

The final step is to initialize the BHM. This is done using the `.initialize()` method, which takes references to the hidden `<input>` and the hidden `<iframe>` elements as its two arguments.

If you now run the application and navigate to a new month on the Calendar, you should see that the back button of the browser becomes available, and that a fragment identifier is appended to the URL in the browser's address bar. This is the mechanism by which the BHM is able to recall the history of the various states the Calendar has passed through. The following screenshot illustrates both the enabled back button, the title bar showing the current page-date, and in the address toolbar, the URL fragment identifier:

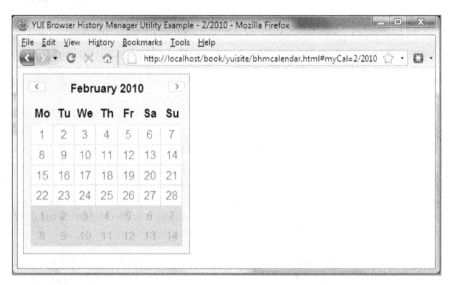

The BHM is not limited to keeping track of the state changes of only one element at a time, you can register any number of elements you want to keep track of by calling `.register()` for each. The ID provided to `.register()`, and used in all other functions, can be any unique string. Using the `id` of an HTML element is a good idea because they should be unique, but any string would do. The elements tracked need not be actual HTML elements. The string provided for each call to `.register()` is a handle, to be used to record state changes (`.navigate()`) or retrieve current or bookmarked states (`.getXxxxxState()`).

The BHM uses the page fragment part of the URL (the part after the #) to store its information. For each element registered there will be an entry with the registered name and the value. Browsers have internal limits on the length of the URLs they accept. Care must be taken when registering several elements or when storing too much information, not to exceed those limits, which change from browser to browser, along versions and are not standardized. The value representing the state is URL-encoded.

Cookies

Cookies have become a fact of life on the Internet, every time we run an antivirus it will warn us about dozens of them used to track where we've been and what we've seen. Cookies, however, have very legitimate uses: when a visitor comes back, it is handy to have him/her remembered, return to where he/she left (something the BHM can help with) and restore his/her preferences.

The Cookies Utility has only one class, `YAHOO.util.Cookie` that cannot be instantiated because, just as with the BHM, as there is only one set of cookies in the browser, it can only have one manager. It has a few methods and no properties or events. The methods are:

- `.exists()`: Tells if a cookie exists
- `.get()`: Reads the value of a cookie
- `.getSub()`: Reads the value of a specific subcookie of a cookie
- `.getSubs()`: Reads the value of all subcookies of a cookie
- `.remove()`: Removes a cookie
- `.removeSub()`: Removes a subcookie
- `.set()`: Sets the value of a cookie
- `.setSub()`: Sets the value of a subcookie
- `.setSubs()`: Sets the value of several subcookies

A cookie doesn't need to be created before being set. Any of the set methods will create one. Browsers impose limits on the number of cookies that can be created per domain, but not on the amount of data a single cookie can carry so a single cookie is often split into sub-cookies. While `.setSub()` will preserve the value of other existing subcookies, `.setSubs()` rewrites all the set of subcookies, deleting any existing subcookie.

All setters take an optional configuration object as the last argument. It can have any of the following options:

- `.domain`: The domain where the cookie can be accessed
- `.path`: The path where the cookie can be accessed
- `.expires`: Tells when the cookie will no longer be valid
- `.raw`: If `true`, prevents URL encoding of the value
- `.secure`: If true, the cookie will only be accessible to `https://` pages

The meaning of these options are as per the corresponding standard (RFC 2965), the YUI simply provides an easy interface to them.

To create/set a cookie you can do:

```
YAHOO.util.Cookie.set("user",userName);
```

To restrict that cookie to a site such as `https://myHost.myDomain.com`, you can do:

```
YAHOO.util.Cookie.set("user",username, {
    domain: "myHost.mydomain.com",
    secure: true
});
```

To set a series of values as subcookies with an expiration date:

```
YAHOO.util.Cookie.setSubs("userInfo",
    {
        user: username,
        lastVisit: new Date(),
        colorScheme: userSkin
    }, {
        expires: new Date("January 13, 2011")
    }
);
```

To read the cookies, you use the get methods:

```
alert(YAHOO.util.Cookie.get("user"));
alert(YAHOO.util.Cookie.getSub("userInfo", "lastVisit",
    function(value) {
        return new Date(value);
    }
);
```

Methods `.get()` and `.getSub()` accepts a final optional argument which is a reference to a converter function. As all cookies are stored as strings, dates, numbers, or Booleans, they might need converting back to their native values. When you use `.getSubs()` you get a hash with all the subcookies at once, and it is up to you to parse them individually as there is no way to specify one parser per item returned, as you wouldn't know what they might be. If the cookie requested does not exist, these methods will return `null`.

The use of the Cookie Utility is quite simple. The only tricks you have to remember are, when removing a cookie or subcookie, you have to provide exactly the same options given when created and that `.setSubs()` will wipe out any previously set subcookies.

Summary

The Animation Utility makes it easy to add a variety of animations covering movement, changes in size, and even changes in color. It's a very easy utility to use and is limited only by your imagination.

The BHM utility is extremely powerful, despite its relatively small supporting class. It gives you the power to define discrete steps or changes in the state of your applications in which the back and forward button functionality is restored. It also allows your visitors to bookmark your application in a particular state and when they return to your application, the state is set so that it resembled their last visit.

The Cookies Utility lets you manage the browser's cookies in a very simple and flexible way so as to preserve bits of information across sessions.

6

Content Containers and Tabs

Content can live in all kinds of containers, usually `<div>` elements, `<p>` elements, and the like. When using the YUI, you have a whole range of new containers in which to keep your content, each of which is designed to meet the needs of a specific implementation. In this chapter we'll be looking at all of them in detail.

A tabbed interface allows you to fit more content together on the same page without cluttering it up, distributing related items across different tabs. Doing this manually can lead to design nightmares, so the TabView control from the YUI Library can really help you to cut corners code-wise without sacrificing presentational style or functionality.

While the Container and TabView controls are completely separate, tabs can still be looked upon as Content Containers, which is why these two controls have been included together in this chapter.

Skills that you will take away from this chapter include:

- The primary purpose of each of the different types of container
- How to implement each container
- Skinning the different containers
- Adding transition animations to applicable containers
- The different methods of adding tabbed content
- Adding content to tabs dynamically

Meet the YUI Container family

The Container control is not in itself a control, but rather a family of container-like controls that can add visual appeal and enhancements to any web page or application. The Container family has been created in order to allow you to easily create different types of content containers, which each serve a specific purpose.

The Container family is split up into six different individual containers, which are:

- Module
- Overlay
- Panel
- Dialog
- SimpleDialog
- Tooltip

You will rarely use the first two directly; they are the basis from which all the others inherit. They are also the basis for other controls such as Menu and all those that use Menu such as Button and the Rich Text Editor, which we'll see later. There is a small include file `container_core-min.js` that contains these first two and we will have to include it when required by those other components that depend on it; as usual, the Dependency Configurator will let us know. If we do need an actual useful container in our application, that is, any of the last four controls in the list, we need to include the full `container-min.js` file in order to function.

The following figure shows a visual representation of the structure of the Container family; the arrows indicate the direction of inheritance:

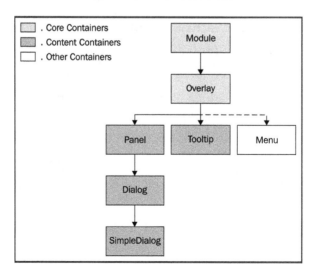

Let's now look at each member of the Container family in greater detail.

Module

Module is the fundamental unit and base class of all the Container classes, and is the foundation from which all of the other containers are derived. Modules can be defined either in your HTML markup or exclusively through JavaScript. They enable us to create a JavaScript object representation of any HTML container defined using **Standard Module Format (SMF)**.

SMF, a Yahoo! standard for defining blocks of HTML content, consists of a container <div> element and three child <div> elements, which correspond to the header, body, and footer of the module. Many components of the library use SMF as well as almost any window in our desktop such as the browser itself, which has a title bar (header) and a status bar (footer) around the content (body).

The YAHOO.widget.Module constructor, used to create the most basic type of container, is very simple and takes just two arguments. If we are doing **Progressive Enhancement** (PE) and reading existing markup, the first argument will be either a reference to a container with the HTML we want to enhance or the id of this container. If we are creating the Module via JavaScript, then it should be a string, which will become the id of the container when it is finally rendered; as we hardly ever care about this value, we would usually call Dom's .generateId() to produce a unique id. The second argument is an optional configuration object used to set different options of the module. We will never use Module directly, but all its subclasses use this same pattern.

The configuration object can take several attributes, but most of them are used by its subclasses and we don't normally care about them, the exception being:

- visible, a Boolean indicating whether the Module's display CSS attribute is set to block or none.

Each subclass adds to this list of configuration attributes and they are all handled in the same way.

Once the Module instance is created, configuration attributes can be changed by accessing the .cfg property and using its methods:

- .cfg.getProperty(): Returns the value of a configuration attribute
- .cfg.setProperty(): Sets the value of a configuration attribute
- .cfg.resetProperty(): Restores the default value
- .cfg.queueProperty() and .cfg.fireQueue(): Allow queuing a batch of configuration attributes and having them applied all at once

The Container family of components is an old-style component, it does not use Element, which provide the far simpler `.get()` and `.set()` methods. At the point when it was devised, the vocabulary used to describe the library was not fully developed, thus we have `.setProperty()` to set a configuration **attribute**, formerly a configuration **property**. The latter expression was dropped to avoid the confusion with native JavaScript object properties, but the names of the methods retained the "property" part for backward compatibility.

Out of the many properties and methods, which all of Module's subclasses inherit, we'll mention just the few that we might use, as most are meant to be used internally by its subclasses. Each control based on Module adds its own to this list, which we'll see as we progress:

- `.header`, `.body`, and `.footer`: Reference to the DOM elements that make each of the three sections of the SMF. They might be `null` if the original markup didn't have the corresponding section or if not using markup at all.

- `.element`: Reference to the overall container.

- `.id`: The ID of the overall container.

- `.setHeader()`, `.setBody()`, and `.setFooter()`: These can receive either a string containing HTML markup or a DOM reference and will create and fill the content of each section. Use these in preference to directly handling the properties pointing to the SMF sections.

- `.appendToHeader()`, `.appendToBody()`, and `.appendToFooter()`: In contrast with the previous methods, these will not create the section if it doesn't exist and they only take a DOM reference, not a string.

- `.show()` and `.hide()`: These have the same effect as changing the `visible` configuration attribute.

- `.render()`: Once configured, this will render the Module.

- `.destroy()`: Deletes and releases all resources taken by the component.

Method `.render()` has an optional argument (two actually, but we don't care about the second), which is a reference to where we want the Module rendered. If we are building the Module via JavaScript then we need to specify where we want it rendered and this argument becomes mandatory. If we are building the Module from markup, we don't need to provide it as it is already in the page.

Lets recap the very minimum we need to do to create a Module or, for that matter, all members of the Container family. If we do it from existing markup, we create the instance providing the `id` or a reference to the existing markup and any configuration attributes we might want to set and then call `.render()` with no arguments.

If we create the component from JavaScript we create the instance providing a unique string for an `id`, possibly using Dom's `.generateId()`, and any configuration attributes we care about. We use any or all of the `.setXxxx()` methods to fill in the three sections and finally we call `.render()` with a reference to where we want it. Most Containers we actually create will float over the page so their actual location is irrelevant; therefore, this object is usually `document.body`.

If we had set `visible` to `false`, we might later call `.show()` to turn it visible. We can also call the `.setXxxx()` methods at any time after rendering to set or change the contents of each of the sections, preferably while it is not visible.

Out of the many events Module offers, we'll just mention `showEvent`, which is the one used most often when loading content dynamically:

```
myModule.showEvent.subscribe(function(type, oArgs) {
    myModule.setBody("whatever");
});
```

The content, being dynamic, would hardly be a literal string, but the principle still holds; right before actually being shown, the Module gets its content from wherever appropriate.

Overlay

An Overlay is a Module that floats over the page. It has many more properties and methods that give us very fine control over its positioning but, for general use, a few configuration attributes are all that we need:

- `constrainviewport`: If this is set, the Overlay will remain in view when the user scrolls.

- `context`: An array of arguments used to anchor a specific corner of an Overlay to a specific corner of the anchor element.

- `fixedcenter`: Originally a Boolean, if `true` it anchors the Overlay to the center of the viewport. If the container is too tall for the viewport, keeping it centered would always leave the header and footer out of the screen so a further setting was added; now it can also have the value of `contained` that acts almost the same as `true` but will not try to center the container if it doesn't fit in the browser's viewport.

- `height` and `width`: The dimensions of the Overlay.

- `autofillheight`: If a `height` is provided and the content of the three sections don't add up to it, this property can be set to `header`, `body`, or `footer` to tell Overlay which section to stretch to reach the requested height.

- x and y: The absolute coordinates of the Overlay.
- xy: An array of the absolute X and Y positions of the Overlay.
- zindex: The CSS z-index of the Overlay.

The context attribute allows us to position the Overlay relative to any other element in the page. It is an array made of up to five parts, though we usually use the first three:

- contextElement: A reference to the element we want to position the Overlay relative to, or its id.
- containerCorner: Aligns the contextElement to whichever corner of the container we want; can be any of tr (top-right), tl (top-left), br (bottom-right), or bl (bottom-left).
- contextCorner: Aligns to whichever corner of the contextElement we want the containerCorner to align to.
- triggerEvents: (optional) Sometimes you change the size or position of the context element as a result of some Overlay event. This might leave the Overlay in the wrong position. This property may have an array of the names of the events we might want to force the position to be recalculated. It can be any of Overlay's own events, plus windowResize, windowScroll, or textResize.
- xyOffset: (optional) An array with [x,y] pixel values we want to offset the corners.

For example, if we want to pop an Overlay right below a button with an id of button1, we would provide the following context:

```
context: ["button1","tl","bl"]
```

Positioning is the big addition of Overlay over Module and is exploited in all its descendants. A very high degree of control can be achieved by manipulating its methods, but looking at them, it becomes obvious that the configuration options shown previously provide the same functionality in a more compact manner.

Panel

The YAHOO.widget.Panel class extends the Overlay class, and allows you to create a floating container, which acts very much like an operating system window, allowing your visitors to drag it around or close it at will. It also adds support for modality to the Overlay.

Unlike the previous two containers that we have looked at so far, the Panel is meant to be used directly, not as the basis for another component, so it comes with pre-defined styling that is controlled by the sam skin and creates a default appearance for Panel elements.

An excellent feature of the Panel is its modal capabilities. When the modal attribute is set, the user cannot interact with anything else in the page but the modal Panel itself.

Most of the functionality is provided by its base class so we will only focus on the few configuration attributes that provide added functionality to the Panel Container; they include:

- close: A Boolean indicating whether a close button should be displayed on the Panel, true by default.

- draggable: Another Boolean, indicating whether the Panel should be draggable. It defaults to true, but requires the Drag & Drop utility to work.

- keylisteners: This attribute makes use of the YAHOO.util.KeyListener class, part of the Event Utility, to specify a keypress or array of keypresses for which the Panel should listen and the functions to execute when a key is pressed. This allows, for example, listening to the *Esc* key to hide the panel when it is pressed.

- modal: This Boolean dictates whether the Panel should be modal or not. Panel will cover the whole window with a semitransparent mask right behind the Panel that prevents any user interaction from reaching the application behind.

- underlay: A string that sets the type of underlay to use for the panel. Your options are shadow, matte, or none, with shadow being the default.

Tooltip

The Tooltip Container is a highly specialized control that generates a Tooltip object that is displayed when the visitor mouses-over a specified element on the page, just like a standard browser tooltip. Like the Panel, the Tooltip class extends the Overlay class, inheriting many of its members, while also adding a few more of its own.

This container is designed to be very easy to implement and configure and therefore, requires a minimal amount of code. The YAHOO.widget.Tooltip() constructor is required of course, but like the other Container elements, it's very simple to use and takes just two arguments. It hardly makes any sense to build a ToolTip from existing markup so the first argument is usually a unique string, which can be obtained from DOM's .generateId() method. The second argument, the configuration object, has many options, most of which deal with timing issues, such as how long to wait before showing the Tooltip, and have already suitable defaults. The most relevant ones are:

- text: A string representing the text displayed in the Tooltip
- context: A string or element reference specifying the element or elements that the Tooltip should be anchored to

The text attribute name is somewhat misleading; actually, it can be any HTML markup that sets Tooltip apart from the native browser tooltip provided by the title attribute, which accepts only plain text. A YUI Tooltip can have images, formatting, tables, and what not.

The context attribute can be either a reference to a single element or an array of such elements. The Tooltip will pop up when the cursor hovers over any of the elements in the list, just like the normal browser tooltip. If no text attribute is given, Tooltip can read the title attribute of the context elements and show it as the native browser tooltip would.

One exceptional thing about Tooltip in relation to the rest of the Container family is that you never call .render(). Tooltip will render and show on its own when the cursor stays long enough over the context element(s).

The text can also be set on the fly. We have already mentioned the showEvent event for this same purpose when we looked at Module. The same thing can be done for ToolTips:

```
myToolTip.contextTriggerEvent.subscribe(function(type, oArgs) {
    var context = oArgs[0];
    this.cfg.setProperty("text", "Tooltip for " + context.id);
});
```

Here, we use the contextTriggerEvent, which is more useful than showEvent because it reports the actual element that is causing the Tooltip to show. This is very handy when context is given as an array of elements because it tells us which was the one causing it to pop up.

Tooltip adds listeners for mouseover, mousemove, and mouseout events automatically for each and every context element. DOM event listeners are costly in terms of memory and too many subscribers will also affect performance. It is not a good idea to have Tooltips on too many context elements. After all, if you don't need any of the fancy formatting features of a Tooltip, using the built-in tooltip facility of the browser, the title DOM attribute, might be wiser.

Dialog

The Dialog Control extends Panel, and the primary difference between the two is that the Dialog is meant to be used to submit data, much like an operating system prompt.

We will usually create a Dialog from existing markup, but this should not be considered straight Progressive Enhancement. Remember PE is meant to allow visitors with older browsers or without JavaScript enabled to still interact with our page. However, a form meant to pop up in a dialog box, to float over the page, seldom has any place to fit in the layout of a non-enhanced page.

We will use Dialog's ability to read existing markup, not to do PE but because it is easier to create the form and all its contents with our regular HTML design tools than doing it via script. We will use the regular SMF layout of three sections, header, body, and footer. We must place the whole of the form in the body section and leave the footer section empty for Dialog to place the buttons in. Our form should not contain submit or reset buttons, these will be provided by Dialog, as we shall see. We will usually place some text in the header as would be expected in any regular pop-up window.

Dialog also allows us to submit the data that it has collected from the visitor using one of three methods: the standard form submission method that relies on the action attribute of your HTML form, via **XMLHttpRequest** (**XHR**) using the Connection Manager Utility (that also uses the action attribute), or leaving it up to us to handle as we see fit.

Dialog has a few important optional dependency files. If submitting via XHR, Connection Manager is required. Dialog will also use YUI Buttons if present, which also requires the matching CSS file; if not, it will still work but the buttons will look very dull. It will also benefit from having drag-and-drop included, as it allows our visitors to drag the Dialog around as would be expected from a floating window.

Besides all other configuration properties inherited from its inheritance chain, Dialog adds the following:

- postmethod: Can be any of async, form, or manual. The default is async, which will do automatic submission via XHR. form will do a normal Web 1.0 submission and manual will expect us to handle it.

- postdata: Allows us to add extra information to the XHR POST.

- hideaftersubmit: Usually true, hides the form once it has submitted its data.

- buttons: An array of buttons to add to the form.

The buttons attribute will usually contain submit and cancel buttons that can be defined as follows:

```
buttons: [
    {text:"Ok", handler: function() { this.submit();},
                                    isDefault:true},
    {text:"Cancel", handler: function() { this.cancel();}}
]
```

This will produce a couple of buttons with labels **Ok** and **Cancel**, the first being the default button that will submit the form and the second that will simply hide (.cancel()) the Dialog. Both handlers are executed in the scope of the Dialog instance, which allows us to use this.

To find out what happens with our submission, we have to set the .callback property as we would do for Connection Manager's .asyncRequest(). Our .callback property can have .success, .failure, .upload, and .argument properties. We cannot set the scope for our callback as Dialog will set it to point to itself.

Before submitting, we can validate the information. Dialog has a dummy .validate() method defined that simply returns true. We can override it with a function of our own to check the fields before submitting. Method .getData() is handy to fetch the values of what the Dialog would submit. Once we check the fields, returning true will let it go ahead while false will cancel the submission. We can also use the .form property to validate the fields or signal the errors to our visitor.

We can also listen to the event beforeSubmitEvent that will fire after .validate(), if it returns true. Returning false from the listener will also cancel the submission.

We've seen methods `.submit()` and `.cancel()` in the brief sample earlier. There is also `.doSubmit()`, which is the one finally doing the submissions after the form has been validated and the corresponding events have been fired. It is better not to use it to avoid bypassing all those previous steps.

To do a manual submission, we would listen to `manualSubmitEvent` and take over from there. We could also hook our manual submission function as a handler for the buttons, but the `.validate()` function would never be called, the events would not be fired, nor would the form automatically hide.

SimpleDialog

The `YAHOO.widget.SimpleDialog` class extends the Dialog class and forms the last link in the subclass chain. It is designed to be used in circumstances where input is required from the visitor, but only in the form of a single answer, such as a simple **yes** or **no**. It is a replacement for the browser's native `window.confirm()` or `window.prompt()` methods.

The main highlights of the class definition are once again the configuration attributes specific to this control. In addition to those inherited, it also defines:

- `icon`: A string that defines the icon to be used in the SimpleDialog, which can be one of six constant properties `ICON_ALARM`, `ICON_BLOCK`, `ICON_HELP`, `ICON_INFO`, `ICON_TIP`, or `ICON_WARN` (they are static constants so they need to be specified with their full names, such as: `YAHOO.widget.SimpleDialog.ICON_HELP`)
- `text`: The text displayed in the SimpleDialog

As with the standard Dialog control, SimpleDialog allows us to create a `button` array of objects whose members represent the buttons we would like to have displayed on the SimpleDialog. When used as a replacement for `window.confirm()` it is usually the handlers for these buttons that are all we care about. We also need to set the `modal` configuration attribute to `true` to block the rest of the page as `window.confirm()` does.

If we want to prompt for a simple piece of data, property `.form` points to the `<form>` element that Dialog automatically creates and we can append an `<input>` element into it.

To set the heading, we need to use method `.setHeader()` as with any other member of the Container family.

The SimpleDialog is the last member of the Container family that represents a control visible to your visitors, but there are a couple of other relevant classes used by the Container family, which we will take a brief look at now.

Container Effects

All members of the Container family accept an `effect` configuration attribute, though it is useless in Module. It allows the container to fade and/or slide in and out.

The `YAHOO.widget.ContainerEffect` class manages these transition effects for us and interacts with the Animation Utility in order to generate them. We could build our own effects as subclasses of `ContainerEffect`, but usually we would use either or both of the two pre-packaged ones, `FADE` and `SLIDE`.

We can add the following configuration attribute to any of the Containers mentioned:

```
effect:[
    {effect:YAHOO.widget.ContainerEffect.FADE,duration:0.5},
    {effect:YAHOO.widget.ContainerEffect.SLIDE,duration:0.5}
]
```

If only one of them is specified, we don't need the square brackets. Attribute `duration` defaults to `1` second if not specified. The same effect will be applied when the Container shows and in reverse when it hides. All effects need the Animation Utility.

OverlayManager

The `YAHOO.widget.OverlayManager` class is used to manage the focus states of multiple Overlay instances or, more often, any of its descendants. An Overlay (or array of Overlays) is registered with the OverlayManager using the `.register()` method. The method returns `true` if the register operation was successful.

Once registered, the Overlay receives `focus` and `blur` methods and events, which allow us to easily change the currently focused Overlay or determine programmatically the currently focused Overlay, as well as detect when the focus changes.

Other methods that we may find beneficial when using the OverlayManager class include:

- `.blurAll()`: Removes the focus from all registered Overlays
- `.find()`: Looks for and returns the specified Overlay if it exists
- `.getActive()`: Returns the currently focused Overlay
- `.hideAll()`: Hides all registered Overlays
- `.remove()`: Removes the specified Overlay
- `.showAll()`: Shows all registered Overlays
- `.toString()`: Returns a string representing the OverlayManager

Two configuration attributes are available for use with the OverlayManager: the `focusevent` attribute, which specifies the DOM event used to focus an Overlay, and `overlays`, which is the collection of Overlays in use.

Creating a Panel

We'll work through examples of each of the out-of-the-box YUI containers that we have just looked at, so you can see exactly how easy they are to implement and work with. Creating custom containers is also possible, but won't be discussed in this book.

To showcase the ease with which Panel objects can be created, we will use our standard template and, besides the ever-present `yahoo-dom-events.js`, we will include `container-min.js` and its associated `container.css` from their corresponding locations as the Dependency Configurator will instruct us. We will also add `dragdrop-min.js` so we can drag the Panel around without any further coding on our part.

The page will contain a couple of image thumbnails and when clicking on them, a full sized version will pop up in a Panel. The actual example, `panel.html`, that is included in the examples download, has some more decoration, supported by an ancillary CSS file, which we won't analyze here; however, the style of the Panel itself is the one built-in for the `sam` skin and required no effort from us. The full example for our Panel will appear like this:

The left-most thumbnail has just been clicked and the full sized version has popped up on a floating panel. The panel that originally was centered within the browser window has been moved to the right to uncover its thumbnail and the dragging cursor can still be seen in the title bar of the panel. The relevant HTML for this example is:

```
<div id="thumbs" class="images">
  <a href="images/image1_full.jpg">
    <img class="thumb" src="images/image1_thumb.jpg"
                title="click for full-size view" alt="thumb1">
```

```
    </a>
    <a href="images/image2_full.jpg">
     <img class="thumb" src="images/image2_thumb.jpg"
                        title="click for full-size view" alt="thumb2">
    </a>
</div>
<div id="panel1" class="panel" style="visibility:hidden;">
   <div class="bd"><img id="fullImage" alt="full-size image"></div>
   <div class="ft">Copyright &copy; The Extremist 2008</div>
</div>
```

The first `<div>` contains the two thumbnails; each is enclosed in an anchor `<a>` element pointing to the full size image, thus, the page will work with or without JavaScript enabled. Without JavaScript enabled the visitor will simply navigate to the full sized image in a plain Web 1.0 style.

The second `<div>` is the markup for our Panel. Note that it lacks a header section, as at this point we have no contents for it. The whole `<div>` is made invisible by applying the style `visibility:hidden`. This is also done for non-JavaScript enabled users; the Panel, once instantiated will immediately be made invisible, but without JavaScript the whole thing will show up. If we don't plan to support non-JavaScript visitors we don't need to hide this nor do we need the anchors in the top `<div>`.

```
YAHOO.util.Event.onDOMReady(function() {
    var Dom = YAHOO.util.Dom, Event = YAHOO.util.Event;

    var panel1 = new YAHOO.widget.Panel("panel1", {
        close:true,
        visible:false,
        modal:true,
        fixedcenter:'contained'
    });

    panel1.render();

    Event.on("thumbs","click", function(ev) {
        var target = Event.getTarget(ev);
        if (target.tagName.toUpperCase() == "IMG") {
            Event.stopEvent(ev);
            var filename = target.src.replace("thumb","full");
            Dom.get("fullImage").src = filename;
            panel1.setHeader(filename);
            panel1.show();
        }
    });
});
```

Our script is quite simple. Once within the sandbox, we create an instance of Panel. We configure it so it has a close icon on to the right of the title bar, it is initially invisible, it is modal so nothing else can be done until it is dismissed, and make it pop up centered though, if the window is too small to hold it, the `contained` setting will allow our visitors to scroll down and see the rest of the image. We then render the panel.

Finally, we set a listener for a `click` on the container for the thumbnail images using event delegation as we've seen before. We first find out the actual target of the click and if it is indeed an image, we call `.stopEvent()` to prevent the default action of the anchor `<a>` element, which we've set just for our JavaScript-challenged visitors.

We find out the file name of the thumbnail from the `src` attribute of the `<img>` and recklessly produce the name of the full-sized image by changing the `thumb` part of the filename into `full`.

We use that filename as the `src` attribute for the `<img>` tag in the body of the panel and also use it as the header for it. We didn't have a header set in the markup of the panel but `.setHeader()` will create one for us. Finally, we show the panel.

Before we go on

Lest we forget, it is worth stressing some of the techniques we've been using so casually in our examples:

- Use the **Reset, Fonts**, and **Base** CSS Tools to ensure a consistent look in all pages.

- Use the **Grids** CSS Tool to help in producing the most standard page layouts, compatible with the ad industry standard banner sizes and display resolutions.

- Use the **Dependency Configurator** to ensure we have all the pieces we need. Remember to check for optional dependencies on each component Developer Guide page.

- Use aggregate and minified files for production.

- Set the `sam` skin class name on the body, unless you have your replacement for it.

- If possible, make your pages accessible to JavaScript-challenged visitors; the YUI supports Progressive Enhancement and it can often be used without much of a burden. Disable the JavaScript interpreter on the browser to test it.

- Place your code right before the end of the `<body>` section of your page so no time is wasted loading code that will not be executed until there is a page to work with. As a matter of fact, for the best performance in terms of what the visitor perceives, all included scripts files should actually go there while the included CSS files should be in the `<head>` section.

- Don't try to do anything on a page until it is ready. Use the Event Utility `.onDOMReady()` function to ensure that.

- Use a **sandbox** to keep all your variables and functions isolated from the Global Namespace but, if needed, don't hesitate to use `YAHOO.namespace()` to define your own branch under the `YAHOO` namespace to hold globally accessible properties or methods.

- Use **shortcuts** and **constants** for strings. This not only reduces our overall typing but also compresses better and makes typos easier to detect.

- Use **Event Delegation** whenever similar actions are to be performed on a range of similar elements. Always check the actual target of the event because it will also fire when clicking on the not-so-empty space in between targets; and never trust the tag name to be reported in uppercase as it should. YUI 2.8 now has a `.delegate()` method back-ported from YUI 3. This requires a couple of extra dependencies, which add several kilobytes of code. If the condition to check for a valid target is easy, it might not be worth the extra code.

- Be generous assigning IDs to HTML elements. Even if you don't assign one explicitly, internally the browser will, so you are not saving any memory by not doing so. Use Dom's `.get()` method to reach any element by ID.

Working with Dialogs

In this section we'll add an AJAX-enabled Dialog box that will let visitors rate either of the images. Using Dialog is very similar in many ways to using the Panel. The underlying markup for Dialog follows the same SMF, and the constructors are also very similar.

One of the benefits of Dialog over Panel is that you can send and receive data asynchronously between the Dialog and an application running on the server. This makes use of all of the AJAX facilities provided by the YUI with very little intervention from us.

We'll also write the PHP code that will carry out the rating request. Like the last time we looked at an AJAX application with the YUI, we need a full web server environment for this example to work correctly.

By the end of this section, we'll have something that looks like this:

We have added a series of buttons, one underneath each image to enable our visitors to rate each image. When pressing that button, a Dialog pops up that is perfectly aligned to the right edge of the image to rate.

This is the HTML we used for each of the thumbnail images:

```
<div class="image-block">
  <a href="images/image1_full.jpg">
   <img class="thumb" src="images/image1_thumb.jpg"
            title="click for full-size view" alt="thumb1">
  </a>
  <button class="rate-button">Rate It!</button>
</div>
```

We enclosed both the image and the button in a <div> and used some CSS styles to vertically align them inside. The button should have been enclosed in an anchor <a> element to support non-JavaScript enabled visitors with a suitable href full of URL arguments to direct the visitor to a separate ratings page, but we omitted this to keep it simple.

We have also added the markup for the rating dialog:

```
<div id="dialog" style="visibility:hidden;">
  <div class="hd">Please Rate This Image</div>
  <div class="bd">
   <form method="POST" action="ratings.php">
     <div class="radioContainer"><input type="radio" name="rating"
                                       value="Great">Great</div>
     <div class="radioContainer"><input type="radio" name="rating"
                                  value="Pretty Good">Pretty Good</div>
     <div class="radioContainer"><input type="radio" name="rating"
                                     value="Average">Average</div>
     <div class="radioContainer"><input type="radio" name="rating"
                                        value="Poor">Poor</div>
     <div class="radioContainer"><input type="radio" name="rating"
                                  value="Very Poor">Very Poor</div>
   </form>
  </div>
</div>
```

The rating form is fully contained within the body section of the SMF block. It has the `method` and `action` attributes set, which the dialog will read and use. This form would not work without JavaScript, lacking a **Submit** button but, anyway, it really has no place in the page layout so there is no point in even trying. The form simply has a set of radio buttons to provide the rating. The container is initially hidden so that JavaScript-challenged visitors won't see it. Dialog will later handle the visibility for those who have JavaScript enabled.

To the code in the Panel example, we have added:

```
var dialog = new YAHOO.widget.Dialog("dialog", {
    width:"200px",
    visible:false,
    draggable:false,
    modal:true,
    postmethod:"async",
    buttons: [
        {text:"Rate!", handler:function() {
                this.submit();
            }},
        {text:"Cancel", handler:function() {
            this.cancel();
        }}
    ],
    effect: {effect: YAHOO.widget.ContainerEffect.FADE, duration: 0.5}
```

```
   });

   dialog.render();

   dialog.callback.success = function(o) {
      alert(o.responseText);
   };
   dialog.callback.failure = function(o) {
      alert("Failure! " + o.status);
   };

   dialog.validate = function () {
      return this.getData().rating !== undefined;
   }

   Event.on("thumbs","click",function (ev) {
      var target = Event.getTarget(ev);
      if (Dom.hasClass(target,"rate-button")) {
         var img = Dom.getElementsByClassName("thumb", "img",
            Dom.getAncestorByClassName(target,"image-block")
         )[0];
         dialog.cfg.setProperty("postdata",
                     "image=" + encodeURIComponent(img.src));
         dialog.cfg.setProperty("context",[img,"tl","tr"]);
         dialog.show();
      }
   });
```

We create the Dialog instance referring to the id of our HTML markup and providing a series of configuration attributes: we set the width, ensure it is invisible and not draggable because we want it to pop up aligned to the image and to keep it there. We set it modal, confirm we will use XHR to post it and set a couple of buttons with their handlers, one making the form submit, the other simply closing it. We have also added a FADE effect, for no particular reason.

Now we go to the real business of what to do with the reply from the server once the form is submitted. Both for the success and failure callbacks we show an alert box with either the reply from the server or an error message. We also add a validator function by overriding the built in .validate() method. In it, we simply read the data that is about to be submitted using .getData() and make sure the .rating property is anything but undefined.

Finally, we add the listener for the button click. We will also use event delegation as seen in the earlier example; in fact, we set the listener to listen to the same event on the same container. Yes, it is perfectly fine to do so. When setting event listeners, the Event Utility will queue them and later call each in sequence. This spares us from having to modify the listener for the other Dialog. In large applications, this provides extra modularity as the two pieces of code are totally independent and can be added and removed at will.

Within the listener we find the actual target and make sure it is the correct one, in this case by checking it has the correct class name. We then locate the image. We do so by first looking for the `<div>` that contains the button and the image, searching for it by its class name and then locating the image by its tag name and class name. Looking at the HTML for each image block, it would seem that the image is the `.firstChild` of the `.previousSibling` of the target. This is a risky way of locating elements; a later change in the design of the page would render our code useless. Using IDs would have been even better; we simply wanted to show alternatives.

Once the image is located, we set two properties of the Dialog. We add some extra information to the data that Dialog will post. In addition to what Dialog reads from the form itself, we add an image argument set to the filename of the image. Whenever we assemble URL arguments, we must encode the values because any un-encoded reserved character will confuse the parser that will have to deal with this URL at the server side.

We also set the context for the Dialog. We tell it to align the top-left corner of the Dialog to the top-right corner of the image. We finally show it.

When the visitor clicks on the **Rate!** button, Dialog will assemble the data from the form and call the `.validate()` method, which we overrode. We read the value for `rating` and return `false` if it is `undefined`, which will leave the Dialog on the screen; however, if we return `true`, Dialog will send an URL such as:

```
rating.php?rating=Pretty%20Good&
         image=http%3A%2F%2Flocalhost%2F [...] ages%2Fimage1_thumb.jpg
```

The URL is rendered even longer by the URL-encoding of the special characters, but that should be of no concern to us as any parser on the server side will deal with it. Our PHP server script is pretty simple:

```php
<?php
  $imageFile = $_POST['image'];
  $newRating = $_POST['rating'];
  echo "Thanks! the new rating for $imageFile is: $newRating";
?>
```

An "Are you sure?" SimpleDialog

The SimpleDialog extends the Dialog. It's used to get the result of a single question, much like a standard JavaScript confirm box, but with a lot more power. It can also be styled, by using the default sam skin, or by overriding this to add custom styling.

The example for this section will make use of the SimpleDialog to replace the built-in window.confirm() prompt. However, we'll fall far short of the full capabilities of the SimpleDialog, after all, like Dialog, this element also has full AJAX capabilities and it can contain very elaborate HTML inside. However, the component is meant to do simple tasks so we'll keep it simple on purpose.

We'll use it to confirm the rating assigned to an image before sending it to the server. We won't add any HTML, the SimpleDialog will be build entirely through code and, in fact, it might well be built as a separate component to add to our own library of tools, by first defining a suitable namespace and placing it there for general use. We've seen how that is done in previous chapters so we won't repeat it here.

We add the following code to that in the previous example:

```
var areYouSureDialog = null;
var areYouSure = function (header, callback, scope) {
    scope = scope || window;
    if (!areYouSureDialog) {
        areYouSureDialog =
            new YAHOO.widget.SimpleDialog(Dom.generateId(),{
                width:"250px",
                fixedcenter:true,
                modal:true,
                visible:false,
                icon: YAHOO.widget.SimpleDialog.ICON_HELP,
                text: "Are you sure?",
                buttons:[
                    {text:"Yes", handler:function() {
                        callback.call(scope,true);
                        this.cancel();
                    }},
                    {text:"No", handler:function () {
                        callback.call(scope,false);
                        this.cancel();
                    }}
                ]
            });
        areYouSureDialog.render(document.body);
    }
    areYouSureDialog.setHeader(header);
    areYouSureDialog.show();
};
```

We don't want to create our SimpleDialog anew every time we need it so, first, we declare the `areYouSureDialog` variable to hold it once created. Then we define the `areYouSure()` function that will produce the prompt. The question will always be **Are you sure?**, but we might want to change the header of the prompt so we set that as an argument to the function.

We must remember that, unlike the built-in `window.confirm()` box that completely stops the execution of any code until a reply is given, SimpleDialog is asynchronous; it will allow execution to proceed once shown, so we have to provide a means for it to tell us when the visitor has replied. We do that by accepting a `callback` argument, a function to be called when the reply is ready, and an optional `scope` for that callback.

Within the function we make sure to have a valid `scope`: if no `scope` is given, we default to `window`. We then check whether we had the Dialog already built; if not, we create it. We won't be using any markup so we ask Dom's `.generateId()` method to produce a valid, unique `id`. We then set the configuration options. The new ones specific to SimpleDialog are `icon`, which allows us to select from a range of built-in icons, and `text`, which is the associated text. Both will be shown in the `body` section of the Dialog.

For the buttons, we set **Yes** and **No** buttons and on each we call the `callback` function, adjusted to the given `scope`, with either a `true` or `false` argument and finally, we close the Dialog.

As we didn't use markup as the basis for this SimpleDialog, we need to tell it where it should be rendered and, as we don't really care, we render it into `document.body`, which is a pretty safe place as it will always be there. Up to this point, we've dealt with creating the Dialog if it hasn't been created previously. All that is left is to set the header and show it.

To use it, we'll change the definition of the buttons on our previous example. Originally, we had:

```
buttons: [
    {text:"Rate!", handler:function() {
            this.submit();
        }},
    {text:"Cancel", handler:function() {
        this.cancel();
    }}
],
```

Now, we change that to:

```
buttons: [
    {text:"Rate!", handler:function() {
        areYouSure("Image Rating: " + this.getData().rating,
            function(result) {
                if (result) {
                    this.submit();
                } else {
                    this.cancel();
                }
            },
            this
        );
    }},
    {text:"Cancel", handler:function() {
        this.cancel();
    }}
],
```

The **Cancel** button remains unchanged, the **Rate!** button, however, instead of calling `this.submit()` straightaway, calls `areYouSure()` providing a `header` made of the rating selected for the image, and defining the `callback` function in place. The callback will receive a `true` or `false` reply and based on it it will call `.submit()` or `.cancel()`. As the third argument to `areYouSure()` we use `this` so that `.submit()` or `.cancel()` gets called with the proper scope set.

Easy Tooltips

The Tooltip control is one of the easiest components of the library to use; with just a couple of lines of code, you can have a custom Tooltip:

```
(new YAHOO.widget.Tooltip(Dom.generateId(),{
    context:Dom.getElementsByClassName("thumb","img")
}));
```

This simple code will create Tooltips for all our images. The `context` configuration attribute accepts an element or an array of elements either by their IDs or actual references to the DOM elements. Here, we use Dom's `.getElementsByClassName()` to locate all the thumbnail images and use the array returned for the `context` attribute.

Tooltip will read the `title` attribute from the elements it monitors and use it for the `text` so we don't really need to concern ourselves with that; however, while the `title` attribute can only be plain text, Tooltip will properly process any HTML it finds. Moreover, we are quite at liberty to change the standard style to whatever we want, such as:

```
.yui-skin-sam .yui-tt .bd {
  background-color:#B3D4FF;
  color:#ffffff;
  border:2px solid #085394;
}
```

The selection of colors or border width is up to our page design, but it is important to know we are quite free to change it as well as the shadow it places underneath, by overriding these selectors:

```
.yui-skin-sam .yui-tt-shadow
.yui-skin-sam .yui-tt-shadow-visible
```

The first provides the color and offset for the shadow, the second the opacity when visible.

We can also explicitly set the text for the Tooltip by using the `text` configuration attribute and we may also set it dynamically, using code such as this:

```
var tt = new YAHOO.widget.Tooltip(Dom.generateId(),{
    context:Dom.getElementsByClassName("thumb","img")
});
tt.contextTriggerEvent.subscribe(function (type, oArgs) {
    var context = oArgs[0];
    this.cfg.setProperty("text", context.title);
});
```

In practice, this code is quite silly because it is what the Tooltip does by default; however, there are times when we might want to change the text of the ToolTip dynamically and the source of that text might be elsewhere. We created the Tooltip as before, but this time we kept a reference to it. Then we subscribed to the event that signals when the Tooltip is about to be shown. In the listener, we set the `text` configuration attribute to the value of the `title` of the element that caused it to show. In practice we would use this code to obtain the text from another source.

The YUI TabView Control

A visit to almost any area of the expansive Yahoo! web portal is practically guaranteed to result in your exposure to a TabView Control in action. It's easy to see why; tabbed content is both attractive and functional, and helps to maximize the content on any one page without overcrowding it.

Unlike manually creating your own tabbed interface, which takes a lot of time, skill, and of course, debugging, using the TabView Control is both quick and easy. It is constructed using a logical unordered list, and like many of the library components, it can be built from underlying markup or entirely from simple JavaScript.

Whether your TabView Control is built from HTML or script, its API provides a rich and varied set of configuration attributes, methods, and events that allow us to programmatically switch between tabs, create, or destroy them, and manipulate the content contained in them with ease.

To make more of a visual impact with our tabbed Content Containers, we can include the Animation Utility and define transition effects that occur when the active tab changes. Using the Connection Manager utility, we can even pull in the data for your tabs asynchronously.

TabView classes

The TabView Control consists of two classes: `YAHOO.widget.Tab` and `YAHOO.widget.TabView`. Both are subclasses of `YAHOO.util.Element` and inherit many properties, methods, and events from it. The TabView class is the class from which the complete TabView Control is derived, whereas the Tab class represents one tab and its content. Both have their uses so let's look at them quickly now, starting with their constructors.

The `YAHOO.widget.TabView()` constructor that is used to create a TabView control on the page takes the usual two arguments, the first a reference to existing markup and the second a configuration object. As the first is optional (the TabView can be entirely constructed via JavaScript), the second argument can be moved to the first slot.

The constructor for `YAHOO.widget.Tab` also follows the same pattern but building a single Tab out of existing markup hardly ever makes any sense so the first argument is never used. In practice, as the second argument can be moved up to the first position, we can assume that the constructor simply takes a configuration object.

We can create a base TabView from markup and still create extra Tabs via script and add them to the TabView at any time. If we didn't use any markup at all, our TabView will be floating in thin air so we need to call `.appendTo()` to point to some empty container that will actually hold the newly built TabView.

Class members

Neither TabView nor Tab has any properties worth mentioning. They are basically string constants with the class names that it will assign to the different HTML elements. Most of the properties and methods that both have are inherited from Element and we will rarely use any of them, except as noted below. Both are mostly handled via their configuration attributes and a few methods, especially in `YAHOO.widget.TabView`:

- `.addTab()`: Used to add a new tab to the control. The tab instance to add to the control should appear as the first argument and the second, optional argument is the index position to add it at; it defaults to the end.
- `.getTab()`: Used to obtain the tab at the index specified by its only argument.
- `.getTabIndex()`: Used to obtain the index of a tab specified in its single argument.
- `.removeTab()`: Removes the specified tab instance.
- `.selectTab()` and `.deselectTab()`: To select or deselect a tab by its index, which is the same as changing the `activeTab` or `activeIndex` configuration attribute.

Both `TabView` and `Tab` have `.get()` and `.set()` methods, inherited from Element, that allow us to change the configuration attributes, which are the same that we specify when creating the instances of each. TabView offers:

- `orientation`: Any of `top` (the default), `bottom`, `left`, or `right` determines where the tabs will be in relation to the contents
- `activeTab`, `activeIndex`: To find out or set the active tab by either Tab instance or index
- `tabs`: Read-only array of Tabs in this TabView
- `element`: The overall container for the TabView

We have far more control over Tab via its configuration attributes:

- `active`: Whether the tab is active. Setting it will activate this tab.
- `content`: The HTML for the content of this tab.
- `contentEl`: The actual `<div>` element that holds the tab contents.
- `label`: The text to be shown in the tab.
- `labelEl`: The element that contains the label text.
- `disabled`: If `true`, the tab cannot be selected.

The content of a Tab can be loaded dynamically via XHR. It requires the Connection Manager to be loaded. This happens every time a Tab is made active, so if the visitor never selects that Tab no effort is wasted, but switching back and forth between tabs, every time the tab is re-activated, its contents will be refreshed. The loaded content can only be passive HTML, any `<script>` or `<style>` tags will be completely ignored. The configuration attributes related to dynamic loading are:

- `dataSrc`: The URL of the content to be loaded.
- `loadMethod`: Defaults to `GET`; can be any method supported by Connection Manager.
- `dataTimeout`: Number of milliseconds to wait before giving up.
- `postData`: Any extra URL arguments to be passed to the server when `loadMethod` is `POST`.
- `dataLoaded`: A Boolean reporting whether the data has been loaded.
- `cacheData`: Tab will fetch the content every time the tab is re-activated. Setting `cacheData` will keep the content once fetched and prevent refreshing it.

Element, from which both TabView and Tab descend, provides events to signal any change in any of the configuration attributes; for every xxx configuration attribute there will be a `beforexxxChange` and an `xxxChange`. The first allows the change to be rejected by returning `false` and with it, the associated action; the second occurs after the change has happened if nobody vetoed it.

Adding tabs

In this example, let's suppose that we're making a website for a computer hardware retailer; on pages that display items for sale we'll use a tabbed interface to provide extended product information displayed on a series of tabs.

We'll just create one page of this imaginary site, and as the data for the products would probably come out of a database, we'll also look at adding content to tabs dynamically using the Connection Manager. The finished page should end up looking something like this:

The underlying markup

For this example we'll need to include the indispensable `yahoo-dom-events.js`, TabView dependencies: `element-min.js` and, as we'll do dynamic loading, `connection-min.js` and, finally, `tabview-min.js` and its CSS file `tabview.css`. Next we can add the underlying HTML for the page.

This will form the foundation of the TabView control:

```
<body class="yui-skin-sam">
  <div id="productTabs" class="yui-navset">
    <ul class="yui-nav">
      <li class="selected">
        <a href="#tab1"><em>Overview</em></a></li>
      <li><a href="#tab2"><em>Extended Specification</em></a></li>
      <li><a href="#tab3"><em>Reviews</em></a></li>
    </ul>
    <div class="yui-content">
      <div>
        <a name="tab1"></a><h1>GeForce 8800 GTS</h1>
        <img src="images/gcard.gif" alt="GeForce 8800 GTS">
        <div class="descText">
          In Stock<br>
          &pound;173.99<br>
```

```
            Interface: PCI-e<br>
            Memory: 320Mb<br>
            Output: Dual DVI<br>
            manufacturer: XFX<br>
          </div>
        </div>
        <div>
          <a name="tab2"></a><h1>Full Spec</h1>
          Memory Interface: 320bit<br>
          Memory Type: DDR3<br>
          RAMDACs: Dual 400 MHz<br>
          Memory Bandwidth: 64GB/sec<br>
          Fill Rate: 24 billion/sec<br>
          Graphics Core: 500 MHz<br>
          Clock Rate: 580 MHz<br>
          Chip Set: GeForce &trade; 8800 GTS<br>
          Interface: PCI-e
        </div>
        <div>
          <a name="tab3"></a><h1>Consumer Reviews</h1>
          <p>The 8800 GTS is the best thing ever, woot. Lorem ipsum
                                                      etc…</p>
          <p>In et lorem, etc…</p>
          <p>Phasellus non erat etc…</p>
        </div>
      </div>
    </div>
  </body>
```

The outer container for the TabView control is a simple <div> element. We can give it an id attribute that will be fed to the constructor and a class so that it can be targeted by the sam skin for styling.

The Tab headings are created from a simple <ul> that has been given the class name yui-nav. Each is made of an anchor <a> element so that, in a Progressive Enhancement situation, the visitor can jump directly to the corresponding section. The content areas of the tabs are created from <div> elements that appear as child nodes of the <div class="yui-content"> element. There must be the same number of <li> elements in the tab headings list as there are <div> elements in the tab content container. The heading of each section has an anchor label (<a name="">) to match the links above; these are only required in a PE situation, otherwise they may be omitted.

The JavaScript needed by TabView

We'll only need a tiny bit of JavaScript to initially build our TabView control. Directly before the closing `</body>` tag, add the following `<script>` block:

```
<script type="text/javascript">
YAHOO.util.Event.onDOMReady(function() {

    //define the TabView object
    var tabs = new YAHOO.widget.TabView("productTabs");

    //add a new tab programmatically
    tabs.addTab(new YAHOO.widget.Tab({
        label:"Accessories",
        content:"SLI bridge<br>4 pin molex to 6 pin " +
                "PCI-e adapter<br>DVI to DSUB converter"
    }));

    //add another new tab
    tabs.addTab(new YAHOO.widget.Tab({
        dataSrc:"altprods.php",
        label:"Alternative Products"
    }));
});
</script>
```

The `YAHOO.widget.TabView()` constructor takes just the `id` of the container element and this one line of code creates the whole TabView control from the above markup! We then create two further tabs via JavaScript. The first one has static content, which is specified as an HTML string. The second is loaded dynamically from a server script `altprods.php`. This script has to return HTML that will be inserted directly into the `.innerHTML` of the tab contents `<div>`.

If the source of data does not produce HTML directly and further processing is needed, the `.loadHandler` property has the `success` and `failure` callback functions that Connection Manager will use and they can easily be overridden to do any required processing of the received data. The full example in the downloadable examples for this book has an extra tab (not shown here) that shows this technique, which we won't discuss here.

Summary

The Container family of controls found in the YUI provides an important series of components that allow us to add elements to our web applications that make them look and feel more like desktop applications.

All of the different containers are highly configurable and come pre-styled for our convenience. Using them takes surprisingly little code, so we can focus more on the content instead of worrying about how to present it.

TabView offers a flexible approach to grouping related chunks of content in an attractive tabbed interface, and gives us full control over the tab headings and tab content, allowing us to add new tabs and new data on the fly from a variety of sources.

7
Menus

In this chapter, we're going to look at a very common web page element: navigation menus. The Menu widget provides a timesaving and code-efficient solution to common website application requirements.

The skills that you will take away from this chapter include:

- How to implement a basic navigation menu
- How to override the default sam skin
- How to create an application-style menu bar
- How to use the ContextMenu type

Common navigation structures

All but the most limited of websites must have a mechanism by which visitors can navigate around the pages of the site from the home page. In order to meet accessibility guidelines, several methods of navigation will usually be available, including at least a navigation menu and a site map.

There have been many different implementation styles that have been popular over the years. Before anyone really worried about accessibility or standards compliance, a common way of designing a navigation menu was to use a series of images that linked to other pages of the site, and there was also the popular frame-based navigation structure. While these methods saved the designer a lot of time, effort, and any real skill, they led to hugely increased page load times and a legacy of bad coding practice.

Thankfully, those days have long since passed, and with the continued development of CSS, it's now possible to design an effective navigation structure based on semantic HTML and styled with CSS.

Designing a navigation menu that is effective, robust, and presented effectively can still pose a challenge, and troubleshooting the compatibility of a menu between different browsers can be a very time-consuming process. This is where the YUI steps in.

Instant menus—just add water (or a Menu Control)

The Menu Control is used to add one of several different menus to your website, saving you the chore of adding this almost essential feature yourself. It's another control that takes a complex, difficult, or time-consuming task, and one which is an almost inherent requirement of any website, and packages it up into a convenient and easy-to-use module. The three different types of menu you can create are:

- A standard navigation menu
- An application-style menu bar
- A right-click context menu

The navigation menu can be implemented as either a vertical or horizontal menu and generates a clean and attractive interface, which your visitors can use to navigate to different areas of your site. The navigation model of any site is key to whether using the site is easy and enjoyable; nothing turns off visitors more than a poorly designed or inconsistent navigation structure.

Another type of menu that the Menu Control is able to create is an application-style menu bar, which stretches across the screen horizontally, building on the current trend in the online world to blur the distinction between the browser and the desktop.

As well as taking care of navigation for you, it can also be used to add right-click context (pop-up) menus to any part of your web application, which again can give a web application a definite desktop feel to it.

The Menu Control is very flexible and can be built from existing HTML markup using a clean and logical list structure, or it can be generated entirely through JavaScript and built at runtime. Each of the different menu types is also given a default appearance with the sam skin so there is very little that is required to generate the attractive and highly functional menus.

We'll be looking at implementing each of the different types of menu ourselves in just a moment. Before we do this, let's take a quick look at the classes that go together to make the Menu Control.

The Menu classes

This component, much like the Container that we looked at in the earlier chapter, is made up of a small family of different types of menu. There is a range of different classes that work together to bring the functionality of the different types of menu to you.

The three main classes behind the Menu family are:

- `YAHOO.widget.Menu`
- `YAHOO.widget.ContextMenu`
- `YAHOO.widget.MenuBar`

Menu is a subclass of Overlay, part of the Container family, and the other two are subclasses of Menu. Just as each TabView is made of several Tabs, each kind of Menu has a different class for its items:

- `YAHOO.widget.MenuItem`
- `YAHOO.widget.ContextMenuItem`
- `YAHOO.widget.MenuBarItem`

`ContextMenuItem` is simply an alias for `MenuItem` created just for the sake of symmetry. All types of menu items can have a `Menu` as a submenu; neither `ContextMenu` nor `MenuBar` can be nested in a menu item, they are only good at the outermost level.

All the menus are coordinated by `YAHOO.widget.MenuManager`, which listens to events at the document body level and dispatches them to the corresponding menus or menu items using the technique of Event Delegation to the limit; after all, the document body is the furthest out an event can bubble.

Like the other members of the Container family, the constructor for Menu and its subclasses take two arguments; first a reference to existing markup or, if built via code, the `id` we want the Menu to have once rendered. The second argument takes the configuration options, if any, and accepts any configuration attribute as would be expected. However, in Menu, it can also take a couple of properties: `itemData` and `lazyLoad`, while `MenuItem` can also take `value`. We will see what they can be used for shortly.

Menus can be built from existing markup or from code or any combination of both. The required markup for a Menu might seem a little complicated at first but it is intended to work in older clients or for users without JavaScript enabled. This, we know, is called Progressive Enhancement and Menu supports it very well; the CSS style sheet for Menu works whether JavaScript is active or not and by using the correct class names the Menus will look just the same for all our visitors regardless of the capabilities of their browsers.

The markup will usually consist of a series of unordered lists <ul>, each of their list items <li> containing an anchor element <a> that leads to the next non-JavaScript enhanced page and optionally followed by a further nested unordered list. Menus will also read <select> elements creating a MenuItem for each <option>.

When building a Menu from code, we may create and add each individual MenuItem to the Menu or we may use the itemData configuration option we've just mentioned, which takes an object literal with the description of the whole Menu at once. This is particularly handy for ContextMenus as they hardly make any sense without JavaScript enabled.

Just as with any container, Menus have to be rendered. ContextMenus are usually rendered into document.body, as they have no place in the normal flow of the page. If the menu structure is too complex and takes too long to render, the lazyLoad option tells the Menu to render just the first level of items, those that would be visible initially, postponing rendering the rest until needed.

Menu subclasses

The ContextMenu is a specialized version of the control that provides a menu hidden from view until the element that it is associated with (the trigger element) is clicked with the right mouse button (except in Opera on Windows and OS X which requires the left-click + *Ctrl* key combination). The trigger element is defined using the trigger configuration attribute; this is the only configuration attribute natively defined by the ContextMenu class, all others are inherited.

The MenuBar is similar to the standard Menu, but is horizontal instead of vertical. It can behave like an application-style menu bar, where the top-level menu items must be clicked in order for them to expand, or it can behave more like a web menu where the menu items expand on a simple mouse over and have submenu indicators. This is controlled with the autosubmenudisplay Boolean configuration attribute.

The MenuItem class

Each menu type has a subclass representing the individual menu items that form choices within the menu. They will be created automatically when a Menu is built from existing markup or by setting the `itemData` configuration option to a menu description. You will only create individual MenuItems when extending the functionality of an existing menu.

MenuItems have several interesting configuration attributes:

- `checked`: Shows a checkmark to the left of the label, useful for items that toggle in between two states.

- `classname`: Added to the existing if any further styling is required. It can read this from existing markup.

- `disabled`: This item cannot be selected and will be grayed out. When built from markup, it can read this attribute from an `<option>` tag.

- `keylistener`: The key combination (*Shift*, *Control*, or *Alt* + character) that will trigger this item. It can be read from markup.

- `onclick`: The method to be called when this item is clicked.

- `text`: A string to be shown in the label.

- `url`, `target`: The destination page for this item when not handled via code.

- `selected`: The item shows highlighted.

- `submenu`: A nested instance of Menu, an object description of a nested Menu, or a reference to the markup that would produce it.

- `value`: A value associated with this item.

MenuItem subclasses

The two subclasses `YAHOO.widget.ContextMenuItem` and `YAHOO.widget.MenuBarItem` both extend the `MenuItem` class, providing a constructor and some basic properties and methods for programmatically working with individual `ContextMenu` or `MenuBar` menu items.

As a matter of fact `ConextMenuItem` is simply an alias for `MenuItem`. `MenuBarItem` has different defaults than `MenuItem` to suit the different layout of the `MenuBar`.

Creating a basic navigation menu

Let's now put together a basic navigation menu and use some of those methods and properties that we looked at in the classes. Our menu will be built from underlying HTML rather than from script.

We'll be enhancing the previous example of the image portfolio by first providing a landing, home page that will welcome us. We'll later add a context menu to the image portfolio itself so that instead of adding an extra button (like **Rate!**) for each option, we'll handle them via menus. Once complete, our landing page should appear like this:

The initial HTML page

Menu requires `yahoo-dom-events.js` and `container-core-min.js` but, as our image portfolio example already contains the full `container-min.js` and all its dependencies, we just need to add `menu-min.js` and its corresponding CSS file, `menu.css`. A nice feature of the Dependency Configurator is that it can also provide us with a customized link to it with our selection set, such as this:

```
http://developer.yahoo.com/yui/articles/hosting/?container&MIN
```

We can save this URL in a comment in our page so that when we need to add extra components, we can start with this URL and then add the new ones. The Dependency Configurator will immediately notice that the full Container files are loaded and will avoid any duplication.

You'll recognize the layout of the image above from *Chapter 2* when we discussed the Grids CSS Tool that was produced by this HTML:

```
<body class="yui-skin-sam">
  <div id="doc" class="yui-t1">
    <div id="hd">
      <h1>DigitalDesigns</h1>
    </div>
    <div id="bd">
      <div id="yui-main">
        <div class="yui-b">
          <h1>Welcome to DigitalDesigns!</h1>
          <p>Lorum ipsum etc...</p>
          <p>Lorum ipsum etc...</p>
        </div>
      </div>
      <div class="yui-b">
        <!-- the menu goes here -->
      </div>
    </div>
    <div id="ft">
      <p class="ftext">Copyright&copy; Mr Freelance 2007</p>
    </div>
  </div>
</body>
```

Except for the textual content in some of the sections this is a boilerplate grid with a narrow 160px sidebar on the left on a 750px document. It has been supplemented by some font choices, background coloring, and borders via CSS besides the styles provided by the sam skin. The menu will go where the highlighted comment shows. It was important to show this part of the HTML because it is easy to get lost once the markup for the menu is thrown in.

The underlying menu markup

There are two good reasons to create the main navigation menu from markup. The first is Progressive Enhancement because the markup Menu uses is perfectly workable for any visitor with even the most primitive browser. The second is to allow search engines to index our site. If we create the main menu via code, no search engine would be able to find the rest of the pages in our site.

We add the menu where the comment above shows:

```
<div id="navmenu" class="yuimenu">
  <div class="bd">
    <ul class="first-of-type">
      <li class="yuimenuitem"><a class="yuimenuitemlabel"
          href="aboutme.html">About Me</a></li>
      <li class="yuimenuitem"><a class="yuimenuitemlabel"
          href="images.html">My Images</a></li>
      <li class="yuimenuitem"><a class="yuimenuitemlabel"
          href="blog.html">My Blog</a></li>
      <li class="yuimenuitem"><a class="yuimenuitemlabel"
          href="contact.html">Contact Me</a></li>
      <li class="yuimenuitem"><a class="yuimenuitemlabel"
          href="imagelinks.html">Image Resources</a></li>
    </ul>
  </div>
</div>
```

We called it `navmenu` but any other name would do just as well. We do have to use the rest of the markup as shown. As Menu inherits from Overlay, it uses the standard SMF format, but it uses no head or footer so we just have a body `bd` section and in it, an unordered list (`<ul>`) where each list item is made of an actual link that should work both for old browsers and search engines and a label. All the class names are mandatory as the CSS file for Menu uses them, even the `first-of-type` class name, which signals that this is the top-level menu and not a submenu.

Our menu wouldn't be a proper navigation menu if there weren't, at least, a couple of submenus; it would just be a list of links. Let's add a couple of submenus now:

```
<div id="navmenu" class="yuimenu">
  <div class="bd">
    <ul class="first-of-type">
      <li class="yuimenuitem"><a class="yuimenuitemlabel"
          href="aboutme.html">About Me</a></li>
      <li class="yuimenuitem"><a class="yuimenuitemlabel"
          href="images.html">Images</a>
        <div id="images" class="yuimenu">
```

```
        <div class="bd">
          <ul>
            <li class="yuimenuitem"><a class="yuimenuitemlabel"
                href="photography.html">Photography</a></li>
            <li class="yuimenuitem"><a class="yuimenuitemlabel"
                href="fantasy.html">Fantasy Art</a></li>
            <li class="yuimenuitem"><a class="yuimenuitemlabel"
                href="Corporate.html">Corporate Logos</a></li>
          </ul>
        </div>
      </div>
    </li>
    <li class="yuimenuitem"><a class="yuimenuitemlabel"
        href="blog.html">My Blog</a></li>
    <li class="yuimenuitem"><a class="yuimenuitemlabel"
        href="contact.html">Contact Me</a></li>
    <li class="yuimenuitem"><a class="yuimenuitemlabel"
        href="imagelinks.html">Image Resources</a>
      <div id="links" class="yuimenu">
        <div class="bd">
          <ul>
            <li class="yuimenuitem"><a class="yuimenuitemlabel"
                href="http://www.flickr.com">Flickr</a></li>
            <li class="yuimenuitem"><a class="yuimenuitemlabel"
                href="http://www.b3ta.com">B3ta</a></li>
            <li class="yuimenuitem"><a class="yuimenuitemlabel"
                href="http://yotophoto.com">Yoto Photo</a></li>
          </ul>
        </div>
      </div>
    </li>
  </ul>
</div>
</div>
```

The submenus take the same format as the top-level menu—an outer container `<div>` with a class of `yuimenu` forms the basis of the submenu, followed by an inner body `<div>`. Each submenu, like the overall Menu, is built from a standard unordered list (`<ul>`) element where each menu item is composed of a single list item (`<li>`). The structure of the menu is very similar to that of the overall page because it has a distinct body section (`<div class="bd">`) and can also be given `hd` and `ft` sections if required.

Formatting options

Menu offers a few formatting options. A menu or submenu may actually be made of several consecutive unordered lists. Menu will produce a thin dividing bar between each group.

A level-6 heading (`<h6>`) can be added before any `<ul>` to create a heading for each group; Menu won't mind any other heading level but the stylesheet has a suitable style only for an `<h6>`. The heading will be bold but slightly grayed out and it will not respond to a click.

When building the menu from code, these groups, whether with headings or not, can be created by using the optional `groupIndex` argument in `.addItem()` or `.addItems()`. Headers can be added with `.setItemGroupTitle()` using those same indexes. The `.addItems()` method, instead of a simple array of menu items, can also take an array of arrays of menu items, each nested array corresponding to a group.

Hints for keyboard shortcuts can be added to each item. Menu will not automatically respond to such shortcuts as read from the markup, a little more code is required afterwards, but the shortcut will be properly presented to the visitor. For example, in the code earlier we could have added a keyboard shortcut hint to an option by doing:

```
<li class="yuimenuitem">
    <a class="yuimenuitemlabel" href="fantasy.html">
        Fantasy Art<em class="helptext">Ctrl + F</em>
    </a>
</li>
```

This image shows an assortment of such options:

The menu has been divided into three groups, each with its heading, the first two have keyboard shortcuts, and the second item is disabled. The **My Blog** option has the `checked` attribute set and the three items in the bottom submenu each have a class name so that they use the default icon (`favicon.ico`) from the target site as a non-repeating background image; the last site offers no default icon but should it offer one, the menu would immediately show it.

Menu will not automatically respond to the keyboard shortcut as displayed; it cannot parse it from the help text as that might be localized. The `MenuItem` object offers the `keylistener` configuration attribute that can be set to the key combination that will activate this item as if it had been clicked. This attribute uses the same format to describe the key combination as used by the `YAHOO.util.KeyListener` object of the Event Utility.

Creating the Menu object

Implementing a basic menu takes just a little bit of YUI-targeting JavaScript. You can add the following `<script>` block to the page directly above the closing `</body>` tag:

```
<script type="text/javascript">
    YAHOO.util.Event.onDOMReady(function() {
        var menu = new YAHOO.widget.Menu("navmenu", {
                                    position:"static" });
        menu.render();
    });
</script>
```

As soon as we detect the DOM is ready, we create the instance of `Menu` using the `id` of the markup as a reference and then we render it. We need to specify `position` as `static` because we want this menu to always be shown in the page, in contrast to `dynamic` menus that float over the contents. This is all we need; links in the terminal nodes of the Menu hierarchy will be active and navigate when clicked. Items having submenus will unfold the corresponding submenu but they won't navigate to the link destination, such links being reserved for non-JavaScript enabled browsers.

This way of navigating, though, is still too Web 1.0 style. Can we change the contents of the main panel without navigating at all? We can certainly do that. We will copy the main content of the image portfolio from the `panel.html` example of the previous chapter and paste it into the current content, enclosing each in its own `<div>`, like this:

```
<div id="yui-main">
    <div class="yui-b">
        <div id="welcome">
```

```
            <a name="welcome"></a><h1>Welcome to DigitalDesigns!</h1>
            <p>Lorem ipsum … vix.</p><br>
            <p>Nec no illud … at ius.</p>
        </div>
        <div id="fantasyart">
            <a name="fantasyart"></a><h1>Fantasy Art Images</h1>
            <div class="images">
                <img class="thumb" src="images/image1_thumb.jpg" …>
                <img class="thumb" src="images/image2_thumb.jpg" …>
            </div>
        </div>
    </div>
</div>
```

The content has been slightly clipped to fit in this page as signaled by the ellipsis. Now we have a `welcome` section and a `fantasyart` section. Each has an `<h1>` heading preceded by an anchor destination. The link in the menu item for this entry is also changed from `href="fantasy.html"` to `href="#fantasyart"`. Thus, in a non-JavaScript situation, both sections would be visible and the link would serve to jump to that section. We then add the following code:

```
YAHOO.util.Event.onDOMReady(function() {
    var Dom = YAHOO.util.Dom, Event = YAHOO.util.Event;
    Dom.setStyle("fantasyart","display","none");
    var menu = new YAHOO.widget.Menu("navmenu", {
                                    position:"static" });
    menu.render();
    menu.subscribe("click",function(type, oArgs) {
        var ev = oArgs[0],
            menuItem = oArgs[1];

        switch (menuItem.cfg.getProperty("url")) {
          case "#fantasyart":
            Event.stopEvent(ev);
            Dom.setStyle("welcome","display","none");
            Dom.setStyle("fantasyart","display","");
            menu.insertItem({text:"Home",url:"#welcome"},0);
            break;
          case "#welcome":
            Event.stopEvent(ev);
            Dom.setStyle("welcome","display","");
            Dom.setStyle("fantasyart","display","none");
            menu.removeItem(0);
            break;
        }
    });
});
```

We are rendering the menu as we did before, but first we are hiding the `fantasyart` section so only the `welcome` section remains. We add a listener to the click event of the menu. We read both parts of the argument, the raw event object (`ev`) and the `menuItem` that was clicked. We read the `url` configuration attribute for that item and if it is `#fantasyart` we stop the propagation of the event (so it does not navigate on its own), toggle the visibility of both sections, and insert an extra item in the menu, which enables the visitor to return to the home page. This newly added menu item is the one handled in the next `case` where we reverse all we did in this one.

Adding menu items to a menu is easy as shown above. Methods `.addItem()` and `.addItems()` let us append new items to the end. These and `.insertItem()` take a freshly created instance of `MenuItem` (or the corresponding subclass for the other types of menu), a literal object with any configuration attributes, or a simple string to be used as the `text` attribute.

Using the ContextMenu

Let's move on to take a look at another menu type—the context, or right-click menu. The navigation menu on our portfolio site provides links to three different image pages. We can use one of these pages to showcase a series of thumbnail images and add right-click functionality to each thumbnail image.

We'll take the page that we used with the Container family controls to show a full view and rate the images and replace that ugly **Rate!** button with a `ContextMenu` with even more options.

ContextMenu scripting

Our custom `ContextMenu` can be created entirely programmatically, without building on existing markup (except for the images of course), making the context menu very easy and quick to implement.

The following screenshot shows how the context menu should appear by the end of this example:

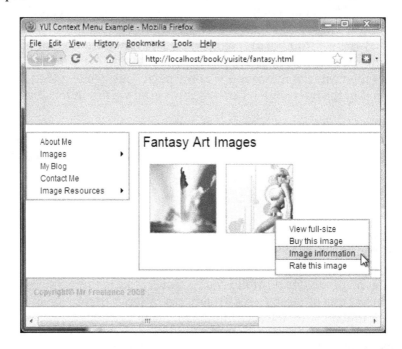

Add the following code to the existing `<script>` block near the bottom of the page. It will create the `ContextMenu`:

```
var context = new YAHOO.widget.ContextMenu(Dom.generateId(), {
    trigger: Dom.getElementsByClassName("thumb"),
    itemData: [
        {text: "View full-size", value:"viewFullSize"},
        {text: "Buy this image", value:"buyImage"},
        {text: "Image information", value:"imageInfo"},
        {text: "Rate this image", value:"rateImage"}
    ],
    lazyLoad:true
});
context.render(document.body);
```

We are creating a new menu, not from markup as we did before, but completely from code. The first argument is not the `id` of an existing section of markup but the `id` we want to give our newly created menu and, as we don't really care, we let the Dom utility's `.generateId()` provide us with one.

The second argument contains the configuration options and we will use the two most important for a ContextMenu, trigger and itemData. trigger can be a reference to an HTML element or an array of them; when the visitor right-clicks on any of them, the ConextMenu will show. As all our images have the class name thumb, it is easy to search for them by using the Dom method .getElementsByClassName(), which returns just the kind of array we need.

The next property is itemData, which takes a definition of the menu; its argument is the same as method .addItems() would take, an array of strings, an array of object literals with menu properties, an array of instances of MenuItem, or an array of arrays, if we wanted grouped items. We have also set the lazyLoad property so that the HTML for the menu is not generated until the menu is requested. If we know the menu will be used only occasionally, it is worth saving the time it takes to render it until it is needed.

Finally, there is nothing left but to render it and as it has no place in the normal layout of the page, we do it in document.body, which is as good as anywhere else. It's interesting to note that the default context menu supplied by the browser is completely replaced by our YUI context menu; right-clicking on an image and anywhere else in the page will produce different results, which is a small step towards protecting the images from being downloaded if this is something that you wanted to do.

As you can see, the context menu has picked up the custom styling of our main navigation menu without any intervention from us. None of the menu items will actually do anything at this stage because we haven't wired in any additional functionality other than displaying the context menu itself.

Wiring up the backend

Adding functionality for the ContextMenu items is extremely easy. The first option in our context menu is to view a full size version of the thumbnail image. We already have this from the Panel example; we triggered it by clicking on the image itself. We'll simply extract the part that actually shows the Panel with the full-size image and call it showFullSize(). We also have the code that shows the ratings Dialog. We'll also extract the part that shows the Dialog and call it askRating(). We then add the following:

```
context.subscribe("click",function(type, oArgs) {
    var ev = oArgs[0],
        menuItem = oArgs[1],
        image = this.contextEventTarget;

    switch (menuItem.value) {
```

```
        case "viewFullSize":
            showFullSize(image);
            break;
        case "rateImage":
            askRating(image);
            break;
        default:
            alert("You've just clicked: " + menuItem.value);

    }
});
```

We listen to the `click` event on the `ContextMenu`. First we extract vital information. The event (`ev`) that we don't use this time as there is no default action to prevent from happening, the `menuItem` to find out what option was selected by the visitor, and finally, what element caused the `ContextMenu` to pop up in the first place, in this case an `image`, upon which to act.

From the `menuItem` we read the `value` property that we assigned to each `menuItem` when we created them. If you were wondering what the purpose of the `value` property was, this is it. It is more reliable than `url` or `text` as any of them might change due to external reasons. The `value` property is our own; if the site is rearranged and URLs changed, or if the site is localized and menu labels get translated, `value` will still remain untouched.

We fork on `value` and call `showFullSize()` or `askRating()` providing the reference to the `image` we want to show or ask the rating about. We really don't have anything to do for all the menu options so we end up with a final `default` to catch the rest of the options.

The application-style MenuBar

The last member of the menu family is the `MenuBar`, which creates a horizontal application-style menu bar. Like both of the other menu types, the menu bar is exceptionally easy to create and work with.

For this example, we can create a basic user interface for a web-based text editor. Creating a fully working online application that can be used to create or open `.txt` files is beyond the scope of this chapter, but we can at least see how easy it would be to create the interface itself. The final page will look like this:

There is not the slightest chance that this application could possibly work without JavaScript enabled so we'll dispense with using any markup. The body of the page should contain:

```html
<body class="yui-skin-sam">
    <div id="doc">
        <div id="hd">
        </div>
        <div id="bd">
          <textarea class="ed" cols="50" rows="12"></textarea>
        </div>
        <div id="ft">
          HTML &amp; JavaScript Text Editor
        </div>
    </div>
</body>
```

The JavaScript code for this example is:

```javascript
YAHOO.util.Event.onDOMReady(function() {
    var Dom = YAHOO.util.Dom, Event = YAHOO.util.Event;

    var menu = new YAHOO.widget.MenuBar(Dom.generateId(), {
        autosubmenudisplay: true ,
        itemdata: [
            {text:"File", submenu:{id:Dom.generateId(), itemdata: [
                {text:"Open",  value:"Open"},
                {text:"Close", value:"Close"},
                {text:"Save",  value:"Save"},
                {text:"Exit",  value:"Exit"}
            ]}},
```

```
        {text:"Edit", submenu:{id:Dom.generateId(), itemdata: [
            {text:"Cut",   value:"Cut"},
            {text:"Copy",  value:"Copy"},
            {text:"Paste", value:"Paste"}
        ]}},
        {text:"Help", submenu:{id:Dom.generateId(), itemdata: [
            {text:"About", value:"About"},
            {text:"Help",  url:"help.html", target:"_new"}
        ]}}
    ]
});

menu.render("hd");
menu.subscribe("click",function(type, oArgs) {
    var value = oArgs[1].value;
    if (value) {
        Event.stopEvent(oArgs[0]);
        alert("You've just clicked: " + value);
    }
});
});
```

When the DOM is ready, we create an instance of `MenuBar`; as we are not using existing markup, we provide generated IDs for all menu instances. In the configuration attributes argument we make submenus display automatically instead of having to click on the main menu for the submenu to show. We then provide the description of our menu structure as an array of object literals, which we assign to `itemdata`.

It is worth noting that `itemdata` and `itemData` are both valid in this context. The property is `itemData` and the configuration attribute, when used with methods `.cfg.setProperty()` or `.cfg.getProperty()` is `itemdata`. When passed as argument in the initial configuration object, it can be either. This is an anomaly that a property, which should use camel-case, can be set as a configuration attribute, which is all lower-case. A similar thing happens with `lazyLoad` and `lazyload`.

All menu items have a `text` property that the visitor will see. Each main item has a `submenu` property, which being a new instance of `Menu` (not of `MenuBar` as neither MenuBars nor ContextMenus can be nested) requires its own `id` and its own set of `itemdata`, each a new array of menu options. The final elements of the menus have a `value` property so we can branch to suitable actions based on them, or a `url` if we simply navigate elsewhere, such as the **Help** item, which will pop up a help text in a new window.

We finally render the menu in the head element of the page, identified with an `id` of `hd` in the three-section SMF format.

To act upon the menu items, we listen for the `click` event, read the `value` property of the item clicked and, if it has any value, we stop the event from propagating and, in this case, we simply show it in an alert box, though in practice this would be a big `switch()` statement or, even more probably, a search into a hash of helper functions indexed by the value.

Keyboard shortcuts can be easily provided, for example, the menu item description for **Edit | Cut** could be given as:

```
{text: "Cut <em class=\"helptext\">Ctrl + X</em>",
          value:"Cut", keylistener: {ctrl:true, keys:88}}
```

Summary

The Menu control is a versatile and easy-to-use control that you'll probably want to implement in many of your web creations. As we've seen, there are three distinct menu types: the standard vertical or horizontal navigation menu, the right-click context menu, and the application-style menu bar. Customizing these different types of menu is as easy as overriding the default styling, if you don't want to stick with the standard skin.

8
Buttons and Trees

In this chapter we are going to look at two very useful controls provided by the library: the Button and TreeView controls. Both provide the rich and engaging functionality expected of web-based interface controls, and both are highly configurable and customizable.

The standard buttons used in practically every web form ever created are an intrinsic part of HTML. These buttons are so ingrained in the average surfer's psyche that they are used without a moment's thought. But don't you ever want to do more than just push them? No? Well the good people at Yahoo! think that you should, and so they've created a new breed of button — the YUI Button Control.

The TreeView control allows us to easily create a variety of hierarchical tree structures in almost no time at all. These are traditionally something that you would expect to find in a desktop application (such as Windows Explorer) rather than a web application, but with the distinction between the desktop and the Web becoming more blurred by the day, this control is only going to get more useful.

In this chapter we will cover the following topics:

- Why we should use YUI's Button Control
- The different button objects that can be implemented and how they can be added to our pages
- The classes behind the buttons
- How TreeView is implemented
- The properties and methods that make up the TreeView classes
- How Trees can be styled
- Dynamic Trees
- Loading remote node data

Why use the YUI Button family?

Standard web buttons are one element whose default appearance can vary wildly between browsers and platforms, and they are also very difficult to style consistently across browsers. Styled buttons also look far less "buttony" to the average web user than unstyled buttons, and they can often just feel not very much like buttons. Styled buttons also often lack the inverted bevel effect that makes them look like they are being depressed when they are clicked.

The YUI Button family overcomes these difficulties with ease, providing rich and attractive buttons, whose styling is consistent across A-grade browsers and whose functionality far exceeds that of traditional buttons. Another important property of the Button Control as opposed to standard HTML buttons is that the Button Control can have a label that is entirely different from its value.

Meet the Button Control

The Button Control gives you the ability to easily create a range of innovative different button types that extend standard HTML form buttons and allow for much more advanced behavior than just submitting or resetting a form.

The Button family consists of eight individual Button types, each with its own advanced behavior:

- A basic push button that acts like a normal web button but looks much better.

- A link button that navigates visitors to a specified URL when clicked.

- A submit button that automatically submits the data entered into its parent form.

- A reset button that automatically clears any input entered into its parent form.

- A checkbox button that shows as a two-state button but acts like a standard checkbox from a programming standpoint.

- Radio buttons that are a group of mutually exclusive two-state checkbox buttons and behave like traditional radio controls so that only one of them can be selected at a time.

- A menu button that can be expanded to show a series of options when clicked.

- A split button with two clickable regions. The first region initiates some kind of action as any standard button would do, but the second region shows a menu when clicked that allows the action of the first region to be changed.

Button controls can be created in one of three ways: from standard HTML form elements such as `<input>` or `<select>` elements, entirely through JavaScript, or by using a special kind of markup, suitable for a Progressive Enhancement situation.

Two classes are defined by the Button Control: `YAHOO.widget.Button` and `YAHOO.widget.ButtonGroup`. Both classes are subclasses of the Element Utility and inherit properties and methods from it.

The `Button` class takes care of all of the different types of button except the radio style button, which is handled exclusively by the `ButtonGroup` class. Let's take a look into each of the classes and see the properties and methods available for us to use.

YAHOO.widget.Button

The `Button` class is huge, as it needs to be in order to cover all those different types of button. Its constructor takes just two arguments, both optional; the first can be a string specifying the `id` of the element used to create the button, or an element reference, while the second is an object with the configuration attributes. When the reference in the first argument is not required, the second argument can be bumped up to that position.

There is a huge range of methods available to you through the `Button` class, including:

- `.addHiddenFieldsToForm()`: To ensure that values selected with Radio, Checkbox, MenuButton, and SplitButton controls are submitted with the form, this method adds the value of each control to a hidden text field.

- `.blur()`: Causes the Button to lose focus and the blur event to fire.

- `.destroy()`: Removes the Button control and any associated event handlers.

- `.focus()`: Causes the Button to gain focus and the focus event to fire.

- `.getForm()`: Gets a reference to the parent form.

- `.getHiddenField()`: Gets the `<input>` used when the form is submitted.

- `.getMenu()`: Obtains the Button's menu control.

- `.hasFocus()`: Returns true if the Button has focus.

- `.isActive()`: Returns true if Button is active.

- `.onFormKeyDown()`: A handler for keydown events of the Button's parent form.

- `.submitForm()`: Submits the form of which the Button is a child.

- `.toString()`: Returns a string representing the Button instance.

Like most other controls provided by the library the Button Control also makes use of a literal configuration object.

Configuration attributes include, but are not limited to:

- `checked`: Indicates whether Radio or Checkbox Buttons are checked by default. The default is `false`.

- `disabled`: Indicates whether the Button should be disabled but does not apply to link buttons. The default is `false` again.

- `href`: If the Button is a link it needs this to define its `href` attribute.

- `label`: The text label or `innerHTML` of the Button.

- `menu`: If the Button is a Menu Button this property allows you to specify the Menu to use. It can take the form of an object specifying a Menu instance, a string or object specifying the `id` of the element used to create the Menu, or finally, an array of object literals like the one we've seen assigned to `itemData` when we saw Menu.

- `name`: The name of the Button.

- `tabIndex`: A number representing the tab index of the Button.

- `target`: If the Button is a link Button, this specifies the target of the link.

- `title`: The `title` (tooltip) of the Button.

- `type`: This is used to specify the different types of Button.

- `value`: The internal value of the Button.

YAHOO.widget.ButtonGroup

As I mentioned before, the `ButtonGroup` class is used solely to define Buttons with the behavior of radio `<input>` elements. To clarify this behavior, out of any number of buttons in a `ButtonGroup`, only one can be selected at any given time.

The `YAHOO.widget.ButtonGroup()` constructor accepts exactly the same arguments as that for the Button. Methods you may wish to make use of include:

- `.addButton` or `.addButtons`: Methods for adding Buttons to the group

- `.check()`: Checks the Button at the specified index

- `.destroy()`: Removes the whole group and handlers (if any have been registered)

- `.getButton` or `.getButtons`: Methods for getting Button instances

- `.getCount()`: Gets the number of Buttons in the group
- `.removeButton()`: Removes a single Button from the group

Like the `Button` class, the `ButtonGroup` class defines a series of configuration attributes for use in an object literal passed into the constructor allowing you to set attributes such as:

- `checkedButton`: Allows you to specify which Button of the group is checked by default
- `container`: Allows you to specify the `id` of the element that the `ButtonGroup` should be rendered into
- `disabled`: Allows you to specify whether the group should be disabled
- `name`: The name for the `ButtonGroup`
- `value`: An object that specifies the value for the group

Using the Button Control

Let's play with some of the available Button controls. During this example, we'll create the page displayed in the following screenshot:

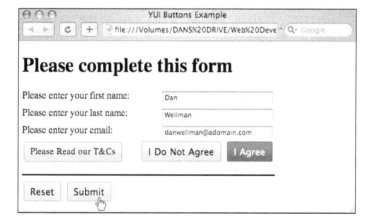

For this example, our template will include the habitual yahoo-dom-events.js, element.js, and button-min.js. In the body of the page, we'll add the following HTML:

```
<h1>Please complete this form</h1>
<form method="post" action="#" id="testform" name="testform">
    <div class="formdiv">
        <label for="fname">Please enter your first name: </label>
        <input id="fname" class="field" type="text" name="fname">
    </div>
    <div class="formdiv">
        <label for="lname">Please enter your last name: </label>
        <input id="lname" class="field" type="text" name="lname">
    </div>
    <div class="formdiv">
        <label for="email">Please enter your email: </label>
        <input id="email" class="field" type="text" name="email">
    </div>
    <div class="formdiv">
        <button id="tacs" name="tacs" type="button">
                            Please Read our T&amp;Cs</button>
        <div id="myButtonGroup">
            <input id="radio1" type="radio" name="termsRadio"
                            value="I Do Not Agree" checked />
            <input id="radio2" type="radio" name="termsRadio"
                            value="I Agree" />
        </div>
    </div>
    <div id="buttons">
        <button id="myReset" name="myReset" type="reset">Reset</button>
        <button id="mySubmit" name="mySubmit" type="submit">
                                                Submit</button>
    </div>
</form>
```

We have a very basic <form> element with some <label> elements, some <input> fields, three of them plain text ones, two radio buttons, and a few standard HTML <button> elements. This will form the basis of our example.

The class names are meant to help in formatting, with the <label> elements styled with float:left and half the width of the form, which is set to a suitable size. None of this formatting is particularly interesting or relevant to this example.

Creating the YUI Button objects

We can now construct our shiny new Button objects to replace the existing, boring, standard <button> elements. Add the following <script> block directly before the closing </body> tag:

```
<script type="text/javascript">
    YAHOO.util.Event.onDOMReady(function() {
        var Dom = YAHOO.util.Dom, Event = YAHOO.util.Event,
            Button = YAHOO.widget.Button,
            ButtonGroup = YAHOO.widget.ButtonGroup;

        //define a submit Button object
        var mySubmit = new Button("mySubmit");
    });
</script>
```

This very simple script uses the YAHOO.widet.Button() constructor, with the name of the standard <button> element that we want to transform into a Button Control passed in as an argument. The constructor is wrapped in our sandbox, where we have defined our shortcuts plus those of the two classes that make the Button component. This is how the two buttons would look at this point:

The one on the right is the YUI button while the left one is the standard one. Admittedly, as most desktops now have 3D shading effects, the built-in buttons no longer look so flat and boring; I actually had to find an old computer to get it to look this bad. But looks are not the only reason to use YUI buttons. We'll explore some of the configuration options available to us.

After creating the submit button, we can add the following to create the reset button:

```
var myReset = new Button("myReset", {
    disabled: true,
    onclick: {
        fn: function() {
            //disable once clicked
            this.set("disabled", true);
        }
    }
});
```

For the reset button we'll have it initially disabled, after all, there would be nothing to reset yet. We'll also add a function to be executed every time it is clicked. In it, we simply disable this button because, after resetting all input fields in the form, there is no point in insisting. The `onclick` event listener has `this` conveniently set to the button itself. We could have had it changed by using the `scope` property to set it to something else. Later on we'll see how to re-enable the button.

Just as with the Submit button, we don't need to tell Button that this one is of `type` `reset`, it already knows from the markup it read. Likewise, we don't need to tell it what its default action should be; we may add extras like the previous function, but each enhanced button will know what to do.

Configuration attributes that are set in the constructor can be easily accessed and changed if necessary using the `.get()` or `.set()` methods, as we just did with `disabled`. This is a feature provided by the Element Utility.

Creating the YUI Buttons for the other elements in the page is just as easy:

```
var myButtonGroup = new ButtonGroup("myButtonGroup", {
    disabled: true
});

//define a link button
var tacs = new Button("tacs", {
        type: "link",
        href: "tacs.html",
        target: "_blank",
        onclick: {
          fn: function() {
              //when the T&C are read, enable the I Agree button
              myButtonGroup.set("disabled", false);
          }
        }
});
```

For the radio buttons we cannot create a single button but instead create a `ButtonGroup`. In this case we don't give the constructor a reference to any individual radio button but to the container that groups them all. There is also some more elaborate markup that we can use to define a set of radio buttons, which gives us more flexibility and control in the visual aspect both with and without JavaScript enabled, so it is more amenable for Progressive Enhancement situations. It is quite lengthy and complicated and it adds little to the concepts discussed in this chapter so we won't cover it.

We had the Agree/Disagree radio buttons initially disabled because we meant our visitor to read the Terms and Conditions page. That is what we do with the `tacs` button. We declare it as of `type: "link"` and provide both an `href` and `target` so, when the button is clicked, a page showing those terms will appear. At the same time, we add a listener to the click event enabling the group of radio buttons so the visitor can explicitly agree to the terms just read.

Let's set a function so that the enabled/disabled state of our buttons changes. **Reset** will be available as soon as any change has been made, while **Submit** will become enabled once all the fields have at least one character and the visitor has agreed to the terms and conditions:

```
var fields = Dom.getElementsByClassName("field");

var setButtonState = function() {

    //check if radio is set to Agree
    var submitReady =
        myButtonGroup.get("checkedButton") == "Button radio2";
    var resetReady = submitReady;
    Dom.batch(fields,function (el) {
        //submit is ready when all fields are non-empty
        submitReady = submitReady && el.value.length;
        //reset is read when any field is non-empty
        resetReady = resetReady || el.value.length;
    });
    mySubmit.set("disabled",!submitReady);
    myReset.set("disabled", !resetReady);
};

//adjust the reset and submit buttons state when the inputs change
myButtonGroup.on("checkedButtonChange", setButtonState);
Event.on(fields, "keyup",  setButtonState);

//set the initial state
setButtonState();
```

First we locate the fields to be filled by their class name and store them in `fields`. Function `setButtonState()` uses two variables to find out the state of the fields, one, `submitReady`, will determine whether the submit button should be enabled, the other, `resetReady`, the reset button. Both are initially set to the same value, whether the visitor has agreed to our conditions. We then loop over all the nodes in the fields array, and here `submitReady` requires all fields to have a non-zero (truish) length while `resetReady` accepts any being non-empty. Once the loop is finished, we set the disabled state for each button.

We call `setButtonState()` for any change in the state of the radio buttons, on any keystroke on the fields or just when the page is loaded to set the initial state.

Using the Split Button type

Using most of the different Button Controls is similar to what we did previously; each Button can be initially configured via a series of attributes, and those attributes can be easily set or obtained at any point in the script. As we saw in the previous example, using the custom events defined by each class is equally as simple.

Two Button types that we didn't cover in the last example were the Menu Button and Split Button types, both of which are highly specialized controls not available natively under HTML.

The Menu Button displays a Menu when it is clicked, allowing us to bundle up a series of related actions into a single `Button` object. The Split Button is similar but its face is split into two sections — the Button itself and a drop-down that allows the Menu to be opened. We won't be looking at the Menu Button as it is simply what the Split Button has on its right-hand side.

By the end of the example, we'll have a page the same as shown in the following screenshot, in which the visitor has just clicked on the down-arrow to the right of the split in the button to unfold the menu and is hovering over the options:

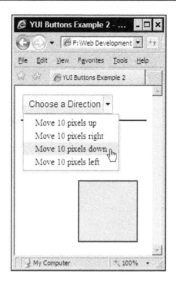

Getting started

The Menu and Split Buttons are really an agglomeration of several components, thus they will have the longest list of dependencies we've had so far. Besides the ever-present `yahoo-dom-events.js`, which should always go first, we'll need to add `element-min.js`, `container-core-min.js`, `menu-min.js`, and `button-min.js` as well as the skin files for Button and Menu. As always, the safest way to ensure we have everything is to check the Dependency Configurator.

Our HTML for this example is also simple:

```
<div id="splitContainer"></div>
<div id="square"></div>
```

The first `<div>` will contain our button while the second is the box we'll move around. We'll use CSS to position and color it:

```
<style type="text/css">
    #square {
        position: absolute;
        width: 100px;
        height: 100px;
        background-color: lightblue;
        border: 2px solid darkblue;
        left: 100px;
        top: 100px;
    }
</style>
```

Scripting the Split Button

Everything is in place, we can now move on to adding the JavaScript that will bring our Split Button control to life. Directly above the closing `</body>` tag we add the following `<script>` block:

```
<script type="text/javascript">
    YAHOO.util.Event.onDOMReady(function() {
        var Dom = YAHOO.util.Dom;

        var direction;

        //define the menuSelect function
        var menuSelect = function(type, args, item) {

            //set the button label to the selected menuitem text
            mySplitButton.set("label", this.cfg.getProperty("text"));
            direction = item.value;
            moveSquare();
        };

        //define an array of menuitem objects
        var splitMenu = [
            {text: "Move 10 pixels up", value:"up",
                            onclick:{fn:menuSelect}},
            {text: "Move 10 pixels right", value:"right",
                            onclick:{fn:menuSelect}},
            {text: "Move 10 pixels down",  value:"down",
                            onclick:{fn:menuSelect}},
            {text: "Move 10 pixels left",  value:"left",
                            onclick:{fn:menuSelect}}
        ];

        //generate a splitButton
        var mySplitButton = new YAHOO.widget.Button({
            type:      "split",
            label:     "Choose a Direction",
            name:      "mySplitButton",
            menu:      splitMenu,
            container: "splitContainer"
        });
    });
</script>
```

Let us look at this code from the bottom up. We create a button `mySplitButton`, which is a Button of type `split`, we give it a `name`, a `label`, and say where it will be contained. We further define the `menu` that it will unfold, `splitMenu`, which is defined right above.

The menu definition is simply an array of configuration objects, one for each menu item, each made of a `text` (the label to be shown), the `value` to be returned by the menu item when asked, and how to handle it. Of course, this is just the same menu definition that Menu's `itemData` configuration attribute would have taken, so we are free to add any attributes we want, even submenus. In this case, all menu options are handled by the same function `menuSelect()`, which is defined right above.

In `menuSelect()` we read the `text` that corresponds to the menu item selected and set it as the `label` for the whole button and also read the `value` of that menu item and assign it to variable `direction`, which we defined right above.

We had to read this code segment from the bottom up because every piece needed to be defined before being used in a later stage. If we had placed everything in the order we've commented on it, many references, (`menuSelect()`, `splitMenu`) would have been `undefined`. We don't face that problem with `moveSquare()` because that function will be called much later, when the visitor clicks the Split Button, and by that time all references will be resolved.

In `menuSelect()` we can see a difference in programming style among components. The Menu component is old style; it is a subclass of the Container family. To read or write any of its configuration attributes, we need to refer to its configuration object, `.cfg`, and use `.getProperty()` or `.setProperty()`. Button, on the other hand, is a new-style component, which inherits from `Element`, so to read or write its properties we simply use `.get()` or `.set()` directly.

Moreover, `menuSelect()` itself is an old-style event listener because it is called by the Menu persona of the Split Button, while the listener for the click event on the button persona of that same button is new style. The most obvious difference is in the number and nature of the arguments each receives; the old-style listener receives the `type` argument that reports the event that was fired.

If we loaded the page at this stage, it would actually look like the screenshot seen earlier, though the square would not move at all. To add movement, we need to add the moveSquare() function:

```
var moveSquare = function() {

  //get the square div and its existing coordinates
  var square = Dom.get("square"),
      x = Dom.getX(square),
      y = Dom.getY(square);

  //move the square
  switch (direction) {
    case "up":
      Dom.setY(square, y - 10);
      break;
    case "right":
      Dom.setX(square, x + 10);
      break;
    case "down":
      Dom.setY(square, y + 10);
      break;
    case "left":
      Dom.setX(square, x - 10);
      break;
    default:
      //there was no direction chosen
      alert("Please choose a direction");
  }
};

//execute moveSquare when button is clicked
mySplitButton.on("click", moveSquare);
```

The moveSquare() function uses the Dom utility methods to locate the square and read its current x-y coordinates and adjust them depending on the value of variable direction, which we've set previously in menuSelect(). If direction is none of the above values, it means none has been selected yet and it prompts the visitor for one.

Finally, we add a listener for a click event on the button (left) part of the Split Button so the square will both move on first selecting the menu option and, once selected, it will keep moving with each click on the button.

Tree-like structures with the TreeView Control

Back in *Chapter 3* when we looked at the Dom utility, we saw the DOM Inspector provided by Firefox (under the heading *DOM concepts*). DOM viewers are an excellent example of a useful tree-like representation of a series of objects (in that example the objects making up a web page), and the TreeView control can be used to create tree-like structures that are just as useful. File system explorers, such as Windows Explorer or the Finder application on the Mac, are also common examples of tree structures at work.

This component is extremely versatile and provides essential methods for adding and removing nodes programmatically, as well as loading node data dynamically. It also has a set of default behaviors that can be manipulated to give you the effects you want.

It even allows you to override the default behavior of allowing several parent nodes to be expanded at once in order to use the tree control as a navigation menu, and has the capability to be combined with the Animation Utility to provide transition effects when opening and closing nodes.

The TreeView is one of the oldest visual components in the library, and it shows. All its formatting is done with HTML tables, one per row because most browsers didn't fully support CSS when it was designed. The component had a big review for version 2.6 (after the first edition of this book) when it got several features added such as Progressive Enhancement, node editing, keyboard navigation, and others. However, when the component was updated, the old interfaces were kept for the benefit of existing applications, thus there are more ways to do something than would make sense, one the old deprecated, but still supported way, the other the new style. This concern for backward compatibility also made it impossible to make TreeView inherit from `Element`, as all newer components do. All this makes TreeView a one-of-a-kind component within the library.

Planting the seed

There are three ways to build a tree; we can point to existing HTML consisting of a series of nested ordered or unordered lists (`<ol>` or `<ul>`) and TreeView will enhance it. We can have a literal object defining the tree, or we can create and append one node at a time.

If we had the following HTML:

```
<div id="markup">
    <ul>
        <li class="expanded">List 0
            <ul>
                <li class="expanded">List 0-0
                    <ul>
                        <li>item 0-0-0</li>
                        <li><a target="_new"
                            href="http://www.elsewhere.com"
                            title="go elsewhere">elsewhere</a></li>
                    </ul>
                </li>
            </ul>
        </li>
        <li>List 1
            <ul>
                <li>List 1-0
                    <ul>
                        <li>02/01/2009</li>
                        <li>item 1-1-0</li>
                    </ul>
                </li>
            </ul>
        </li>
    </ul>
</div>
```

This is all the code we would need to enhance this static HTML into a full TreeView:

```
<script type="text/javascript">
    YAHOO.util.Event.onDOMReady(function() {
        var myTree = new YAHOO.widget.TreeView("markup");
        myTree.render();
    });
</script>
```

We just need to provide the constructor with a reference to the container of the HTML to be enhanced and then render it. Each <li> element will be turned into a tree node. The text content of each <li> element will become its label and, if followed by an <ul> or <ol>, a branch will be created. TreeView will recognize a few things in it. If an <li> element has a class name of expanded that branch will be expanded when enhanced, otherwise, they will all be collapsed. TreeView also accepts an anchor <a> element instead of plain text and it will preserve its functionality. The tree would look like this:

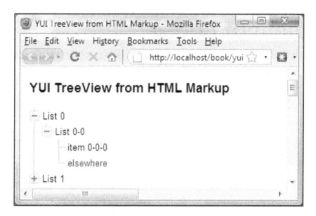

The second way of building a tree is by using a literal definition. Assuming an empty container, the above tree could be build by the following code:

```
var myTree1 = new YAHOO.widget.TreeView("emptyContainer", [
    {label:"List 0", expanded:true, children:[
        {label:"List 0-0", expanded:true, children:[
            "item 0-0-0",
            {label:"elsewhere", title:"go elsewhere",
                href:"http://www.elsewhere.com/", target:"_new"}
        ]}
    ]},
    {label:"List 1", children:[
        {label:"List 1-0", children :[
            "02/01/2009",
            "item 1-1-0"
        ]}
    ]}
]);
myTree1.render();
```

This code will produce in an empty container the very same tree as before. The definition is made of a series of nested arrays of nodes. Each item in the array can either be a plain string, if no other options are required, or an object with values for each property to be set. An extra property, `children`, takes a further array of nodes to be nested to that node.

Method `.getTreeDefinition()` returns an object such as the one seen earlier, which can be saved and used later on to rebuild the same tree.

An assortment of nodes

So far, we have dealt with text nodes, which are the most basic type of node, but TreeView supports several types:

- `TextNode`: The most basic, plain node.
- `HTMLNode`: Instead of plain text, it contains HTML.
- `DateNode`: A `TextNode` containing a date. It only makes a difference when editing because it will pop up a Calendar to edit its label.
- `MenuNode`: A `TextNode` that allows only one node expanded at a time.

They all inherit from `YAHOO.widget.Node`, which provides the basic behavior for any node. You never create an instance of `Node`, it is what in other languages we would call an "abstract" class. A further node type is `RootNode`, which is automatically created alongside the `TreeView` and is the root of the entire tree. The `RootNode` is hidden; it is an invisible container.

We will create an assortment of nodes in an empty container:

```
<script type="text/javascript">
   YAHOO.util.Event.onDOMReady(function() {
      var TreeView = YAHOO.widget.TreeView,
          TextNode = YAHOO.widget.TextNode,
          HTMLNode = YAHOO.widget.HTMLNode,
          MenuNode = YAHOO.widget.MenuNode,
          DateNode = YAHOO.widget.DateNode;


      //create a TreeView object
      var tree = new TreeView("treeDiv");

      //find the root of the tree
      var root = tree.getRoot();

      var text = new TextNode({label:"first text node"}, root);
```

```
            var text1 = new TextNode("first text child", text);
            var text2 = new TextNode({
                label: "second child text",
                href: "http://yahoo.com",
                target: "_new"
            }, text);

            var HTML = new HTMLNode(
                {html:"first HTML node <img src='icons/script.png' />"}
                                                        ,root);

            var menu = new MenuNode("first menu node", root);
            var menu1 = new MenuNode("first menu child node", menu);
            var menu2 = new MenuNode("second menu child node", menu);

            var date = new DateNode(
                        {label:"01/02/2010",editable: true}, root);

            tree.subscribe("clickEvent", tree.onEventEditNode);

            tree.render();
        });
    </script>
```

In our customary sandbox, we create shortcuts for all the node types TreeView offers, at least those we can create. We then create the `TreeView` instance in a container, `treeDiv`, which is empty, there is no markup to read from it, and locate the `root` node, which is part of the `tree` instance.

We create a set of three text nodes. The second argument to each constructor points to the parent for each new node. The first node branches off the `root` while the other two are its children; this is the way we can nest nodes next to one another. The first argument for any type of node is a configuration object. For a `TextNode`, the main attribute to set is `label`. Text nodes accept a plain string instead, which will be used for the `label` property. Text nodes take an optional third argument, `expanded`, which is the same as setting the `expanded` property to `true` in the configuration object.

The last of the text nodes has the `href` and `target` properties set so it will open the Yahoo home page in a new window. This is one of the anomalies kept for backward compatibility, a `TextNode` with `href` set behaves differently than without; it should be a completely different type of node, a LinkNode, if you will, but that doesn't exist.

After the text nodes, we create an `HTMLNode` that doesn't have a `label` property but an `html` property instead. The first argument can also be a string, which will be assigned to the `html` property. Can you put an anchor `<a>` element in it? You can, but it will be inactive, it won't navigate anywhere. The TreeView captures all clicks in its nodes and prevents all default actions except for text nodes with `href` set.

We then create a series of menu nodes. The only difference in between them and plain text nodes is that if you expand **first menu node**, any other node at that same depth in the tree will collapse. However, if you expand the **first text node**, the `MenuNode` won't collapse. Menu nodes have ego problems, text nodes are fine. Menu nodes are not meant to be created in isolation as in this example but when you want a tree that acts like a menu, where expanding one branch collapses all others.

Finally, we create a `DateNode` with a literal string for a date and make it `editable`. We do so because otherwise, a `DateNode` is no different from a `TextNode`. A `DateNode` is a `TextNode` that uses a Calendar component as its editor, if editable. There is no further difference. To control the Calendar, `DateNode` has a `calendarOptions` property that will be passed through to the Calendar when created. This allows us, for example, to change from the default `mm/dd/yyyy` format to any other date format.

Date nodes and text nodes (or menu nodes) with the `href` property not set are editable. For text nodes, a simple textbox will pop up, for Date nodes, if the Calendar component has been loaded, a full Calendar will appear. However, setting the `editable` property is not enough; we need to let the TreeView know how we intend to trigger the editor. For that, we subscribe to `clickEvent` and set `.onEventEditNode()` as its listener. We could attach the editor to a double-click or pop it up with a context menu. Any node with `editable` set will then become editable, except `HTMLNodes` and those that have `href` set.

Finally, we render the tree.

Reading from markup

When creating a node from markup, TreeView will create a `TextNode` for all nodes starting with text or an anchor element and, in the latter case it will fill in the `href` and `target` properties. If the first element it finds is not text or an anchor element, it will create an `HTMLNode`. TreeView will only read in a single DOM element from each list item; if more than one is needed, we have to wrap it in a `<span>` or `<div>` to hold them.

As the amount of information that TreeView can read from existing markup is limited, TreeView will parse an extra custom `yuiConfig` attribute on an `<li>` element and read extra property values from it. For example, TreeView cannot create a `DateNode` from markup directly because a date string looks pretty much like plain text. We can force a `DateNode` by using the `yuiConfig` attribute like this:

```
<li yuiConfig='{"type":"DateNode","editable":true}'>02/01/2009</li>
```

This will make TreeView create a `DateNode` instead of a `TextNode` and make it `editable`. The value of the `yuiConfig` property should be in JSON format and the JSON Utility must be included if this option is used.

When building a tree from an object literal, the `type` property can be used to set the node type. If it is not present, a `TextNode` will be assumed. This would make a `MenuNode`:

```
{type:'MenuNode',label:'branch 3',title:'this is a menu node'}
```

The `type` property can also take the strings `text`, `menu`, or `html` as shorthand.

TreeView members

Unlike components that inherit from `Element`, when you change a property on a node, it will not be reflected in its appearance. If I locate a node and set its `href` property, the label won't turn blue and underlined. If I set the `expanded` property on a node that is already rendered, it won't expand, I would have to call the `.expand()` method to make it change. This is an old-style component; we have to use its methods:

- `.expandAll()`: Expands the whole tree.
- `.collapseAll()`: Collapses the whole tree.
- `.getNodeByXxxx()`: A family of methods that allow us to locate a node in a tree by several criteria.
- `.getTreeDefinition()`: Returns a full definition of this tree, which can be used to rebuild the tree.
- `.removeNode()` and `.removeChildren()`: To remove a node and all its children or only its children.
- `.popNode()`: Removes a node that we can then add elsewhere.
- `.setNodesProperty()`: Sets a property on all nodes at once.
- `.setExpandAnim()` and `.setCollapseAnim()`: Lets us set an animation from those in `YAHOO.widget.TVAnim`.
- `.onEventEditNode()`: An event listener to edit an editable node. Not meant to be called directly.

- `.onEventToggleHighlight()`: An event listener to toggle the highlight state of a node. Not meant to be called directly.

- `.setDynamicLoad()`: To set a function to load nodes on demand.

TreeView has a few properties worth mentioning. Some of the properties listed in the API docs should be marked private and shouldn't be shown, we'll only mention:

- `.currentFocus`: This property shows the node that currently has the focus.

- `.singleNodeHighlight`: When highlighting is enabled, this property allows only one node to be highlighted at a time.

- `.validator`: A validating function can be set to validate any node when saved after having been edited.

As for events, the most useful are:

- `expand` / `collapse`: This event tells when a node is about to be expanded/ collapsed. The listener receives a reference to the node being changed and, if it returns `false`, the operation will be cancelled.

- `expandComplete` / `collapseComplete`: This event tells that the operation has just completed successfully.

- `clickEvent, dblClickEvent`: They report those same browser events with the node that was (dbl) clicked already, resolved and passed as an argument.

- `enterKeyPressed`: When navigating via keyboard, pressing the *Enter* key is much like clicking on the node that currently has the focus.

- `focusChanged`: This event reports when the focus has changed from a node to another, via mouse or keyboard. Either the new or old nodes might be `null` if the focus comes from or goes outside the tree.

- `editorSaveEvent, editorCancelEvent`: This event is used to keep track of changes done by the editor.

- `highlightEvent`: This event reports changes in node highlighting.

The TreeView will always respond to clicking on the plus (+)/ minus (-) (toggle) icon by toggling the expand/collapse state of the node. On `TextNodes` with the `href` property set, clicking on the label or pressing *Enter* while that node has the focus will navigate as expected; we cannot change that behavior.

As users will expect some sort of response from clicking on the labels; TreeView provides a default one, the only one it knows: toggling. However, we can easily prevent that. When listening to either `clickEvent` or `enterKeyPressed` after doing whatever we want, we just need to return `false` to cancel that default behavior.

Tree nodes

Most of the interesting activity occurs on the nodes. It is easy to get a hold of a node; all of the events report which node was affected by the event they signal. The `.getNodeByXxxx()` set of methods also allow us to find any nodes. The list of methods and properties for nodes is large; half of those methods should actually be private, but nobody did that in the old days; newer additions are correctly marked as private when they need to be, but the old ones have to be kept alive because plenty of applications use them. So, don't be surprised when I mention so few of them. A few others I'll discuss in later sections. As for the properties, we have:

- `.children`, `.nextSibling`, `.previousSibling`, and `.parent`: These properties are used to move around to neighboring nodes.

- `.className`: This property allows us to add extra class names to particular nodes.

- `.depth`: This property informs us how deep this node is, the root being 0.

- `.editable`: This property is used to edit node, but ignored on `HTMLNodes` or `TextNodes` with `href` set.

- `.expanded`: This property reports whether a node is expanded.

- `.hasIcon`: This property defaults to `true`, if `false`, the node will not have the toggle icon.

- `.multiExpand`: This property, if `false`, collapses the node's siblings when the node is expanded. A `MenuNode` is a `TextNode` with this property set to `false`.

- `.nowrap`: This property adds a `nowrap` attribute to the label cell to prevent it from wrapping to the next line.

- `.renderHidden`: TreeView will not waste time rendering nodes that are not visible until the parent node is expanded. When this is `true`, they will be rendered even if collapsed.

- `.tree`: This property refers to the TreeView instance this node belongs to.

Properties `.className`, `.editable`, `.expanded`, `.hasIcon`, `.multiExpand`, `.nowrap`, and `.renderHidden` can be set when creating the node instance. Once the tree is rendered, they have no or limited effect. Each specific node type may have extra properties: Text nodes have `.label`, `.href`, `.target`, and `.title` (tooltip text), HTML nodes have `.html`, and date nodes have `.calendarConfig`.

As for methods, we have:

- `.appendTo()`: This method appends a node, possibly popped from elsewhere, as the last child of this node.

- `.applyParent()`: This method after appending allows a branch to receive properties that trickle down from the tree.

- `.collapse()`, `.collapseAll()`, `.expand()`, `.expandAll()`, and `.toggle()`: These methods quite predictably do what their names suggest.

- `.editNode()`: This method brings up the node editor.

- `.focus()`: This method sets the focus on this node.

- `.getAncestor(n)`: This method reaches up to the nth parent.

- `.getNodeCount()`: This method returns the number of nodes in this branch, at all levels.

- `.getNodeDefinition()`: This method returns an object definition of this node and its descendants. TreeView's `.getTreeDefinition()` calls this function on the root node.

- `.getSiblings()`: This method returns an array of the contiguous nodes at this same level, except for itself.

- `.hasChildren()`: This method reports if the node has children. It can report on nodes loaded dynamically.

- `.insertAfter()`, `.insertBefore()`: This method inserts younger or older siblings to this node.

- `.isRoot()`: This method reports if the node is the root.

- `.setNodesProperty()`: This method sets a property on all nodes in a branch.

Additionally, `HTMLNode` has `.setHtml()` to force new content into the node and have it shown.

Custom information

When creating a node we can set many of the properties that define the node. TreeView further allows us to add extra, custom properties to any node. When TreeView parses the `yuiConfig` attribute of existing markup, when it reads an object definition, or when a node instance is created, the values for existing properties will be read and set. Any property TreeView doesn't know about will be saved in each node in an object under the `.data` property. All these three fragments:

```
var node = new YAHOO.widget.TextNode(
                                {label:"root", dir:"/", …}, parent);
{type:"text",label:"root", dir:"/", ….. }
<li yuiConfig='{"dir":"/"}'>root</li>
```

will produce a `TextNode` so that `node.label` will return `root` and `node.data.dir`
will return `/`. Custom properties will always be found as subproperties of property
`.data`. Method `.getNodesByProperty()` can locate both; it will first search for the
requested property amongst the node's native properties and then it will also look
for custom properties under `.data`.

Dynamic loading

When a tree might be too big to build all at once, we can do so on demand as the
branches expand. TreeView already avoids rendering nodes that are in collapsed
branches, but the node is still created in the browser's memory though it won't be
rendered until its parent is expanded. With dynamic loading we can retrieve the
information for a node as needed.

To set up a tree for dynamic loading we have to call method `.setDynamicLoad()`
either for the full tree or for a specific node, and provide it with a function that will
do the loading. When a node is expanded for the first time, it will look for a dynamic
loader, either of its own or a generic one for the whole tree. If there is one it will call
it pointing to itself, so the loader knows which node is being expanded, and will
also provide a function for the loader to signal when it is done. The following simple
script will keep expanding the tree with three new children forever:

```
YAHOO.util.Event.onDOMReady(function() {

    //create a TreeView object
    var tree = new YAHOO.widget.TreeView("treeDiv","0");

    //set the dynamic loader
    tree.setDynamicLoad(function (node, onCompleteCallback) {
        //always add three nodes
        for (var i = 0; i < 3; i++) {
            (new YAHOO.widget.TextNode(node.label + '-' + i , node));
        }
        //signal we're done after a little suspense
        window.setTimeout(onCompleteCallback, 500);
    });

    //generate the tree
    tree.render();
});
```

Each time a node is expanded, our dynamic loader will be called, which will add three new nodes to the tree using the node being expanded, the one received as an argument, as their parent. Each has its `label` set to that of its parent plus an index suffix. In a real-world scenario, we would probably need to call `YAHOO.util.Connect.asyncRequest()` to retrieve the node information and we wouldn't be able to call `onCompleteCallback()` until the reply came back from the server. We have used `.setTimeout()` to simulate this delay.

For a more real-world example, the downloadable examples (see the Preface) have a working script that does call a small PHP script that sends information back.

A couple of properties are important for dynamic loading. TreeView cannot know beforehand if a node actually has children or not; by default it always offers an expand icon assuming that there might be more children to fetch. If we know that a node has no further children, we can set the `.isLeaf` property to `true` so TreeView knows there won't be any further children. In the associated example, we list the files in the `examples` directory. If the name belongs to a directory, we leave `.isLeaf` as `false`, so it can be expanded further. For files, we set `.isLeaf` to `true` as we cannot go any further.

Sometimes we want to mix static and dynamic nodes. If we set a dynamic loader, TreeView will try to load extra nodes when expanding any node, even those that are already loaded with static children. To signal that a node is done and needs no further loading, we can set `.dynamicLoadComplete` to `true`.

TreeView will not drop nodes loaded dynamically when their branch is collapsed. Don't expect nodes to be refreshed by toggling them; once loaded, their children remain loaded. However, we can listen to `collapseComplete` and remove all the children, and also set `.dynamicLoadComplete` back to `false` so TreeView will attempt to load them again.

It is a good idea to avoid calling `.expandAll()` when there is dynamic loading. TreeView disables the *Shift* + keystroke on dynamic trees. After all, if the tree was deemed too large to load all at once, we wouldn't want our visitors to inadvertently request a full expansion. Moreover, dynamic trees may not be finite, such as when they have loops; trying to expand them in full would not be possible and would be fatal to an application that attempts it.

Highlighting

TreeView supports node highlighting/selection (they are treated as one). These are different from simply setting the focus on a particular node, a feature common to all elements on a page. Any number of nodes may be highlighted or selected at once. TreeView also supports branch highlighting; selection of a node may propagate down so that when a node is selected all its children are selected as well. It can also propagate up so that if a node is highlighted, its parent and all its ancestors will also be highlighted; however, on each ancestor, TreeView will check the state of the rest of the children. If all children are highlighted, the parent will be fully highlighted, if only some of the children are highlighted, the parent will be partially highlighted. Propagation stops on nodes not enabled for highlighting.

Highlighting and propagation are set on a per-node basis. Method `.setNodesProperty()` is very handy so we can set these options on all the tree at once. The following would set a tree for highlighting in response to clicking on a node and set propagation in both directions:

```
myTree.subscribe('clickEvent',myTree.onEventToggleHighlight);
myTree.setNodesProperty('propagateHighlightUp', true);
myTree.setNodesProperty('propagateHighlightDown', true);
```

We first decide on which event will produce the highlighting and then set the built-in listener to handle that event. Then we set the propagate properties on all nodes of the tree or a specific branch. Property `.enableHighlight` is always on by default on all nodes.

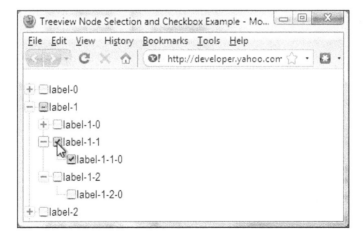

The screenshot shows a random tree after clicking on node **label-1-1**. The highlighting has propagated down to **label-1-1-0** and up to **label-1**, which shows as partially highlighted as only one of its children is highlighted.

Highlighting simply sets a class name on each node; it is up to the designer to provide the visual clue to the visitor. The skinned CSS file provided along with TreeView offers two styles of highlighting. To activate either of them we just need to set the class name on the overall container for the tree. To have the above highlighting, we just need to use the `ygtv-checkbox` class name, and there is a plainer `ygtv-highlight` that simply colors the nodes.

All nodes have `enableHighlight` set to `true` because if you don't specify any highlighting skin no highlighting will be apparent, so it doesn't really matter. To make highlighting visible in a similar way to the above, a designer might add:

```
.myHighlightingStyle .ygtv-highlight0 .ygtvcontent {
    padding-left:1em;
    background:url(check0.gif) no-repeat;
}

.myHighlightingStyle .ygtv-highlight1 .ygtvcontent {
    padding-left:1em;
    background:url(check1.gif) no-repeat;
}

.myHighlightingStyle .ygtv-highlight2 .ygtvcontent{
    padding-left:1em;
    background:url(check2.gif) no-repeat;
}
```

The suffixes on both the `ygtv-highlight` class name and the icon file name correspond to the three possible highlight states: 0: no highlight, 1: normal highlight, and 2: partial highlight.

TreeView offers several methods and properties to handle highlighting.

- `.singleNodeHighlight`: When `true`, only one node can remain active at once. Propagation is disabled.
- `.getHighlightedNode()`: This method returns the highlighted node, only when `.singleNodeHighlight` is set.
- `.onEventToggleHighlight()`: Built in listener to toggle highlighting in response to an event such as `clickEvent`, `dblClickEvent`, or `enterKeyPressed`.

No method is provided to return the highlighted nodes when `.singleNodeHighlight` is `false` because when propagation is enabled there are several possible interpretations on what should be returned. Calling `.getNodesByProperty("highlightState",1)` would return an array of fully highlighted nodes, but what about partially highlighted ones? Often times we need only highlighted leafs, not intermediate nodes. TreeView leaves this open to us.

TreeView will fire the `highlightEvent` event reporting the node that has caused the change. It does not report on nodes that have received the highlight by propagation.

At the node level, we have:

- `.enableHighlight`: Whether the node is amenable to be highlighted and propagate the highlight.
- `.highlightState`: Which can be `0`: not highlighted, `1`: highlighted, or `2`: partially highlighted.
- `.propagateHighlightUp` and `.propagateHighlightDown`: Enables propagation of highlight. A partially highlighted state can only be achieved by upward propagation from its children.
- `.highlight()`, `.unhighlight()`, and `.toggleHighlight()`: Once rendered, highlighting should be handled via these methods.

On a dynamically loaded tree, if a node being expanded has `.propagateHighlightDown` set, the freshly loaded children will inherit its highlight state, regardless of their configuration when created. Partial highlighting never propagates down.

The property `.highlightState` can be set when creating a node instance, but it will not propagate when the tree is rendered.

Summary

The Button family of controls is a versatile replacement to the dusty old native HTML Button element, providing enhanced features and functionality, wrapped up in an attractive and aesthetically appealing package.

The TreeView control is an important component of the library that creates an object with no analogous native counterpart. It creates a tree-like control, which enables you to show the relationship between different objects in an intuitive and easy-to-use interface.

Both controls are backed up by rich and feature-packed classes that add the functionality and behavior that you'd expect from web design aids of the calibre found in the YUI Library.

9
DataSource and AutoComplete

We've seen how to retrieve remote information via the Connection manager. A lot of the information we use is structured as tables; anything coming from a database server is likely to be tabular. In this chapter, we're going to look at the DataSource, which allows us to fetch tabular data from different sources, both local and remote, and in different formats, extract the fields, parse them if necessary, and deliver them to the component that requested them. We will also see one of these clients, the AutoComplete control, which offers a list of choices based on what you type. Two more components use DataSource: DataTable, which we'll see shortly, and Charts, which is still beta and won't be covered.

The skills that you will take away from this chapter include:

- The different sources DataSource can reach
- The various data formats supported
- How to tell DataSource what to extract and how to parse it
- How to implement an autocomplete text field linked to a live data source

Tabular data sources

Once upon a time the concept of a table was somewhat harder to explain. Nowadays it is easy to say that a data table is like a spreadsheet, and if that doesn't work, you simply mention the brand of whatever spreadsheet program happens to be popular at the time. Still, that is not exactly a good analogy; in a spreadsheet, any cell can contain anything you want, completely unrelated the contents of its neighbors.

In a database table, each row will contain assorted information about an item, students on a class, passengers on a tour, tracks in a music album, or departing flights, while each column will contain similar information about each of the items such as names, destinations, departure times, grades, and so on. We call each row a record, each column a column, and the data at each intersection a field. All the fields in the same column will be of the same data type. In the names column, they will all be strings; if grades, they will be letters or numbers (it varies as per country). Any of the cells might contain a special value that is neither a number nor a string and that is null, which says that there is no information at all.

Tabular information can be available in several formats. DataSource can handle the following:

- Delimited text: Data is a single stream of characters with two special characters reserved, one to mark the end of each record, another to mark the end of each field.

- HTML table: The data is in the body of a table, each table row containing a record, each cell a field.

- Array: The data is an array where each array item is a record, each one composed of either a further array or an object literal containing the fields.

- XML: The data is stored as repeating occurrences of a DOM element and each field is either an attribute or a nested DOM element.

- JSON: A representation of an array, serialized into a string, usually nested within an "envelope".

The last three formats are capable of having nested fields. A single field such as an address might be broken into city, state, zip, street name, street number, floor, and door number, each having its own subcell within the larger cell.

DataSource classes

Data can be local or remote and if remote it might be within the same domain or have to be reached across domains. For each, DataSource has a specific class:

- `LocalDataSource`: Used to access data, such as arrays or HTML tables that are already in the client

- `XHRDataSource`: Used for remote data accessible via XHR, using Conection Manager's `.asyncRequest()`

- `ScriptNodeDataSource`: Used for accessing remote data in JSONP format from other domains

- `FunctionDataSource`: Used when a function will provide the data

All these classes are subclasses of `DataSourceBase` which is an "abstract" class. There is also the handy `DataSource`, which is not really a class but a factory. DataSource will try to guess from its arguments what kind of DataSource you actually need and return that one. You actually never get a DataSource when you try to create an instance of DataSource, you'll always end up getting one of the four listed earlier.

For some obscure reason, a few more classes have been packed along with the DataSource component, they are:

- `Number`: This class contains a single static function `.format()` used to format numbers with decimal and thousand separators, fixed number of decimals, prefix and suffix, all of them configurable.

- `Date`: This class contains a single static function `.format()` used to format dates in several formats and locales.

- `DateLocale`: This class is used by `Date` to store locale information. The default is American English (`"en-US"`, used also as `"en"`) but it also contains British and Australian (`"en-GB"` and `"en-AU"`).

We won't discuss these additional classes as they are pretty simple to use and are otherwise unrelated to DataSource itself.

All classes of this component reside under `YAHOO.util` as none of them has any visible interface.

All DataSource subclasses are used very much alike. Unless we need to highlight something about one of them, we will always refer to them by the generic DataSource.

The DataSource constructor takes two arguments, the first a reference to the data and the second, optional, a configuration object. The first argument can be:

- A string: DataSource will assume it is a URL and return an `XHRDataSource`.

- A function: DataSource will return a `FunctionDataSource`.

- A JavaScript array: DataSource will return a `LocalDataSource`.

- A reference to an HTML table: DataSource will return a `LocalDataSource`.

DataSource will never produce a `ScriptNodeDataSource` by guessing, as both an `XHRDataSource` and a `ScriptNodeDataSource` take a URL as an argument.

The second argument can be used to set any of DataSource's properties; the most useful are:

- `.dataType`: Any of DataSource's own static constants, one per subclass; avoids the guesswork DataSource does. You can either create a particular subclass or create the generic DataSource and use `.dataType` to tell it what you want. The default, `.TYPE_UNKNOWN`, forces DataSource to guess; otherwise we may use `.TYPE_LOCAL`, `.TYPE_XHR`, `.TYPE_SCRIPTNODE`, or `.TYPE_JSFUNCTION`.

- `.liveData`: This is the source of data; the first argument of the constructor ends up here.

- `.maxCacheEntries`: DataSource can keep a cache, beyond what the browser itself might cache. It is set to `0` by default, so it is disabled.

- `.responseType`: Can be any of DataSource's own constants to define the format of the data retrieved. We'll see each one in detail.

- `.responseSchema`: This gives information on how the data is structured; it depends on the `.responseType`.

- `.useXPath`: If the data is in XML format, this enables the use of XPath syntax to locate information.

Just as Connection Manager has a single method `.asyncRequest()` that is used most of the time, DataSource has its own, `.sendRequest()`, which initiates the retrieval. `.sendRequest()` takes two arguments (a third one is now deprecated); the first depends on the data source and we'll see it later; the second is a callback object very similar to the one we've seen for `.asyncRequest()`. It may contain:

- `success`: A function to be called upon a successful return
- `failure`: A function to be called upon a communication failure
- `scope`: Allows adjusting the scope of the success and failure functions
- `argument`: An additional argument that the callbacks will receive

Both callbacks will receive the same arguments:

- `oRequest`: Is whatever value or object `.sendRequest()` received in its first argument.
- `oParsedResponse`: Is an object containing the parsed response data.
- `oPayload`: Is whatever was passed as `argument` in the callback object.

The parsed response itself is an object made of several properties:

- `tId`: This property is the handle to the underlying communication transaction.
- `results`: This property contains the actual data.
- `error`: If this property is true, `results` will be empty.
- `cached`: This property shows a flag indicating that the data was retrieved from the cache.
- `meta`: This property has additional information retrieved from the source.

DataSource can also handle repetitive connections by calling `.sendRequest()` at regular intervals. Methods `.setInterval()`, `.clearInterval()`, and `.clearAllIntervals()` deal with this.

The configuration of a DataSource is very dependent on the source and format of the data to be retrieved so we'll see it case by case.

HTML table

The server-side scripting environment might make it very easy to generate HTML tables making this a useful data format for tabular data. We might also be in a Progressive Enhancement situation where we want to present the data to the user as a plain HTML table if JavaScript is not enabled.

DataSource can read from such a table by passing a reference to it. We are used to referencing elements in the DOM either by their id or by actual DOM reference. We cannot use the id with DataSource because, being a string, it will assume it is a URL.

For the following table:

```
<table id="sourceTable">
    <thead>
        <tr>
            <th>Driver</th>
            <th>Team</th>
            <th>Championships</th>
        </tr>
    </thead>
    <tbody>
        <tr>
            <td>Michael Schumacher</td>
            <td>Mercedes</td>
            <td>7</td>
        </tr>
```

```
        <tr>
            <td>Fernando Alonso</td>
            <td>Ferrari</td>
            <td>2</td>
        </tr>
        <tr>
            <td>Jenson Button</td>
            <td>McLaren</td>
            <td>1</td>
        </tr>
    </tbody>
</table>
```

We could retrieve it with the following code:

```
YAHOO.util.Event.onDOMReady(function () {
    var Dom = YAHOO.util.Dom, Event = YAHOO.util.Event,
        Lang = YAHOO.lang, DS = YAHOO.util.DataSource;

    var format = "<p>{driver} has won {championships}" +
                    "championships and now runs for {scuderia}<\/p>";

    var myDS = new DS(Dom.get("sourceTable"),{
        // responseType: DS.TYPE_HTMLTABLE,
        responseSchema: {
            fields: ["driver","scuderia",
                        {key:"championships",parse:"number"}]
        }
    });
    myDS.sendRequest(null, {
        success: function(oRequest, oParsedResponse) {
            if (oParsedResponse.error) {
                alert("Something went wrong");
            } else {
                var r = oParsedResponse.results,
                    output = ["<h2>F1 Pilots:</h2>"];
                for(var i = 0,len = r.length;i < len;i++) {
                    output.push(Lang.substitute(format, r[i]));
                }
                Dom.get("destination").innerHTML = output.join("\n");
            }
        },
        failure: function(oRequest, oParsedResponse) {
          alert(oParsedResponse.status + ": " +
                                    oParsedResponse.statusText);
        }
    });
});
```

For an HTML table we need to provide the DataSource constructor with a reference to the table, which Dom's `.get()` method provides us. We don't need to tell it that it needs to use a `LocalDataSource` or that the `.responseType` is of `TYPE_HTMLTABLE` (the setting is commented out) as it can find that out on its own. We need to specify the `responseSchema`, in particular the list of `fields` we want to retrieve. The first two fields are strings and we can just name them, but the third one, being a number, we need to indicate both the `key` and the `parser` to be used. This is all we need for the setup.

To actually retrieve the data, we call method `.sendRequest()`. For HTML tables, the first argument is ignored and for the second, we provide the two callback functions. In the `success` function we check if the parsed response had any errors and if not, we loop over the `results` array and format the output to be shown.

There are several important things about HTML tables: DataSource will read everything in the `<tbody>` section; headings, if any, should be in the `<thead>` section or stripped before parsing.

Fields are detected by their position in the table; the `fields` array specifies the names that those fields will be given once read; they are completely unrelated to the values in the header cells (`<th>`) of the original table. DataSource ignores headers.

DataSource gets confused if any cell spans more than a single column.

DataSource provides three built-in parsers that can be specified by their shorthand names, `number`, `string`, and `date`; this last one uses the JavaScript native `Date.parse()` method that offers limited options and is not localizable; however, a parser can be any function that receives the value to be parsed and returns it already parsed. It is very easy to define your own parsers.

Simple array

This is such a simple case that is best seen in code:

```
YAHOO.util.Event.onDOMReady(function () {
    var Dom = YAHOO.util.Dom, Event = YAHOO.util.Event,
        Lang = YAHOO.lang, DS = YAHOO.util.DataSource;

    var data = [
        ["Michael Schumacher", "Mercedes", 7],
        ["Fernando Alonso", "Ferrari", 2],
        ["Jenson Button", "McLaren", 1]
    ];

    var myDS = new DS(data,{
```

```
        // responseType: DS.TYPE_ARRAY,
        responseSchema: {
            fields: ["driver", "scuderia", "championships"]
        }
    });

    myDS.sendRequest(null,{
        /*
         *  No change in this section
         */
    });
});
```

The code is very similar to what we've seen before; the difference is that now the data resides within the code itself as an array of arrays. The `responseSchema.fields` array has no parser for the `championships` field as now it is really a native JavaScript number. Once again, the association is made by their ordinal position; the names in the fields array are not the names of the fields to fetch, as they have none, but the names to be given to those fields.

Complex array

While in the previous case, the data was made of an array, where each record was a further array with each field as an item within each record, in a complex array, each record is represented as an object with its fields named. The previous code will run exactly the same if we use this data:

```
var data = [
    {driver: "Michael Schumacher", scuderia: "Mercedes",
                                        championships:7 },
    {championships:2, driver: "Fernando Alonso",
                                        scuderia: "Ferrari"},
    {scuderia: "McLaren", championships:1, driver: "Jenson Button"}
];
```

The code is exactly the same because we've been careful to name each value with the names listed in the `fields` array. Now, as each value is named, they can be scrambled as we did; their position is now irrelevant as they are located by name. Fields might even be missing; DataSource will return `null` for them.

FunctionDataSource

Sometimes getting the data is beyond what DataSource can manage. Perhaps the data has to be merged from two different sources or somehow pre-processed. A `FunctionDataSource` is a DataSource where you can plug in whatever extra processing is needed.

```
var dataFunction = function(argument) {
    alert(argument);
    return [
        {driver: "Michael Schumacher", scuderia: "Mercedes",
                                            championships:7 },
        {championships:2, driver: "Fernando Alonso",
                                            scuderia: "Ferrari"},
        {scuderia: "McLaren", championships:1,
                                    driver: "Jenson Button"}
    ];
};

var myDS = new DS(dataFunction,{
    // responseType: DS.TYPE_ARRAY,
    responseSchema: {
        fields: ["driver","scuderia","championships"]
    }
});

myDS.sendRequest("Ok?", {
        /*
         *  No change in this section
         */
});
```

Here we define function `dataFunction()`, which, when called, should return an array like the one we saw in the previous section; in fact, we used exactly the same one. When creating the DataSource instance we provide a reference to this function as the first argument.

There is a further difference, the first argument passed to `.sendRequest()` is now used as the single argument to the function. We've used it here to show it in an alert box. So far this argument served no purpose; now it can help to tell the fetching function what it is meant to retrieve.

Remote DataSource with text

So far, all sources of data were in the page itself, whether an HTML table to progressively enhance, a local array, or a function. This function might need to connect somewhere remote to access the data but, as far as DataSource cares, it is local. Now we will deal with remote sources, that is, sources that are not in the page itself. Remote doesn't need to be too far; when developing the "remote" source is the developer's own machine, and a "remote" file is anything outside of the HTML page in the browser. So, for our example, we'll use a plain text file:

```
Michael Schumacher   Mercedes           7
Fernando Alonso      Ferrari            2
Jenson Button        McLaren            1
```

It contains the same information as we've been using this far, with the fields separated by tab characters (you can't tell spaces and tabs apart in print) and with a record per line. This simple text is in a separate file, `F1Drivers.txt`. It really doesn't matter to the browser whether this is a passive file or produced by some scripting engine; as far as the browser is concerned, this has a URL just like any other Web resource.

As the resource is remote, we now need to include `connection-min.js` in our dependencies. It is an optional dependency; we haven't used it in the previous examples. The Dependency Configurator won't include it if you don't ask for it (or add all optional dependencies, which is not a good idea).

To handle this file, we will use basically the very same script we've been using so far, the only difference is how we declare the DataSource:

```
var myDS = new DS("F1Drivers.txt", {
    responseType: DS.TYPE_TEXT,
    responseSchema: {
        fieldDelim : "\t",
        recordDelim : "\n",
        fields:
            ["driver","scuderia",{key:"championships",parse:"number"}]
    }
});
```

The argument to the constructor is now the relative URL of the "remote resource", which is the file. As it is a URL, DataSource will actually return an `XHRDataSource`. Now, we do need to specify the format of the response by setting `.responseType` to the correct constant. This is important: all data transferred remotely is just a stream of bytes; DataSource can no longer do any guessing as in the previous examples, a byte is just as good as another one, and we have to tell it what it is it's retrieving for us.

For textual information, the .responseSchema must have two properties set, .fieldDelim and .recordDelim, specifying which characters are used to separate one field from the next and one record from another. The .fields array is the same as it was originally, where we must tell it to use the number parser because everything is nothing more than a string.

Remote DataSource with JSON

We've already used JSON in *Chapter 4* reading news from Yahoo's own site via the Yahoo Query Language (YQL) service. Before we go on, I'd like to clarify a few misunderstandings about what JSON is.

Though JSON is based on JavaScript notation, it has been restricted with the specific purpose of making it portable to other systems and languages. It is often believed that JSON is whatever the JavaScript eval() function can read. That is not correct. JSON is a restricted, portable subset of what eval() can parse. These are the main differences:

- JSON uses double quotes only, it does not use single or double quotes interchangeably.
- Identifiers should be enclosed in double quotes.
- Numbers and the special values null, true, and false should not be enclosed in quotes.
- JSON must not contain executable instructions.

It is a very bad idea to try to encode JSON without the assistance of a suitable library. Besides the above pitfalls, encoding Unicode characters above the standard ASCII set is not trivial and at any point, an otherwise perfectly valid new entry in the database containing a "funny" character might ruin your application. There is an online JSON validator at: http://www.jsonlint.com/.

The JSON site at http://json.org/ maintains a list of libraries for those languages that do not yet provide JSON services natively. The newer browsers have JSON encoders/decoders. This might sound strange as an eval() can decode JSON, but with eval() you run the risk of getting extraneous code executed and in some environments eval() is not allowed.

How does our previous example look in JSON? Here we have both the
`F1Drivers.json` file and the instantiation of the DataSource:

```
{"results":{"drivers":[
    {"driver":"Michael Schumacher",
                        "scuderia":"Mercedes","championships":7},
    {"driver":"Fernando Alonso",
                        "scuderia":"Ferrari","championships":2},
    {"driver":"Jenson Button",
                        "scuderia":"McLaren","championships":1}
]}}
var myDS = new DS("F1Drivers.json",{
    responseType: DS.TYPE_JSON,
    responseSchema: {
        resultsList: "results.drivers",
        fields: ["driver","scuderia","championships"]
    }
});
```

As before, we have to tell the DataSource what `.responseType` to expect. In contrast
with previous examples, the data in the JSON file is not on the surface but nested
two levels deep in `results.drivers`. DataSource accepts this sort of "dot" notation
to specify deeply nested structures. It can also take square brackets, useful when
the data comes as one item in an array. The previous could have been written:
`resultsList: "results['drivers']"`. The same "dot" (and square bracket)
notation can be used for the fields as well.

We don't need to specify a parser for the numeric field as it is not enclosed in quotes.

Remote DataSource with XML

Once again, a new version of the same information:

```
<?xml version="1.0"?>
<results>
    <result championships="7"><driver>Michael Schumacher</driver>
                            <scuderia>Mercedes</scuderia></result>
    <result championships="2"><driver>Fernando Alonso</driver>
                            <scuderia>Ferrari</scuderia></result>
    <result championships="1"><driver>Jenson Button</driver>
                            <scuderia>McLaren</scuderia></result>
</results>
```

It is worth noticing that the `championships` field is now an attribute, not a separate XML element. DataSource will always search for a field name both as an attribute and as a separate element. The code for this is:

```
var myDS = new DS("F1Drivers.xml", {
    responseType: DS.TYPE_XML,
    responseSchema: {
        resultNode : "result",
        fields:
            ["driver","scuderia",{key:"championships",parse:"number"}]
    }
}
```

The `.responseType` has been changed and in the `.responseSchema` we use `.resultNode` instead of `.resultsList` as with JSON. While in JSON, `.resultsList` specifies the name of the property that contains the array of records, in `.resultNode` we specify the tag names of the records themselves.

Another difference is that in JSON we have to specify the full path from the root to the array, but with XML we need to specify the tag name of each record and it doesn't matter how deep it is. This might seem a good thing at first, but what happens if the same tag name repeats itself at different places with different meanings? That is when you have to enable the `.useXPath` option and then you can be just as precise with your specification as with JSON.

News reader examples

The downloadable examples also contain the news reader examples that we've seen in *Chapter 4*, now redone using the DataSource instead of directly using Connection Manager's `.asyncRequest()` or the Get Utility. One of those examples uses a `ScriptNodeDataSource`, which we haven't covered in the previous sections.

It might be of interest to compare all these examples to one another to see the differences. Something that is immediately apparent from such comparison is that the processing code remains the same. In the previous sections, looking at how to define the DataSource for each response type, we've only seen how to create the DataSource instance; we didn't show the rest of the code, the part that processes the response, because it is always the same. That is the whole point of the DataSource Utility, it normalizes the way we retrieve information from any source, in any format.

Meta information

Besides the data we want to retrieve, it often happens that the same package of information carries information about that data. In the news reader examples, we have also asked for no diagnostic information, but perhaps we might find that information useful or even vital for our application. When you have data about the data, it is called metadata and DataSource can also help extracting it.

One characteristic about metadata is that it is not of tabular nature. While the data itself is made of a series of records, metadata is often simple scalar information such as the number of records returned, the time it took the query to be processed, whether there is more information available or any such ancillary information.

We can use, once again, the Yahoo Query Language service (YQL) to do a query, which we define like this:

```
var YQL_QUERY = 'select name, country.content, admin1.content ' +
                'from geo.places where text="{query}"',
    YQL_URL_ARGS = "format=json&diagnostics=false&q=",
    YQL_SERVICE = "http://query.yahooapis.com/v1/public/yql?",
    FORMAT = "<p>{name} in {admin1}, {country}</p>",
    META =
"<p><i>Found: {count} records, updated: {updated}<\/i><\/p>"
```

We are using the same structure we did for our news reader back in *Chapter 4*, defining several of the string constants we will use in the code. The YQL_QUERY is the one that interests us. We are searching Yahoo's geographical database for names of places. When asked for Barcelona that search produces a result like this:

```
{
 "query":{
  "count":"10",
  "created":"2010-02-03T02:44:55Z",
  "lang":"en-US",
  "updated":"2010-02-03T02:44:55Z",
  "uri":"http://query.yahooapis … t%3D%22barcelona%22",
  "results":{
   "place":[{
     "name":"Barcelona",
     "country":"Spain",
     "admin1":"Catalonia"
    },
    {
     "name":"Barcelona",
     "country":"United Kingdom",
     "admin1":"England"
    },
 }
```

We use the following DataSource to retrieve data from it:

```
var myDS = new DS(YQL_SERVICE,{
    dataType: DS.TYPE_SCRIPTNODE,
    responseType: DS.TYPE_JSON,
    responseSchema: {
        resultsList: "query.results.place",
        fields: ["name","country","admin1"],
        metaFields: {
            count: "query.count",
            updated: "query.updated"
        }
    }
});
```

We create an instance of DataSource using the URL of the YQL service as the first argument and then declaring the `.dataType` of `TYPE_SCRIPTNODE`, which will make DataSource return a `ScriptNodeDataSource` to us. The `.responseType` will be JSON and the data is to be found in the array located by using dot notation at `"query.results.place"`. Each individual place will be reported by the fields `"name"`,`"country"`, and `"admin1"` (that is state, province, or other main administrative division within a country).

However, we also want to read some metadata, the number of places found and when the query was updated. We do so by declaring the `.metaFields` property, an optional part of the `.responseSchema` telling it, via dot notation, where to locate those two fields and how we want them named once fetched.

We can then call `.sendRequest()` (after doing some manipulation of the URL arguments, which we have discussed already in *Chapter 4* and can be seen in the downloadable examples) and in the success handler, we do:

```
var responseHandler = function(oRequest, oParsedResponse) {

    if (oParsedResponse.error) {
        alert("Something bad happened");
    } else {
        var output = [],
            places = oParsedResponse.results,
            meta = oParsedResponse.meta;

        for (var i = 0; i < places.length; i++) {
            output.push(Lang.substitute(FORMAT, places[i]));
        }
```

```
            Dom.get("listing").innerHTML = output.join("\n");

            meta.updated =
                     YAHOO.util.Date.format(new Date(meta.updated),"%D");
            Dom.get("ft").innerHTML = Lang.substitute(META,meta);
       }
   };
```

If there was an error, we report it (DataSource is not very generous in the error information it provides), otherwise, we set an array for the output to be piled up into, and we locate within the parsed response the `places` (the data) and the metadata. We simply push the results into `output` using the format we defined at the beginning.

For the metadata, we first need to do some conversion because the updated field is really in an unreadable format. We use `YAHOO.util.Date.format()`, which comes with DataSource for no logical reason. Then we send it to the footer of our three section SMF page along with the count, all after inserting into the `META` template we defined previously.

Massaging unruly data

Sometimes we have no control over the source of our data and the way it is produced is not suitable for us to process. We can intervene in the processing of the data when it misbehaves. There are several points in the processing of the data where we can manipulate the data so that if fits into something more reasonable. The table `search.suggest` in the YQL service produces a result like this:

```
{
  "query":{
   "count":"10",
   "created":"2010-02-03T03:38:39Z",
   "lang":"en-US",
   "updated":"2010-02-03T03:38:39Z",
   "uri":"http://query.yahooap … barcelona%22",
   "results":{
   "Result":["fc barcelona",
     "barcelona hotels",
     "barcelona spain",
     "barcelona weather",
     "barcelona hostels",
     "barcelona airport",
     "barcelona map",
     "barcelona apartments",
```

```
          "barcelona restaurant",
          "custo barcelona"
        ]
      }
    }
  }
```

The result is a simple array. In DataSource it could be defined as of TYPE_JSARRAY, but this .dataType does not accept an array nested deep into query.results.Result, like in this case. It could be defined as TYPE_JSON, but then, it needs an array of named values, not raw, unnamed values. However, we can manage by doing the following:

```
var myDS = new DS(YQL_SERVICE, {
    dataType: DS.TYPE_SCRIPTNODE,
    responseType: DS.TYPE_JSARRAY,
    responseSchema: {
        fields: ["suggestion"]
    }
});
```

We declare our DataSource as of being of TYPE_JSARRAY and in the .fields array we name those fields suggestion. Being unnamed fields, we don't fetch them by name but by ordinal position and then give them a name.

Now we do the massaging. We can intervene at several points, listed in the order in which they occur:

- responseEvent: An event that fires when the data has just been received
- .doBeforeParseData(): A function called before parsing
- .doBeforeCallback(): A function called after parsing and before returning the data
- responseParseEvent: Fired right after .doBeforeCallback()

The events receive as arguments the live data being processed. You can change the data, and whatever you set is what DataSource will carry on processing. In both events, the property `.response` in its single argument is the one we would be looking for. In the first, it is still very raw, completely unprocessed, while in the latter, it has already been fully parsed.

In the methods, whatever we return is what DataSource will continue to process from then on. DataSource contains dummy functions for them, which return the relevant argument unchanged, the second argument for `.doBeforeParseData()`, the third for `.doBeforeCallback()`. To fix our data, we can easily override `.doBeforeParseData()` to extract the array DataSource is expecting from deep down to the surface:

```
myDS.doBeforeParseData = function ( oRequest , oFullResponse) {
    return oFullResponse.query.results.Result;
};
```

In contrast with `responseEvent`, by the time `.doBeforeParseData()` is called, the JSON parser has already been applied so the data is no longer a raw string, which makes `responseEvent` hard to use. Of course it all depends on your data and how bad it is; the further we can manage to get with DataSource alone before intervening, the better. At times, the only alternative is to use a `FunctionDataSource` and do all the preprocessing completely outside of DataSource.

Look ahead with the AutoComplete Control

The AutoComplete control allows you to add a useful typing suggestion facility that presents a drop-down list, which holds suggested words when a visitor types into a text field. It's just the frontend, so you'll need to consume third-party web services or construct your own backend data source, from which the suggestion engine receives data.

The following screenshot shows an example of an AutoComplete control that has been interacted with in this way:

Here, the visitor has found a suitable suggestion and has moved down with the down arrow to select **javascript tutorial**, ready to hit the *Enter* key, which would fold the dropdown and execute the associated action.

AutoComplete Constructor

The YAHOO.widget.AutoComplete constructor takes up to four arguments:

1. A reference to an HTML input element that the AutoComplete control is associated with and can be either an ID string or DOM reference

2. A reference to a container element, usually a <div>, that will house the suggestions and again can be either an ID string or DOM reference

3. A reference to a DataSource instance

4. (Optional) Additional configuration parameters

The first two arguments are references to two HTML elements that are to be used by AutoComplete, such as these:

```
<div class="yui-b">
    <input id="myInput" type="text">
    <div id="myContainer"></div>
</div>
```

In this case the first two arguments would be `myInput` and `myContainer`. They will usually be within a container so they are both kept together in a suitable place in your layout. The `<input>` element may have a `value` preset. The auxiliary container may be anywhere; it will be floated to unfold right below the `<input>` element, but there is no reason not to keep them together.

The reference to a DataSource instance might be to any of the DataSource classes we have seen in the previous sections. Not surprisingly the last of those examples queries a YQL table called `search.suggest` and we will use that one in the example in the next section.

Any of the many AutoComplete properties can be set in the last argument, amongst them:

- If the Animation Utility is loaded, the `.animxxx` options let you control the way the suggestions box unfolds and folds.

- The `.queryxxx` options let you control when a query will be sent to the server. For example, `.minQueryLength` is set to 1 by default. This means that as soon as the visitor types a single character (if not followed by another within an interval you can also control), AutoComplete will send a query. Such a low number might uselessly tax your server with pointless requests.

- `.delimChar` lets you define a delimiter so that several queries can be processed in the same input box. The most frequent case is with e-mail recipients, where you want to search for each entry separately.

- Several options deal with presentation such as the use of shadows, additional class names to decorate the suggestion box, and so on.

- `.forceSelection` limits what the input box can contain to items in the suggestion box.

- `typeAhead` will fill the input box with the first suggestion of the list while still allowing the visitor to go on typing.

From the many methods, we'll just mention the few used most often:

- `.generateRequest()`: Allows us to tailor the request sent to the server based on the typed input. The return of this function will be used as the first argument in the call to the DataSource `.sendRequest()` method. It defaults to `query={query}`.

- `.formatResult()`: AutoComplete assumes the result is an array of plain strings. If the result is made of several fields, this method lets us format those fields into something useful to show in the suggestion box.

- `.filterResult()`: This method is basically an alias for the DataSource `.doBeforeCallback()` method so you can filter the results to be presented to the visitor.

- `.setHeader()` and `.setFooter()`: The suggestion box is structured as a three-section SMF container; AutoComplete uses the body section of it so it is better to stay away from that one, but you are free to use the other two sections. These methods let us set their contents.

Method `.formatResult()` is particularly interesting because the suggestion box is a plain container capable of accepting all sorts of HTML, so it is not limited to a regular drop-down box as it might seem to be. If the server providing your suggestions can send more information beyond plain strings, there is a lot you can play with by using this method. The YUI examples for AutoComplete contain an example that offers suggestions taken from Flickr, which includes images in the suggestion box, by assembling an `<img>` tag with the URL for the thumbnail pointing to Flickr itself, and active links to navigate to the full-size image.

AutoComplete abounds in events, but we'll only mention `itemSelectEvent`, which is the one you are most likely to use. It is the one fired when a selection has been made either by hitting the *Enter* key or clicking on one of the suggestions. The default action, as would be expected, is to fill the input box with the selected suggestion, but you are free to use that data to perform any additional action.

Implementing AutoComplete

Let's jump straight into the coding with no further ado. We'll use the page and code of our previous example for this one. Out of the code, we'll keep this section, which we have already discussed.

```
var YQL_QUERY = 'select * from search.suggest where query="{query}"',
    YQL_URL_ARGS = "format=json&diagnostics=false&q=",
    YQL_SERVICE = "http://query.yahooapis.com/v1/public/yql?",
    FORMAT = "Your selection was: <b>{0}<\/b>";

var myDS = new DS(YQL_SERVICE,{
    dataType: DS.TYPE_SCRIPTNODE,
    responseType: DS.TYPE_JSARRAY,
    responseSchema: {
        fields: ["suggestion"]
    }
});
```

```
myDS.doBeforeParseData = function ( oRequest , oFullResponse) {
    if (parseInt(oFullResponse.query.count,10)) {
        return oFullResponse.query.results.Result;
    } else {
        return [];
    }
};
```

The only difference with our previous version is that in .doBeforeParseData() we've been a little more careful because there might not be any suggestions offered so we return an empty array. With the DataSource defined, we can create the instance of AutoComplete:

```
var myAC = new YAHOO.widget.AutoComplete(
                    "myInput","myContainer", myDS);

myAC.generateRequest = function(sQuery) {
    var yqlQuery = Lang.substitute(YQL_QUERY,{query: sQuery});
    return YQL_URL_ARGS + encodeURIComponent(yqlQuery);
};

myAC.itemSelectEvent.subscribe(function(sType, aArgs) {
    Dom.get("listing").innerHTML = Lang.substitute(FORMAT,aArgs[2]);
});
```

We create the AutoComplete instance pointing it to the two HTML elements, the first being the <input> box, the second the container that will become our suggestion box and the last argument being the DataSource instance we've just created.

Our suggestion server, the YQL service, needs the URL arguments in a particular format, the same we've been using in our previous example for the call to .sendRequest(). We've simply cut and pasted the code to assemble those arguments into .generateRequest().

Finally, we subscribe to itemSelectEvent, where we simply show the text for the selected item in a suitable place. If the purpose of this AutoComplete instance had just been to help filling the input box with a suitable value, this would not even be necessary as that is the default action.

That was it. That's how hard AutoComplete is; not a big deal, is it?

Just remember to include all the necessary files, as the Dependency Configurator will tell you, plus all the optionals depending on what kind of DataSource is required for your data. Also, as this is a control and has a skin, the AutoComplete suggestion box needs to be within a container that has the yui-skin-sam class name in it, usually the <body> element.

Summary

The DataSource is a very flexible utility that lets you retrieve tabular data from many sources, local and remote, in many formats, extract and parse its fields, detaching the code that uses this data from the means of obtaining it. DataSource is used by several YUI components such as AutoComplete, DataTable, and Charts.

The AutoComplete control can transform any regular input box into a search box, easing the process of data entry and allowing our visitors to avoid typing errors by offering suitable entries from those we have already stored. We no longer have to offer a separate search functionality attached to an input box; AutoComplete can turn any input box into a full search box.

10
DataTable

Tabular data is one of the most frequent forms of information we usually deal with. In the previous chapter we've seen how such information can be retrieved from various sources via the DataSource Utility. In this chapter we will see how to present that information to our visitors in a highly interactive way. A YUI DataTable can be sorted, paginated, its cells edited, its columns resized, reordered, hidden or shown, its records selected, and various actions can be associated with user interaction with the table.

In this chapter we will see how to:

- Define a DataTable
- Use and add cell formatters
- Respond to user interaction
- Enable cell editing
- Enable sorting and paging on the client side and through the server

DataTable is the largest component measured in the size of its source file and also that of its documentation, which provides a good representation of the options it offers. To this, it is fair to add the size and features provided by the DataSource that is a required dependency. We will certainly not see everything that DataTable can do, as that would require a whole book, but we'll be able to get a good look at its most popular features.

DataTable dependencies

DataTable is a subclass of Element as most modern YUI components are, so it needs `element-min.js`. Like any other YUI component, it also requires `yahoo-dom-events.js`. It also needs `datasource-min.js` to retrieve the data it is to display, plus any dependencies DataSource might need depending on the source of data. Resizing columns or moving them around also requires `dragdrop-min.js`. Finally, if date information is to be edited, the Calendar component would also be needed.

As usual, the Dependency Configurator will provide all the required dependencies, but it is up to us to check for the optional ones, as we are the only ones who know what our intentions are.

DataTable classes

DataTable has two main classes that we will regularly create, `YAHOO.widget.DataTable`, the most basic DataTable, and `YAHOO.widget.ScrollingDataTable`, a subclass of the regular DataTable suitable for small spaces that allows the data to scroll vertically and horizontally while keeping the headers always visible and in sync with the data. Whatever we say about DataTable also applies to ScrollingDataTable, except where noted.

We may also create instances of any of the built-in cell editors, all of them subclasses of `YAHOO.widget.BaseCellEditor`. There are six of them for different kinds of data.

We may use, though we'll never create, instances of `RecordSet`, `Record`, `ColumnSet`, and `Column`, all in the `YAHOO.widget` branch of the library, which are indissoluble parts of the DataTable.

DataTable stores its data in a single RecordSet that contains an array of Record objects, each made of a series of fields containing the values to be shown. The data is never stored in the DataSource, as it is often assumed. DataSource simply retrieves the data and hands it to its client, be it AutoComplete, DataTable, or Chart, it does not save the data itself; each client component is responsible for keeping the data in whatever form suits it best.

Each DataTable has one associated ColumnSet containing instances of Column, each storing the information about the data to be stored in the Records. This is the metadata, as we've discussed earlier: information about information.

Creating a DataTable

The constructor for DataTable takes the following arguments:

1. A reference to a container that will hold the DataTable, either by its `id` or a DOM reference

2. The column definitions that define the data to be shown and how it will be presented

3. The instance of DataSource that will retrieve the data

4. An optional object containing configuration attributes

The first argument can be any container in the page. Contrary to other controls we've seen previously, the DataTable is unable to read existing markup from the page. It is the DataSource that can read HTML tables so, in a way, the container referenced in the first argument may contain markup, but it will reach the DataTable via a roundabout route, through the DataSource. The DataTable will completely obliterate any previous contents of the container so, in a way, the effect is pretty much the same.

For our example, we'll read another of the YQL tables via this query:

```
select abstract, date, width, height, thumbnail_url, size,
    title, url from search.images({count})
    where query="{query}" and mimetype like "{type}"
```

The words in between curly brackets are placeholders for the variable parts of the query. The number of records (`count`), the search term (`query`), and the type of image file (`type`) after stripping off diagnostics information, may produce a response like this:

```
{"query":{
  "results":{
   "result":[{
     "date":"2009/02/08",
     "height":"500",
     "size":"233400",
     "thumbnail_url":
         "http://thm-a01.yimg.com/nimage/d6735ce6d54d5a42",
     "title":"Earflap Hat",
     "url":
         "http://farm4.static.flickr.com/3369/
                                 3261853861_fe042ded97.jpg",
     "width":"500"
   },
   /* … more records here … */
   }
}
```

This will be our DataSource for such a reply:

```
var myDS = new DS(YQL_SERVICE,{
    dataType: DS.TYPE_SCRIPTNODE,
    responseType: DS.TYPE_JSON,
    responseSchema: {
        resultsList: "query.results.result",
        fields: ["title",{key:"date",parser:parseYMDDate},
          {key:"width", parser:"number"},
          {key:"height", parser:"number"}, "thumbnail_url",
          {key:"size", parser:"number"}, "url"]
    }
});
```

The date field is in **YYYY/MM/DD** format, which the built-in date parser (that is the native `Date.parse()` method) does not handle, so we first need to define a function such as `parseYMDDate()` to convert that field into a native JavaScript Date object:

```
var parseYMDDate = function (value) {
    if (!YAHOO.lang.isString(value)) { return value; }
    var aDate = value.split('/');
    return new Date(aDate[0], aDate[1], aDate[2]);
};
```

Many of the other fields are numbers and we specify the number parser by its shorthand `number`. Note that there are quotes around the short name for the `number` parser while there are no quotes around `parseYMDDate` as that is an actual function reference.

We will define our columns like this:

```
var colDefs = [
    {key:"title",label:"Title"},
    {key:"date",label:"Date"},
    {key:"width",label:"Width"},
    {key:"height",label:"Height"},
    {key:"size",label:"Size"}
];
```

From the fields that our `myDS` DataSource instance will retrieve, we are listing only those we want to show. The `key` property has to match the name given in DataSource's `fields` array. Though usually there will be a one-to-one correspondence between the fields retrieved by the DataSource and those displayed by the DataTable, this doesn't need to be so. In this case, the DataSource will retrieve all the fields listed in the query, but in `colDefs` we list only those fields that we mean to show. We'll use those extra fields later. We may also display more columns than fields; we can add columns calculated from other fields, for example, a total price resulting from multiplying the unit price by the quantity, or made up in some other way. In our most basic example, we simply name the fields to be displayed and provide a label for the column. If no explicit `label` is provided, the value for `key` will be used.

Finally, we create the DataTable instance:

```
var myDt = new YAHOO.widget.DataTable("bd", colDefs, myDS, {
    initialRequest:yqlUrl
});
```

We are building our table in the body section of a typical three part SMF page, with the `colDefs` and `myDS` shown previously. We are using the `initialRequest` configuration attribute; its value will be the first argument to DataSource's `.sendRequest()` method, the same `yqlUrl` that we have used in previous examples and we already know how to calculate. The DataTable will call `.sendRequest()` for us and will use the value of the `initialRequest` configuration attribute for it. The resulting table will look like this:

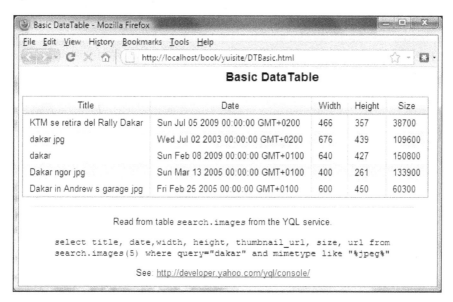

Cell formatting

The DataTable in the previous screenshot doesn't really look good. There is nothing much we can do about the image titles, those are entered by the users themselves, but the dates are far from "user friendly" and all the numbers are left-justified. The `size` could also improve if we expressed it in kilobytes, and we might group the `width` and `height` under a common header, and, of course, it would be nice to see the picture. We can fix this by changing our columns definitions:

```
var colDefs = [
    {key:"thumbnail_url",label:"Image",
                          formatter:showThumbnail},
    {key:"title",label:"Title"},
    {key:"date",label:"Date", formatter:'date'},
    {label:"Dimension", children:[
        {key:"width",label:"Width",
                          className:'right-aligned'},
        {key:"height",label:"Height",
                          className:'right-aligned'}
    ]},
    {key:"size",label:"Size", className:'right-aligned',
                          formatter: byteSizeFormatter}
];
```

We have now added an extra column for the `thumbnail_url` that Flickr reports using the `formatter` option to specify a suitable formatter. We've also specified the `'date'` formatter for the `date` field, added the `right-aligned` class name to the numeric fields, nested the `width` and `height` columns as `children` of an unkeyed column labeled `Dimension` and used `byteSizeFormatter()` to format the `size` field. While the `date` is the short name for an existing, pre-packaged formatter, we have to define `byteSizeFormatter()`:

```
var byteSizeFormatter =
            function (elLiner, oRecord, oColumn, oData) {
    var i = 0, units = ['B','kB','MB','GB','TB'];
    while (oData > 1000) {
        i++;
        oData = Math.round(oData / 1000);
    }
    elLiner.innerHTML = oData + units[i];
};
```

Cell formatters, such as the one discussed earlier, receive four arguments:

1. `elLiner`: A reference to the `<div>` element that will contain the value. Table cells have a further container within, the liner, where the value is actually stored.

2. `oRecord`: A reference to the Record object corresponding to the row where the cell to be formatted resides. This allows us to access other fields in the same record that might influence the formatting or the value, such as colors, or the value itself; for example, unit price and quantity to produce a total price.

3. `oColumn`: A reference to this column and, consequently, all its properties.

4. `oData`: The internal value to be formatted.

Having access to the liner containing the value makes the cell formatter very flexible. Instead of just being limited to returning a formatted value, it can alter other properties of the container such as its font or background colors.

The record instance lets us access other information from the same row, like in the `showThumbnail()` function:

```
var showThumbnail =
        function (elLiner, oRecord, oColumn, oData) {
    elLiner.innerHTML = '<img src="' + oData +
            '" alt="' + oRecord.getData('title') + '" />';
};
```

Here we are building an `<img>` tag out of the `thumbnail_url` field that comes in `oData` as a string value. We are also adding an `alt` attribute to that image using the `title` field we read from `oRecord`. Method `.getData()` gives us access to the value of any field in the Record instance by its name. In a similar way, we could also have read the `width` and `height` fields to add them to the `<img>` tag.

For those numeric fields, we wanted aligned to the right, we added the `right-aligned` class name that we have to define, like this:

```
.yui-skin-sam .yui-dt td.right-aligned {
    text-align:right;
}
```

The CSS selector might seem a little complicated, but we have to beat the default style set by the `sam` skin for the DataTable, thus we need to be very specific so our selector gets higher priority over the default. How the CSS processor determines the priority of each attribute is out of the scope of this book, but in a rich component like the DataTable or almost any other in the YUI Library, it is not always easy to get it right. A good DOM inspector is always a helpful tool to find out.

The resulting table will look like this:

Dates are being shown in **MM/DD/YYYY** format, which might not be suitable for all locales; however, DataTable uses the `number` and `date` formatters, included, for some mysterious reason, in DataSource, which is a required dependency of DataTable, so we can always count on its being there. There are two ways to define the format for dates; we can add the `dateOptions` property to the definition of any column, like:

```
{key:"date", label:"Date", formatter: "date",
dateOptions: {format: "%x", locale: "es-ES"}},
```

This would display the date in the preferred date format for Spain, if it were defined. The other is by defining a generic date format for all columns that use the `date` formatter for this DataTable. When creating the DataTable instance, along with any other configuration options, we may add a generic `dateOptions` property, like this:

```
var myDt = new YAHOO.widget.DataTable("bd", colDefs, myDS, {
    initialRequest:yqlUrl,
    dateOptions: {format: "%x", locale: "es-ES"}
});
```

This would immediately apply to all columns in the DataTable. The same two alternatives exist for the `'currency'` formatter by using the `currencyOptions` either on a per column basis or for the whole DataTable, and for the `'number'` formatter using `numberOptions`.

If we moved all our formatters to a separate file along with our custom library functions, we would need to assign them globally accessible names by using the `YAHOO.namespace()` function to create a branch for our formatters and creating them with names such as `YAHOO.myLibrary.dtFormatters.showPicture()`. Such a name would be a nuisance to specify every single time. We can do better; we can add them to the short-name list of formatters:

```
YAHOO.widget.DataTable.Formatter.showPicture =
            function (elLiner, oRecord, oColumn, oData){ … };
```

We can do for DataSource parsers the same as we just did for DataTable formatters. SQL servers usually produce dates in **YYYYMMDD hh:mm:ss.nn** format and a parser for that would be very handy, we can add `parseYMDDate()` to the list of parsers like this:

```
YAHOO.util.DataSourceBase.Parser.SQLDate = function (value)
  {…};
```

We could then use it in any DataSource instance by simply writing `parser:'SQLDate'`.

DataTable contains the following built-in formatters:

- `button`: Produces a button with the field value as its label.

- `checkbox`: Shows a checkbox checked if the field value is truish.

- `currency`: Uses `YAHOO.util.Number.format()` along with `currencyOptions` to display a number. It defaults to US Dollars.

- `date`: Uses `YAHOO.util.Date.format()` along with `dateOptions` to display a date, defaulting to **mm/dd/yyyy**.

- `dropdown`: Creates a standard `<select>` box using the `dropdownOptions` property to provide its options. `dropdownOptions` should be an array of strings that will be used both for the `<option>` value and label, or of object literals with label and value options, like `{label:"xxxx",value:"yyyy"}`.

- `email`: Produces a `mailto:` link using the field value both for the text displayed and the link value. It cannot produce a link showing a name with the e-mail address in the link.

- `link`: Creates a regular link using the value of the field both as the link and the label.

- `number`: Uses `YAHOO.util.Number.format()` along with `numberOptions` to display a number. It defaults to no decimals and a comma as thousands separator.

- `radio`: Draws a radio button that will be checked according to the truish value of the field. All radio buttons in the same column get a common name, so they form a single mutually exclusive group. If more than one record has a truish value in this field, our visitor will only see the last one checked, which will be inconsistent with the underlying RecordSet.

- `text`: Escapes fields containing `<`, `>`, and `&` characters so they can be safely displayed.

- textarea: Produces a <textarea> field containing the field value.

- textbox: Produces an <input type="text" /> field with its value set to the that of the field.

The default formatter replaces undefined, null, or NaN (Not-a-Number, a special value numbers might have in JavaScript) with a single non-breakable space.

Responding to DataTable events

The DataTable has certain events already wired to predictable actions, and simple configuration settings allow our visitors to sort a column when its header is clicked, or resize a column when its edges are dragged. Other events are left for us to respond to as we see fit.

DataTable has too many events to enumerate here, but they can be grouped into a few categories:

- Before and after configuration change events: For each configuration attribute xxxx there is a beforeXxxxChange and an xxxxChange event. The change can be cancelled by returning false from the before listener. They are all automatically created and handled by the Element Utility that deals with the configuration attributes.

- Key and mouse events: (click, double-click, over, out, down, and up) on the DataTable's table, table body, table head, row, cell, and header cell elements.

- Rendering events, first time (initEvent) and subsequent: beforeRenderEvent, renderEvent, and postRenderEvent.

- User input events, related to elements produced by the different formatters: buttonClickEvent, checkboxClickEvent, dropdownChangeEvent, linkClickEvent, and radioClickEvent. There are no events associated with the user typing in either a textbox or a textarea nor when entering or leaving them; tbodyKeyEvent, theadKeyEvent, or tableKeyEvent are all we have for them.

- Cell editor events, signalling when the editor is shown, cancelled, saved, and a few other editorXxxxEvent events.

Several events signal when other actions occur such as sort, highlight, select, disable the UI (block the table), rows or columns added or removed, and such. They usually signal actions initiated by our own application and are more useful to those customizing the DataTable itself than to application developers.

Let's see the most frequent kind of interaction: responding to a click on a cell. We'll show a full-size image of the picture when its thumbnail is clicked. To the earlier example, we will add the code to create an instance of a Panel (along with its dependencies) that we'll fill with the full-size image. To respond to the click we add the following code:

```
myDt.on('cellClickEvent', function (oArgs) {
    var event = oArgs.event,
        target = oArgs.target,
        oRecord = this.getRecord(target),
        oColumn = this.getColumn(target);
    switch (oColumn.key) {
        case 'thumbnail_url':
            Event.stopEvent(event);
            myPanel.setHeader(oRecord.getData('title'));
            myPanel.setBody('<img src="' +
                    oRecord.getData('url') + '" />');
            myPanel.show();
            break;
    }
});
```

The highlighted code above is DataTable panacea; it is probably the most frequent code segment that appears in the YUI support forums. In response to a cell being clicked, we read from the argument the native `event` object as provided by the browser itself and the event `target`. From that we find the Record and Column instances the cell belongs to. The scope of the listener is set to the DataTable instance so we can use `this` instead of `myDt`, as we just saw. As we are listening to a cell-based event, the target will always be a table cell (`<td>`) reference. Based on which column was clicked, identified by its `key`, we decide what to do, normally using the values read from the rest of the Record.

A couple of details are worth mentioning: we have finally used the `url` field that we had never shown so far. We can ask the DataSource to read more fields than we will actually show; all those extra fields remain available for our application to use. Second, when we decide to deal with the event ourselves, we use `.stopEvent()` to prevent the default action from happening; in rare circumstances we might want both, our custom response and the default, but usually it is an either-or option. The `event` object can also provide us with access to the status of the *Shift*, *Alt*, or *Ctrl* keys, should that be relevant to decide what our response should be.

Quite frequently developers add inline code to DataTable cells, like
`<a href="javascript:_do_something_()">` or `onclick="_do_something_()"`.
These calls often have to carry complicated arguments concocted by the cell formatter
from other fields in the record. This is totally wasteful and not recommended at all.
There is no point in wasting resources filling the table cell with code that might never
be used; even under the best circumstances few cells will ever be clicked. Delaying
the rendering of the DataTable by adding complex calls when all can be handled,
when and if needed, by a centralized dispatcher like the function shown earlier is
hardly ever justified.

Earlier we've mentioned that the number of columns shown and the number of fields
retrieved might not match and that the difference might be either way. Here we had
fewer columns than fields, but we might also go the other way, we may add columns
containing calculated values and we may also add columns to allow for user
interaction. A typical example is a column of checkboxes for multiple row selection.

We might code the column like this:

```
{key:'Select',formatter:'checkbox'}
```

This would immediately freeze our interface to having those checkboxes there for
good. We may, instead, define the column like this:

```
{key:'Select',className:'unselected'}
```

Then, we may define the `unselected` class name as:

```
.yui-skin-sam .yui-dt td.unselected {
    background: transparent url(http://yui.yahooapis.com/
        2.8.0r4/build/assets/skins/sam/check0.gif)
        no-repeat center center;
    width:16px;
    text-align:center;
}
```

The `background` image used above looks like a checkbox so our visitor wouldn't
notice the difference, except that it matches more closely the look of the rest of the
page. We are free to use whatever image, icon, or color that we want. Moreover, the
style is completely separate from the code. Any graphics designer may, in the future,
change the `selected`/`unselected` style at will.

A minor detail remains and that is keyboard accessibility: checkboxes are natural tab
stops, empty cells are not, so the trick is to place an invisible element that can serve
as a tab stop. A cell formatter can be added to insert the following into the liner:

```
'<a style="text-decoration:none;" href="#"> </a>';
```

In fact, you might save the string above as a constant in your own custom library because it usually proves handy.

To respond to a click on that cell, we need nothing more than adding another `case` statement to the panacea code earlier:

```
case 'Select':
   Event.stopEvent(event);
   if (Dom.hasClass(target, 'selected')) {
      Dom.replaceClass(target, 'selected', 'unselected');
      oRecord.setData(oColumn.key, false);
   } else {
      Dom.replaceClass(target, 'unselected', 'selected');
      oRecord.setData(oColumn.key, true);
   }
   break;
```

It is important to note here that we are not only concerned with updating the user interface by changing the style of the cell but we are also ensuring the change is reflected in the underlying Record instance by using `.setData()` to set the value of the corresponding field. Where did that `Select` field come from? Nowhere, we are creating the field on the fly. Non-existing fields are falsy by default and can be set to anything we want at any time.

All changes must always be reflected in the underlying RecordSet. We should never rely on the user interface. The UI might be re-rendered at any time, and if it is, it is always done from the values in the RecordSet. A sort produces such re-rendering. A change in design might force us to use paging, and the marked table rows might go off-screen at any time. The data should always be in the RecordSet and the HTML table should only be a reflection of it.

Some of the custom events bubble; a `buttonClickEvent` will be followed by a `cellClickEvent` that will always be followed by a `rowClickEvent` and finally a `tableClickEvent`. This bubbling can be prevented by returning `false` in any of these. There is a similar bubbling in all the events that start at the `<thead>` section.

The DataTable offers built-in event listeners, all starting with the `onEvent` prefix. They are designed so that we can plug a user action into a DataTable response. For example, do we want to highlight a row on a simple click or on a double-click? The `.onEventXxx()` methods allow us to do such wiring, like:

```
myDT.on('rowClickEvent', myDT.onEventHighlightRow);
```

We might have used `rowDblclickEvent` instead and, if we wanted to be more selective, we might have used the panacea code earlier and, based on whatever criteria we wanted, we may simply call method `.highlightRow();` after all, the `.onEventXxx()` methods are simply glue code to wire the events to the actual methods that carry on the desired action, translating the required arguments in the process.

Care must be taken with all the formatters that allow user input such as drop-down boxes, radio buttons, checkboxes, and such. Formatters are one way: though they reflect the values in the associated field when drawn, any change made by our visitor does not get saved back into the RecordSet. It is always up to us to make sure the changes in the user interface are saved in the RecordSet. Or better just use the cell editors, which we'll see shortly. Remember that the DataTable might get re-rendered if the visitor sorts by any column or, in a paged DataTable, goes to another page. We cannot count on the UI to store information.

The `radioClickEvent` is just as hard to use as the radio formatter itself. The problem is that the browser already makes radio buttons sharing the same name mutually exclusive. Thus, if more than one record has a `true` value for the radio button, only the last one will be shown checked. This has the potential of leaving the user interface out of sync with the underlying RecordSet. The `radioClickEvent` does little to solve this, though it reports the button being clicked, it does not report which button gets automatically unchecked thus, we have to keep track of which was the last one checked so that when it gets unchecked, we can record that in the RecordSet.

More column properties and methods

We've already seen a few column properties and methods and we'll see some more in the coming sections; we'll just mention some that don't deserve a section of their own. Some of those properties are:

- `.field`: Sometimes the field name of the incoming data is inconvenient, usually because it is too long. We can then use `.field` to do the matching between the column to be shown and the value retrieved by the DataSource, and then use `.key` as an internal alias for that field within the DataTable. In the example above, we could have specified:

    `{key:'thumb',field:'thumbnail_url', ...`

- `.hidden`: The column will be shown in a collapsed state. A small vertical gap will be shown to indicate that a column lies hidden. This attribute is used when we want this column to be available and eventually shown. If we don't mean to show the column at all, we simply don't list it in the column definitions.

- `.maxAutoWidth`: Intended to limit the width a column might reach when no width is specified. DataTable will try to adjust the width of a column to accommodate its longest content, which may ruin the layout of the rest of the table. As with all widths, it should be an integer with no units specified and it is always in pixels.

- `.minWidth`: Sometimes both the heading and the contents are too small, this will limit how small the column can get.

- `.width`: The fixed width, in pixels, for the column.

- `.resizeable`: If the Drag & Drop Utility is included, this option will enable our visitor to resize the column by dragging the line separating this column from the next.

- `.getTreeIndex()`: Returns the position of the column within the table. Valid only for non-nested or top-level columns.

There are not many useful properties or methods in ColumnSet; the useful ones also have aliases at the DataTable level, so there is hardly ever a reason to reach to the ColumnSet. The methods DataTable offers related to columns are:

- `.getColumn()`: Returns a Column instance based on its key (`oColumn.key`), a reference to one of its elements such as a table cell (as we've seen in the panacea code), or ordinal position in the table.

- `.getThEl()` and `.getThLinerEl()`: Return a reference to the table header cell `<th>` for the column or the label container.

- `.hideColumn()` and `.showColumn()`: Collapse or expand the given column.

- `.insertColumn()` and `.removeColumn()`: Add new Column instances at the index given (or at the end of none) or remove an existing one.

- `.reorderColumn()`: Reorders the columns in the DataTable, so the one specified gets into the given position.

- `.setColumnWidth()`: Forces the column to the width specified, in pixels. If the argument is null it will resume the normal autoadjustment between the given limits.

Column sorting

One of the most popular features of the DataTable is that it can sort its data by column on the client side. A column can be enabled for sorting by adding the `.sortable` property set to `true` to the column definitions. After clicking on the header for such a column, a DataTable might look like this:

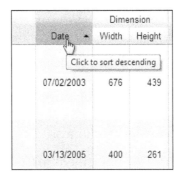

The DataTable is already wired to respond to a click on the header of a sortable column by sorting and changing the color scheme of the affected column; we may also sort it by calling `.sortColumn()`. It is often the case that the original data comes already sorted; we may signal that to our visitor by setting the `sortedBy` configuration attribute. Setting this attribute will neither sort the column nor will it verify that the data is actually sorted; it will simply produce the color scheme and other visual clues to make it obvious to the visitor. Only one column can be highlighted as sorted at any time.

An important requirement for sorting to work is that the data in the RecordSet must be represented in a way so that can be processed by JavaScript's own `Array.sort()` method. In the example above, the dates are sorted in ascending order. If they had been stored as strings, the rows shown would be reversed. That is why it is important to parse the data when retrieving it via the DataSource. Even if the data seems fine to display as-is, you always have to parse it at the receiving end and then format it on displaying it. The usual symptoms when you have forgotten a parser are when numbers sort like: **1, 12, 13, 2, 20, 3, 31**… or dates sort by month.

When a column header is clicked for the first time, the column will be sorted in the direction set by the `.sortOptions.defaultDir` Column property. With dates, it is often set to `YAHOO.widget.DataTable.CLASS_DESC`, so the most recent entries appear at the top. The second time the same column header is clicked, the order will be reversed.

Sometimes the values shown are not the ones that determine the sort order; the
`.sortOptions.field` property lets us name the field that will actually control the
sorting, which might not even be visible.

Finally, there are times when the data is not amenable to being sorted by
`Array.sort()` or we may need to do a complex multiple-column sort; for example,
day, month, and year might be in separate fields, though shown in a single column
thanks to a custom formatter. The `.sortOptions.sortFunction` property accepts a
function that will compare the records and decide on their order. The function will
receive four arguments:

1. `a`: Reference to the first Record to be compared
2. `b`: Reference to the second Record to be compared
3. `desc`: A Boolean, when `true` indicates that the sort direction is descending
4. `field`: The key for the field being sorted

The function must return 0 if the values of the fields to be sorted are the same, less
than zero if the first Record `a` should go before the second one `b` when the third
argument `desc` is `false` or greater than zero otherwise.

Cell editing

Another popular feature of the DataTable is the ability to edit its cells. The following
is an image of a DataTable with an assortment of cell editors active at once. There
can only be a single cell editor active at any one time, so the following screenshot is
composite of the same DataTable at different times:

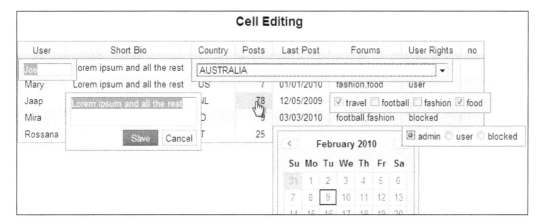

- `TextboxCellEditor`
- `TextareaCellEditor`
- `DropdownCellEditor`
- `DateCellEditor`
- `CheckboxCellEditor`
- `RadioCellEditor`

All the editors reside in the `YAHOO.widget` branch of the library. Except for the `TextareaCellEditor` on the **Short Bio** column, all the rest of the editors have their **Save/Cancel** buttons explicitly disabled by using the `disableBtns` option. For all editors, pressing the *Enter* key is equivalent to the **Save** button while the *Esc* key works as **Cancel**, and for editors where the value is selected by clicking, doing so will also save and close. For the `TextareaCellEditor` it is not practical to suppress the **Save/Cancel** buttons because you would prevent the user from entering a new line into the text. Editors are declared along with the column definitions:

```
{key:"user", label:"User", editor:
        new YAHOO.widget.TextboxCellEditor({disableBtns:true})},
{key:"bio", label:"Short Bio", editor:
                    new YAHOO.widget.TextareaCellEditor()},
```

Besides deciding on what editor we want to use we must also decide how to bring it up. Do we want a single click or a double-click? Sometimes the single click is used for selection and the double-click for editing; at other times a context menu might be used. To show the cell editor with a single click on a DataTable instance called `myDt`, we would add the following:

```
myDt.on("cellClickEvent", myDt.onEventShowCellEditor);
```

All cell editors accept configuration options, such as the `disableBtns` above, amongst them:

- `asyncSubmitter`: Accepts a function that may asynchronously update the saved value on a remote server.
- `defaultValue`: Value to be shown if the field to be edited is `undefined`.
- `disableBtns`: Prevents the **Save/Cancel** from being shown. Defaults to `false`.
- `LABEL_CANCEL` and `LABEL_SAVE`: Text to show in the buttons, usually for localization.
- `resetInvalidData`: On invalid data, the input box will revert to the original value instead of keeping the invalid value; `true` by default.

- `validator`: A function that validates and/or parses the value entered. It may return the parsed value or `undefined` to signal an invalid value.

- `checkboxOptions`, `radioOptions`, `dropdownOptions`: Contain an array of options to be displayed by their respective editors. The options can be an array of string values or of object literals in the form `{value:"CA",label:"Canada"}`.

- `calendarOptions`: A configuration object passed verbatim to the Calendar widget.

- `multiple`: For `DropdownCellEditor`, allows multiple selection.

- `size`: For `DropdownCellEditor`, how many rows to show; defaults to one (classic dropdown).

- `textbox`, `textarea`, `dropdown`, `radios`, `checkboxes`, `calendar`: For each type of cell editor, a reference or array of references to the actual input element(s).

The **Posts** column has a `TextboxCellEditor` assigned that would look exactly like the **User** column, but it has the `YAHOO.widget.DataTable.validateNumber()` validator assigned so that it will refuse to close unless a valid number is entered or the editor is dismissed by hitting the *Esc* key. A `validator` not only serves to validate the value but also to parse it; as everything returned from a textbox is a string. Numbers not passed through `.validateNumber()` would be saved as strings and end up in the wrong place should the column be sorted.

Though some editors and formatters have similar names, they are mostly unrelated. None of the formatters update the RecordSet value automatically, while all the editors do. The `checkbox` formatter shows one checkbox per cell, while the `CheckboxCellEditor` allows for several Boolean options on a single cell. The same goes with the `radio` formatter and the `RadioCellEditor`.

The previous screenshot shows an issue with such a mismatch. In the **Country** column, the `DropdownCellEditor` shows the full name of the country but the table shows only the two letter code, which is the value stored in the server-side database. Sometimes using such abbreviation is convenient as it keeps the column to a predictable size; country names may be quite long and may ruin the layout of the whole page. Otherwise, depending on how our data is structured, we might have to add a formatter. How this formatter is implemented depends on several factors and preferences, so the DataTable does not provide any.

Server-side updating

The DataTable provides several events to signal different stages of the editing process. If we are to update the server-side database with the data being edited on the cell the editorSaveEvent might be good enough. The listener to that event is provided with enough information for us to assemble a suitable message to notify the server via a call to Connection Manager's .asyncRequest(). However, there is a problem: while we can send the update request to the server, the event listener cannot wait for the confirmation from the server or, more worrying, a rejection. By the time the reply comes our visitor might be doing something else and any reply might be lost.

The cell editors offer the .asyncSubmitter property to handle updates on the server side. This property is null by default but may be set to a function that will handle the remote updating. We may define a column like this:

```
{key:"posts",label:"Posts",className:"right-aligned",
    editor:new W.TextboxCellEditor({
        validator:YAHOO.widget.DataTable.validateNumber,
        disableBtns:true,
        asyncSubmitter:submitPosts
    })
},
```

where the function submitPosts() is declared as:

```
var submitPosts = function (fnCallback, newValue) {
    YAHOO.util.Connect.asyncRequest("GET",
      "no_odd.php?value=" + encodeURIComponent(newValue),
      {
        success: function (o) {
            var reply = Lang.JSON.parse(o.responseText);
            if (reply.error) {
                fnCallback(false);
            } else {
                fnCallback(true, reply.result);
            }
        },
        failure: function (o) {
            alert(o.status + ': ' + o.statusText);
            fnCallback(false);
        }
    });
};
```

This function will receive two arguments, a `callback` function and the value as returned by the `validator` function. The function will run in the scope of the cell editor so it can access any other piece of data it might need. In this example, `submitPosts()` uses `.asyncRequest()` to send the server the new value just edited and locally validated by `.validateNumber()`. We assume the server reply will be JSON formatted and will contain a `.error` property and, if `.error` is `false`, a `.result` property. On an error reply, we'll call the callback function with a `false`, indicating that the value cannot be accepted. On a valid reply we will call the callback function with `true` in the first argument, indicating that the value has been accepted, and the actual value as confirmed by the server as the second argument.

The DataTable will remain blocked while the confirmation is received, so our visitor can't do anything else. The downloadable example has a simple server-side script that simply rejects odd values and accepts even ones but returns them doubled. It also has a one second delay so the blocking is evident. A real server-side script would probably do some sort of validation and database updating.

DataTable methods

The DataTable has a very long list of methods that we can only summarize. A whole family of `.getXxxxEl()` methods allow us to reach the HTML elements (hence the "El" suffix) that make up the table. We should be cautions when accessing these elements; the HTML should always be a reflection of the underlying data residing in the DataTable's RecordSet; the on-screen representation should never be considered the original, but a formatted copy of the data.

Both the `.onEventXxx()` and `.onDataXxx()` families of methods are the entry points from events fired by our visitor's actions and by the DataSource when data arrives. Several `.onEventXxx()` are not attached to any particular event and are available for us to decide what to hook them to. For example, we might trigger cell editing by clicking on a cell or by double-clicking on it. Most of them are bridges to map the arguments received from the fired event to the method actually performing the action. For example, `.onEventSelectRow()` resolves the event target to a DataTable row and then calls `.selectRow()`.

Methods `.getColumn()` and `.getRecord()` let us reach the main subcomponents of the DataTable by a variety of means, be it an index, a name, or other ways. Method `.getRecordSet()` gives us access to the whole of the data stored in the DataTable and lets us manipulate it via its own methods, among them RecordSet's `.getLength()` to know how many records we've got or Record's `.getData()` to reach the value of any field by name.

Method .addRow() lets us add a row of data at a given index position or at the end of the table if none is given. The data must be given as an object literal where the property names correspond to the field names. Several consecutive rows can be added at once via .addRows() by providing an array of object literals. The following would append a row with the given data to an existing DataTable. If a value is not specified for a given field, it will be set to null.

```
myDataTable.addRow(
    {partNo:'99-99', description:'new item', unitPrice:10});
```

Methods .deleteRow() and .deleteRows() let us delete one or several consecutive rows. Both methods are quite flexible in the way to specify the first or only row to delete.

Methods .updateCell(), .updateRow(), and .updateRows() let us update a specific cell, a whole row, or a set of consecutive rows. The last two take an object literal or an array of such literals, with the property names matching the field names to be updated.

```
YAHOO.util.Event.on('raise10Percent','click', function() {
    var len = this.getRecordSet().getLength();
    for (var index = 0; index < len; index++) {
        var data = this.getRecord(index).getData();
        data['unitPrice'] *= 1.1;
        this.updateRow(index, data);
    }
}, myDataTable, true);
```

In the code above we are raising all the prices on a given DataTable by 10% when a button with the id of raise10Percent is clicked. We first find the number of records in the table, so we can loop through them. We use a numerical index to fetch each Record instance. Method .getData() with no arguments will return the values for all fields in the Record as an object literal. We update the value for the unitPrice property on this data object and call .updateRow() to update it on the DataTable. We could have used .updateCell() instead:

```
var oRecord = this.getRecord(index);
this.updateCell(oRecord, 'unitPrice',
                        oRecord.getData('unitPrice') * 1.1);
```

Method `.updateCell()` uses the Record instance as a reference to the Record and row to be updated.

All these add, delete, and update methods refresh the screen immediately. If several changes need to be made in a batch, such as in the example earlier, it may be wiser to manipulate the underlying data in the RecordSet and then call `.render()` just once. Some browsers are very slow in recalculating the layout of the elements on the screen, so it is always a good idea to minimize the number of screen updates by doing the entire background job first and updating the screen only once.

We'll cover other methods in the following sections as they are associated with specific features.

Paging

Some tables might be too big to show all at once. Besides the layout issue that a long DataTable would present, tables might take quite a long time to render. Some old browsers still in use take a very long time to render HTML tables, as much as 10:1 in relation to more modern ones. We might reduce the visual impact and the delay by paging long tables.

Paging is handled by the DataTable along with the `YAHOO.widget.Paginator` class. Both `paginator-min.js` and `paginator.css` become required dependencies. A paged DataTable may look like this:

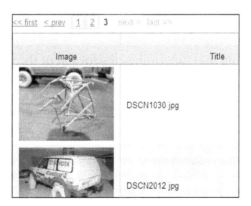

The image shows the last of three pages of a query to the YQL service for images of the Dakar rally. The **next >** and **last >>** links are grayed out as there are no further pages to show. A similar set of paging controls are drawn at the bottom of the DataTable. This has been achieved by simply adding the `paginator` configuration attribute when creating the DataTable instance:

```
var myDt = new YAHOO.widget.DataTable("bd", colDefs, myDS, {
    initialRequest: yqlUrl,
    paginator: new YAHOO.widget.Paginator({
        rowsPerPage: 10
    })
});
```

Paginator is a separate component and has plenty of class members. When used along with the DataTable, we can use the following configuration attributes:

- `alwaysVisible`: Defaults to `true`; makes the paging controls visible even when there is only one page.
- `containerClass`: A class name to assign to the paging controls.
- `containers`: An array of references to HTML elements that will contain the paging controls. By default, DataTable sets this property so that two paging controls appear, one above and one below the DataTable. This attribute may be set to make Paginator show a paging control in any number of containers, anywhere in the page.
- `initialPage`: The page number to show; defaults to `1`, the first.
- `rowsPerPage`: The number of rows to display per page.
- `template`: A string that determines the format of the paging controls.

Most other members of Paginator are handled directly by the DataTable and we should use them with caution if at all.

The default template is set to:

```
"{FirstPageLink} {PreviousPageLink} {PageLinks} {NextPageLink}
{LastPageLink}"
```

This produces a set of links as shown in the previous screenshot. The names in between curly braces correspond to the names of individual formatters. The Paginator contains several of these under the `YAHOO.widget.Paginator.ui` branch, including one, `YAHOO.widget.Paginator.ui.YourComponent` that serves as a model for creating other paging elements.

The Paginator gives us a perfect example of why the data should always be stored in the RecordSet while the screen should not be trusted. If we had checkboxes or other input controls in a page and their values were not saved in the RecordSet, they would be lost when paging elsewhere.

While data is shown just one page at a time, all of it has to be transferred from the server and remains in the browser memory. Counterintuitively, it is not the transmission that takes the longest; with current bandwidths it is often the rendering that takes the longest share of the time, and Paginator can improve the speed of the application without much trouble. With long tables, however, the transmission time might be unacceptable.

Server-side sorting and paging

When the amount of data is too large to transmit all at once to the browser, we need to go for server-side paging, which also involves sorting, after all, the content of a page depends on the way the whole set of data gets sorted. In contrast with client-side sorting or paging, this requires assistance from the server.

This is an advanced topic, which can be skipped and left for another time; there is nothing here that is required to be able to follow the rest of the book. You may jump to the next heading.

The server will receive a URL specifying the index for the first record it expects to receive, the number of records it should receive, and, possibly, the field name for sorting, and the direction of the sort. The server has to produce the requested records and it should also inform the client of the total number of records that make up the requested table. This allows the Paginator to calculate the total number of pages and to display the correct number of page links in the paging controls.

To enable a DataTable for server-side sorting and paging we have to add a few configuration attributes:

```
var myDt = new YAHOO.widget.DataTable("bd", colDefs, myDS, {
    dynamicData:true,
    paginator: new YAHOO.widget.Paginator({
        rowsPerPage: 10
    }),
    generateRequest: myRequestBuilder,
    initialRequest: myRequestBuilder(),
    sortedBy: {
        key:'date',
        dir: YAHOO.widget.DataTable.CLASS_DESC,
    }
});
```

First, we set `dynamicData` so that the DataTable switches to request one page at a time. We need, of course, to provide a `paginator` control just as with client-side pagination.

When set to handle `dynamicData`, the DataTable will request each page by using the following URL arguments, appended to the base URL used to instantiate the DataSource:

```
"sort={SortColumnKey}&dir={SortColumnDir}&startIndex={PaginationStartI
ndex}&results={PaginationRowsPerPage}"
```

The words enclosed in curly braces would be replaced by properly URL-encoded values in each request. We may code our server-side script to respond to these arguments, but quite often, we have no control over the server and we need to tailor the URL-arguments to suit what the server expects. The `generateRequest` configuration attribute accepts a reference to a function that will, on demand, produce those arguments. In this case, we will be using a custom function `myRequestBuilder()`.

For the first request, DataTable will not use the `generateRequest` function, it will still use the argument set in the `initialRequest` configuration attribute. Sometimes the first request has a different format from subsequent ones, so DataTable allows for an `initialRequest` that might be different from that generated dynamically. In this case, we will use the very same one and we call `myRequestBuilder()` with no arguments so it will return a default request.

Finally, we know that the data will come already sorted by date, in descending order, so we let DataTable know by setting the `sortedBy` configuration attribute. This will allow the DataTable to use the correct visual clues on the `date` column so our visitor knows.

As we will be using the YQL service to produce the images, our `myRequestBuilder()` function is somewhat complicated. We need to produce a valid YQL statement based on the following template:

```
var YQL_QUERY = 'select title, date,width, height, thumbnail_url,
size, url from search.images({initialIndex},{finalIndex}) where
query="dakar" | sort(field="{sortField}") {desc}';
```

The `myRequestBuilder()` function is as follows:

```
var myRequestBuilder = function(oState) {
    oState = oState || {
        pagination: {
            recordOffset:0,
            rowsPerPage:10
        },
```

```
                sortedBy: {
                    key:'date',
                    dir:DT.CLASS_DESC
                }
        };
        var query = {
            sortField: oState.sortedBy.key,
            desc: (oState.sortedBy.dir === DT.CLASS_ASC) ?
                                "" : " | reverse()",
            initialIndex: oState.pagination.recordOffset,
            finalIndex: oState.pagination.recordOffset +
                        oState.pagination.rowsPerPage
        };

        var yqlQuery = Lang.substitute(YQL_QUERY, query),
        return YQL_URL_ARGS + encodeURIComponent(yqlQuery);
    };
```

As we are going to use the same function to provide both the `initialRequest` and the following ones, it will be called both with and without arguments. The first thing is to ensure that the `oState` argument has valid default values. If `oState` is undefined, it will be replaced by the object literal that follows. This object literal is a good example of the information we are to expect in `oState`:

- `.pagination`: Contains the information returned by Paginator's `.getState()` method. The most useful properties are `.recordOffset`, `.rowsPerPage`, `.page`, and `.paginator`, which contains a reference to the Paginator instance itself for whatever extra information we might need.

- `.sortedBy`: The same information provided by DataTable's `sortedBy` configuration attribute. It contains the `.key` and `.dir` properties stating the name of the field and the direction of the sorting expected.

To build `yqlQuery` we need to create an object literal that `YAHOO.lang.substitute()` can merge into the `YQL_QUERY` template. We use the values from `oState` to create such an object. This is basically the same process that we've been using all along in this series of examples with the YQL service so we won't discuss it further. At the end, we simply return the string that is what DataTable will use when calling DataSource's `.sendRequest()` method. The downloadable example shows the result of this process in the footer section below the DataTable.

We still have to deal with the total number of records so that Paginator knows how many pages to offer. We already know how to extract metadata from the incoming data in the DataSource, where we might have defined the retrieved data like this:

```
myDataSource.responseSchema: {
    resultsList: "query.results.result",
    fields: [ … ],
    metaFields: {
        totalRecords: "query.diagnostics.totalRecords"
    }
}
```

The above code allows us to extract the `totalRecords` meta-information from the incoming data, but we still have to do something more to get it to the DataTable. We need to override the `.handleDataReturnPayload()` method to insert the extracted information into the `oPayload` object. The payload is what the DataTable uses to keep track of its state in between transactions. It contains plenty of information besides the total number of records, but we will only deal with that one.

```
myDataTable.handleDataReturnPayload =
            function (oRequest, oResponse, oPayload) {
    oPayload.totalRecords = oResponse.meta.totalRecords;
    return oPayload;
}
```

Method `.handleDataReturnPayload()` receives all the information about the data just received, the request used to retrieve it (a string with the URL arguments), the full response, and the payload containing lots of properties. We read the actual `totalRecords` from the metadata and update it in the payload. The DataTable will use this information and pass it over to the Paginator for it to update the page count it shows.

In the example, as the YQL service does not provide the total number of records for a query, we opted to change the template for the paging controls so that it simply doesn't show the link to the last page. We assumed that the visitor would get bored before the end of the pages. If we do reach close to the end, the paging controls will offer page numbers that don't really exist and will fail, but the YQL service doesn't give us any better alternative.

There is also another failure in handling the YQL Service for this purpose: the sorting is applied after the set of records for the page is already selected. Actually, it should be sorted first and then the records selected from this sorted set. There is little we can do about this and the code on the client side, which is the code we care about, is basically correct; however, it helps to show that doing server-side sorting and pagination needs lots of support on the server side and it is not trivial.

Selection and highlighting

We'll cover these two features in the same section for no other reason than to make it clear that they are two separate and different things. Highlighting is simply a visual clue presented to our visitor and is usually associated with the cursor hovering over a certain element; no record is kept of the elements being highlighted and it serves no other purpose than providing some visual feedback to our visitor.

The following samples handle cell, row, and column highlighting. Only one cell at a time can be highlighted, but multiple rows and columns can be. It is up to us to unhighlight the elements, as shown in the following code. Combining highlighting modes is not recommended, it mostly works, but the combination of the styles that provide the visual clues can be a little confusing.

```
// Enables cell highlighting
myDt.on("cellMouseoverEvent", myDt.onEventHighlightCell);
myDt.on("cellMouseoutEvent", myDt.onEventUnhighlightCell);

// Enables row highlighting
myDt.on("rowMouseoverEvent", myDt.onEventHighlightRow);
myDt.on("rowMouseoutEvent", myDt.onEventUnhighlightRow);

// Enables Column highligting
myDt.on("theadCellMouseoverEvent",
                        myDt.onEventHighlightColumn);
myDt.on("theadCellMouseoutEvent",
                        myDt.onEventUnhighlightColumn);
```

We can do some more elaborate highlighting, for example, the following code will only highlight editable cells:

```
myDt.on('cellMouseoverEvent', function(oArgs) {
    var target = oArgs.target,
        oColumn = this.getColumn(target);
    if(oColumn.editor) {
        this.highlightCell(target);
    }
});
myDt.on('cellMouseoutEvent', myDt.onEventUnhighlightCell);
```

Remember that for any .onEventXxxx() listener there is an .xxxx() method, so instead of simply passing the event through, we might be more selective in what we highlight and what not. We could highlight rows based on the contents of a particular field of the underlying record or any other condition we wanted. Unhighlighting can be done more indiscriminately as asking to unhighlight something that is not highlighted causes no harm.

In contrast to highlighting, DataTable does keep track of selection and it follows stricter rules. Row and cell selection is controlled by the selectionMode configuration attribute, which can take the following values:

- standard: Standard row selection with multi-row selection enabled via clicks combined with the *Shift* and *Ctrl* keys.

- single: A single row can be selected at a time. The *Shift* and *Ctrl* modifier keys are ignored.

- singleCell: A single cell can be selected at a time. The modifier keys are ignored.

- cellBlock: Multiple cell selection. The *Shift* modifier key will select all the cells in a rectangular block where the previous and currently clicked cells are the corners.

- cellRange: Multiple cell selection. The *Shift* modifier key will select a sequential group of cells, in normal reading order, much like dates in a calendar.

The following screenshot shows two DataTables where the user has clicked on the cell containing number **377** and then *Shift*-clicked on the cell containing number **12**. The one on the left has selectionMode set to cellBlock, the one on the right to cellRange.

col1	col2	col3	col4	col1	col2	col3	col4
20	400	44	657	20	400	44	657
24	377	97	567	24	377	97	567
32	548	42	543	32	548	42	543
8	465	12	946	8	465	12	946
0	0	0	0	0	0	0	0

In both cases, more cells can be added to or removed from the selection set by doing *Ctrl* + click. Only one range or block can be selected at any one time. Ranges can also be extended by using the arrow keys in combination with the modifier keys.

There is no particular setting for column selection nor does it accept modifier keys. Only non-nested columns or bottom-level columns can be selected.

Besides setting the `selectionMode` we need to decide what event we want to use to trigger selection that is: single or double-click, context menu, or action buttons. For example:

```
myDt.on("rowClickEvent", myDt.onEventSelectRow);
myDt.on("cellClickEvent", myDt.onEventSelectCell);
myDt.on("theadCellDblclickEvent", myDt.onEventSelectColumn);
```

We would never have all these at once; the first two are actually incompatible; we must use the element selection method according to the chosen `selectionMode`.

As always, there are matching `.xxxx()` methods for each `.onEventXxxx()` method, plus the matching `.unselectXxxx()` ones.

Selected elements can be found by using any of the `.getSelectedXxx()` methods:

- `.getSelectedCells()`: Returns an array of object literals like: `{recordId:sRecordId, columnKey:sColumnKey}`

- `.getSelectedColumns()`: Returns an array of Column instances

- `.getSelectedRows()`: Returns an array of strings corresponding to the Record IDs

- `.getSelectedTdEls()`: Returns an array of references to the selected `<td>` elements

- `.getSelectedTrEls()`: Returns an array of references to the selected `<tr>` elements

When using client-side paging, selected elements will be preserved when moving across pages. The last two methods only return references to HTML elements in the current page; they cannot return references to selected elements that are not present on the screen. Cell and row selection is not preserved across pages when server-side paging is used.

The record ID returned in some of these methods is a string that serves as a unique reference both to the row and/or the Record. It can be used in methods `.getTrEl()` and `.getRecord()` to find the corresponding object.

More DataTable configuration attributes

DataTable has few properties worth mentioning, most of it is controlled by configuration attributes that can be set initially in the fourth argument of the constructor or via .get() and .set() methods inherited from Element. We have already mentioned many of them.

- caption: Adds a <caption> tag to the <table> holding the DataTable.

- currencyOptions, dateOptions, and numberOptions: These set the default options for the corresponding formatters, as we've seen earlier.

- draggableColumns: If the Drag-and-Drop component is loaded, it will allow columns to be dragged around the table so the order of the columns can be changed. Only top-level columns can be dragged.

- dynamicData, generateRequest: Associated with server-side paging and sorting, as seen in the corresponding section.

- formatRow: Just as a formatter can be set for each column, we can set a formatter for all rows. We can set formatRow to a function that will receive a reference to a table row and the Record object it is meant to show. It is often used to add class names to the table row to signal particular conditions based on the data. This function must return true for the cells to be filled, otherwise an empty row will show up.

- initialLoad: If this is set to false, the DataTable will not be automatically loaded with data on instantiation; we are responsible for loading it whenever we want. Defaults to true.

- initialRequest: Values that will be passed on to DataSource's .sendRequest() method when the DataTable is first loaded.

- MSG_xxxx: Several strings displayed to the user, such as MSG_EMPTY, which is set to No records found. They can be customized or localized.

- paginator: Takes an instance of YAHOO.widget.Paginator for either client or server-side paging.

- renderLoopSize: For long tables, it allows rendering the table in batches. After each batch, the DataTable will unfreeze the user interface so our visitor will perceive a more responsive interface, though the DataTable will still continue rendering. For tables with a few hundred rows, setting this attribute to at least a hundred is the minimum that makes any difference; for smaller tables, it will not show any improvement.

- selectionMode: Determines how to handle row/cell selection.

- `sortedBy`: May contain `null` or an object literal with two properties, `key` and `dir`. The first names the column that will have the visual clues to signal to the visitor that it is sorted, and the second, the direction of the sort. It must be set when the data comes already sorted from the server to provide the correct clues to the visitor. It can be read to find out what the current sort is.

- `summary`: Sets the summary HTML attribute on the `<table>` element.

ScrollingDataTable

ScrollingDataTable is a subclass of DataTable that adds vertical and horizontal scroll bars to the data section of the DataTable. It will always keep the table header visible, in sync with the columns. ScrollingDataTable adds to the configuration attributes that we just saw the attributes `width` and `height`, which can be set to a string specifying the size and the units for each dimension. Setting `width` creates the horizontal scrolling bar; setting `height` creates the vertical scrollbar.

ScrollingDataTables take a lot of resources as the headers are contained in a completely separate `<table>` that has to be kept in sync with the `<table>` element that holds the data. To avoid degrading the user experience, it is best to specify column widths on all the columns, disable column resizing, and limit the overall amount of data.

A ScrollingDataTable can be defined like this:

```
var myDt = new YAHOO.widget.ScrollingDataTable(
                           "bd", colDefs, myDS, {
    width: "400px",
    height: "20em"
});
```

Such a ScrollingDataTable would have both vertical and horizontal scroll bars. There is no other difference between a DataTable and a ScrollingDataTable, the rest of the arguments and configuration attributes are the same.

As the question often comes up in the forums, it is worth mentioning that the DataTable cannot freeze columns or data rows in place while the rest of the data cells scroll; the only ones that can be frozen in place are the header rows.

Summary

The DataTable component enables us to display tabular data in many flexible ways. It can be further enhanced with many features that allow our visitor to interact with the data: column sorting, cell editing, or element selection, with little or no help from the server.

A rich collection of events allow us to trigger additional actions. Mouse and keyboard events can be detected at any level: cell, cell content, row, or table and hooked via the built-in `.onEventXxxx()` methods to perform several actions: cell, row, or column selection or highlighting or cell editing. Data arrival events can be hooked to add, replace, or update rows.

The DataTable uses the DataSource to fetch the data so it can reach any of the supported sources either local or remote and in several data formats.

For large sets of data, DataTable can break the data into pages so just a part of the whole set is shown at a time and, with help from the server, it can also fetch a page at a time, so in principle, it can handle an unlimited amount of data split into manageable chunks via paging. We learned server-side paging and sorting, along with selection and highlighting.

DataTable is the largest and most complex component in the YUI Library; however, to draw the most basic table or enhance an existing one, it only requires a few lines of code, half of them for the DataSource.

We also saw the ScrollingDataTable, a version of the regular DataTable that can be set to fit within a fixed width and/or height and provides scroll bars to see the contents beyond this region.

11
Rich Text Editor

Long gone are the days when we struggled to highlight a word in an e-mail message for lack of underlining or boldfacing. The rich graphic environment that the Web provides has extended to anything we do on it; plain text is no longer fashionable.

YUI includes a **Rich Text Editor (RTE)** component in two varieties — the basic `YAHOO.widget.SimpleEditor` and the full `YAHOO.widget.Editor`. Both editors are very simple to include in a web page and they enable our visitors to enter richly formatted documents, that we can easily read and use in our applications. Beyond that, the RTE is highly customizable and allows us to tailor the editor that we show the user, in any way we want.

In this chapter, we'll see:

- What each of the two editors offers
- How to create either of them
- Ways to retrieve the text entered
- How to add toolbar commands

The two editors

Nothing comes for free, features take bandwidth, so the RTE component has two versions — `SimpleEditor`, which provides the basic editing functionality, and `Editor`, which is a subclass of `SimpleEditor`. `Editor` adds several features at a cost of close to 40% more size, plus several more dependencies, which we might have already loaded and might not add to the total.

A look at their toolbars can help us to see the differences:

The preceding screenshot shows the standard toolbar of `SimpleEditor`. The toolbar allows selection of fonts, sizes, and styles. Also, it lets you select the color both for the text and the background, create lists, and insert links and pictures.

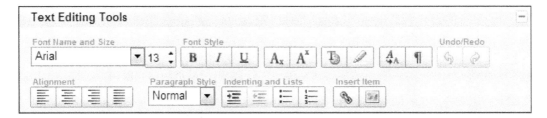

The full editor adds subscript and superscript, remove formatting, show source, undo, and redo to the top toolbar and text alignment, `<Hn>` paragraph styles, and indenting commands to the bottom toolbar. The full editor requires, beyond the common dependencies for both, Button and Menu so that the regular HTML `<select>` boxes can be replaced by a fancier one:

Finally, in the `SimpleEditor`, when we insert an image or a link, RTE will simply call `window.prompt()` to show a standard input box asking for the URL for the image or the link destination. The full editor can show a more elaborate dialog box such as the following for the **Insert Image** option:

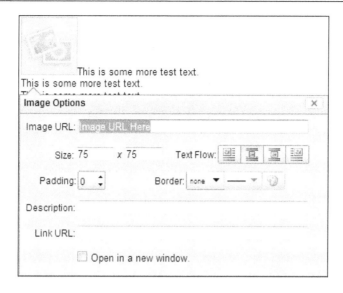

A simple e-mail editor

It is high time we did some coding; however, I hope nobody gets frustrated at how little we'll do, because even though the RTE is quite a complex component and does wonderful things, there is amazingly little we have to do to get one up and running. This is what our page will look like:

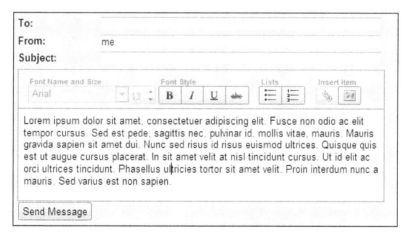

This is the HTML for the example:

```
<form method="get" action="#" id="form1">
    <div class="fieldset"><label for="to">To:</label>
                        <input type="text" name="to" id="to"/></div>
    <div class="fieldset"><label for="from">From:</label>
            <input type="text" name="from" id="from" value="me" /></div>
    <div class="fieldset"><label for="subject">Subject:</label>
                <input type="text" name="subject" id="subject"/></div>
    <textarea id="msgBody" name="msgBody" rows="20" cols="75">
            Lorem ipsum dolor sit amet, … and so on
    </textarea>
    <input type="submit" value=" Send Message " />
</form>
```

This simple fragment of HTML, assisted by a little CSS, would produce something pretty much like the preceding screenshot, except for the editing toolbar; this is by design. The RTE uses Progressive Enhancement to turn the `<textarea>` into a fully featured editing window, so if you don't have JavaScript enabled, you'll still be able to get your text edited, without any fancy formatting and only plain text.

The form should have its method set to `post`, as the body of the message might be quite long and might exceed the browser limit for a `get` request, but using `get` in this demo will allow us to see in the location bar of the browser what would actually get transmitted to the server.

Our page will require the following dependencies: `yahoo-dom-event.js`, `element-min.js`, and `simpleeditor-min.js` along with its CSS file, `simpleeditor.css`. In a `<script>` tag right before the closing `</body>` we will have:

```
YAHOO.util.Event.onDOMReady(function () {
    var myEditor = new YAHOO.widget.SimpleEditor('msgBody', {
        height: '300px',
        width: '740px',
        handleSubmit: true
    });
    myEditor.get('toolbar').titlebar = false;
    myEditor.render();
});
```

This is all the code we need to turn that `<textarea>` into an RTE; we simply create an instance of `SimpleEditor` giving the ID of the `<textarea>` and a series of options. In this case, we set the size of the editor and instruct it to take care of submitting the data on the RTE along with the rest of the form. What the RTE does when this option is `true` is it sets a listener for the form submission and dumps the contents of the editor window back into the `<textarea>` so it gets submitted along with the rest of the form.

The RTE normally shows a title bar over the toolbar; we don't want this in our application and we eliminate it simply by setting the `titlebar` property in the toolbar configuration attribute to `false`. Alternatively, we could have set it to any HTML string we wanted shown on that area.

Finally, we simply render the editor. That is all we need to do; the RTE will take care of all editing chores and when the form is about to be submitted, it will take care of sending its data along with the rest.

Filtering the data

The RTE will not send the data unfiltered, it will process the HTML in its editing area to make sure it is clean, safe, and compliant. Why would we expect our data to contain anything invalid? If all text was written from within the RTE, there would be no problem at all as the RTE won't generate anything wrong, but that is not always the case. Plenty of text will be cut from somewhere else and pasted into the RTE, and that text brings with it plenty of existing markup.

To clean up the text, the RTE will consider the idiosyncrasies of a few user agents and the settings of a couple of configuration attributes.

The `filterWord` configuration attribute will make sure that the extra markup introduced by text pasted into the editor from MS Word does not get through.

The markup configuration attribute has four possible settings:

- `semantic`: This is the default setting; it will favor semantic tags in contrast to styling tags, for example, it will change `<b>` into `<strong>`, `<i>` into `<em>` and `<font>` into `<span style="font: ....`

- `css`: It will favor CSS style attributes, for example, changing `<b>` into `<span style="font-weight:bold">`.

- `default`: It does the minimum amount of changes required for safety and compliance.

- `xhtml`: Among other changes, it makes sure all tags are closed such as `<br />`, `<img />`, and `<input />`.

The default setting, which is not the default, offers the least filtering that will be done in all cases; it will make sure tags have their matching closing tags, extra whitespace is stripped off, and the tags and attributes are in lower case. It will also drop several tags that don't fit in an HTML fragment, such as <html> or <body>, that are unsafe, such as <script> or <iframe>, or would involve actions, such as <form> or form input elements. The list of invalid tags is stored in property .invalidHTML and can be freely changed.

More validation

We can further validate what the RTE sends in the form; instead of letting the RTE handle the data submission automatically, we can handle it ourselves by simply changing the previous code to this:

```
YAHOO.util.Event.onDOMReady(function () {
    var Dom = YAHOO.util.Dom,
        Event = YAHOO.util.Event;

    var myEditor = new YAHOO.widget.SimpleEditor('msgBody', {
        height: '300px',
        width: '740px'
    });
    myEditor.get('toolbar').titlebar = false;
    myEditor.render();

    Event.on('form1', 'submit', function (ev) {
        var html = myEditor.getEditorHTML();
        html = myEditor.cleanHTML(html);
        if (html.search(/<strong/gi) > -1) {
            alert("Don't shout at me!");
            Event.stopEvent(ev);
        }
        this.msgBody.innerHTML = html;
    });
});
```

We have dropped the handleSubmit configuration attribute when creating the SimpleEditor instance as we want to handle it ourselves.

We listen to the `submit` event for the form and in the listener we read the actual rich text from the RTE via `.getEditorHTML()`. We may or may not want to clean it; in this example, we do so by calling `.cleanHTML()`. In fact, if we call `.cleanHTML()` with no arguments we will get the cleaned-up rich text; we don't need to call `.getEditorHTML()` first. Then we can do any validation that we want on that string and any of the other values. We use the Event utility `.stopEvent()` method to prevent the form from submitting if an error is found, but if everything checks fine, we save the HTML we recovered from the RTE into the `<textarea>`, just as if we had the `handleSubmit` configuration attribute set, except that now we actually control what goes there.

In the case of text in boldface, it would seem easy to filter it out by simply adding this line:

```
myEditor.invalidHTML.strong = true;
```

However, this erases the tag and all the content in between, probably not what we wanted. Likewise, we could have set `.invalidHTML.em` to `true` to drop italics, but other elements are not so easy. RTE replaces a `<u>` (long deprecated) by `<span style="text-decoration:underline;">` which is impossible to drop in this way. Besides, these replacements depend on the setting of the markup configuration attribute.

This example has also served us to see how data can be read from the RTE and cleaned if desired. Data can also be sent to the RTE by using `.setEditorHTML()`, but not before the `editorContentLoaded` event is fired, as the RTE would not be ready to receive it.

In the example, we wanted to manipulate the editor contents, so we read it and saved it back into the `<textarea>` in separate steps; otherwise, we could have used the `.saveHTML()` method to send the data back to the `<textarea>` directly. In fact, this is what the RTE itself does when we set `handleSubmit` to `true`.

Improving the looks

Moving from the `SimpleEditor` to the full editor requires very few changes. We need to add a few dependencies—Container Core, Button, and Menu, and their corresponding CSS files, and load `editor-min.js` instead of `simpleeditor-min.js`. We would then create an instance of `YAHOO.widget.Editor` instead of `YAHOO.widget.SimpleEditor` as we did so far. As usual, the most trusted source for this is the Dependency Configurator, which will probably produce a shorter list of dependencies by aggregating or combining whatever it can.

However, we might want less than the full editor but still want to improve the looks. We can do so by going half way — load Container Core, Button, and Menu as for the full editor, but still load `simpleeditor-min.js` and create an instance of `SimpleEditor` (we wouldn't be able to create an instance of `Editor` since we haven't loaded it). Then, we need to add the following right before rendering the editor:

```
myEditor.get('toolbar').buttonType = 'advanced';
```

This option would bring the fancy dropdown with the font names each in its own font; this is nothing much. The **Insert Image** or **Insert Link** options would still show a plain `window.prompt()` dialog box.

Changing the toolbar

Customization is one of the great advantages of YUI's RTE in contrast to other editors. In our previous example we refused to accept text in boldface. It doesn't make much sense for us to have the big boldface button in the toolbar if we are not going to accept its outcome. Remember, we have no control over what gets pasted from other sources so removing the button, or any other command, cannot prevent text in boldface appearing in the text we retrieve from the RTE; we still do need to filter it afterwards.

We have already changed a couple of things in the toolbar, we have dropped the title bar and we changed the buttons to the advanced version. Going from the `SimpleEditor` to the full editor also changes the toolbar significantly though it is not just a matter of changing the looks; `Editor` also adds the code to execute the commands those buttons represent.

The template for the toolbar is represented by an object that describes its features. As we've seen so far, it can be reached by using the `.get()` method inherited from Element. We can change the object that describes the toolbar before we call `.render()` to show the editor. To have an idea of what the toolbar template looks like, the downloadable examples for this chapter contain a page that does a dump of the toolbars for both the `SimpleEditor` and the full editor.

We can also change the toolbar once it has been rendered. As the toolbar can take a while to set up, it has to be done after the `toolbarLoaded` event fires. Then, the `.toolbar` property of the `Editor` can be used, not the `toolbar` configuration attribute, which is only the template for the toolbar before it actually gets rendered.

For example, these two are equivalent:

```
// change the template before it gets rendered
myEditor.get('toolbar').titlebar = false;

// change the actual toolbar once it has been rendered
myEditor.on('toolbarLoaded', function() {
    this.toolbar.set('titlebar', false);
});
```

The `toolbar` configuration attribute (`myEditor.get('toolbar')`) corresponds to the template. Later, once rendered, this will become the `.toolbar` property (`myEditor.toolbar`). What in the template are plain properties (`.titlebar`), in the actual toolbar become configuration attributes (`.get('titlebar')`). This is a bit confusing.

On a first level, the toolbar template has these properties, which then turn into configuration attributes:

- `.titlebar`: Contains either the text to be shown on the title bar, or `false` to hide it.

- `.collapse`: Whether it should show a minimize icon on the top right corner of the title bar to collapse the toolbar. It requires `.titlebar` to be `true`.

- `.buttonType`: Can be `advanced` or `basic` to change the type of element to be used for the buttons.

- `.grouplabels`: Whether it should show the labels for the button groups.

- `.disabled`: Disables the toolbar.

- `.draggable`: Whether the toolbar can be dragged. It simply sets the toolbar as a draggable element; it is up to the developer to set suitable drop targets and actions when they are reached. As a curiosity, the editable area is a valid drop target, which will accept dragged elements, such as the text on the title bar itself.

- `.buttons`: The actual collection of buttons on the bar.

The `.buttons` collection is the most interesting of all because it describes all the buttons and separators in the toolbar. It is easy to change them in the template; for example, to drop the boldface button, we can do:

```
myEditor.get('toolbar').buttons[2].buttons.splice(0,1);
```

It is basically a matter of looking at a dump of the toolbar template and using plain JavaScript to manipulate the object literal. Likewise, to add a button to the end, we could do this:

```
toolbar.buttons.push({type:'separator'});

toolbar.buttons.push({
    group:'mine',
    label:'my button',
    buttons:[{
        type: "push",
        label: "Bold CTRL + SHIFT + B",
        value: "bold"
    }]
});
```

This makes a boldface button appear at the end, in a separate button group called "mine" and labeled **my button**. This new button just added will act just like our original boldface button, though it is in a different location.

Once the RTE is rendered we can add or remove buttons and groups by using the methods provided by the `Toolbar` object:

- `.addButton(config, after)`: Adds the button described in `config`, after the given button in the same group

- `.addButtonGroup(config)`: Adds a button group

- `.addButtonToGroup(config, group, after)`: Adds the button described in `config`, in the named group, after the referenced button

- `.addSeparator()`: Adds a small gap in between groups or buttons

- `.destroyButton(id)`: Deletes the button

- `.getButtons()` and `.getButtonByXxx()`: Methods to find all buttons or specific buttons by different search criteria

The `config` arguments in all cases are object literals like the one shown in the example earlier. For groups, `.group` and `.label` properties are important; for buttons we have:

- `type`: Any one of `push`, `menu`, `color`, `select`, or `spin`.
- `value`: A unique string value assigned to the button.
- `title`: A string to be assigned to the `title` HTML attribute (tooltip).
- `label`: A text to show in the button (unless replaced by an image). It will be used as the `title` if none is given.
- `menu`: The same as for a Button of the menu type.
- `disabled`: Sets the disabled, grayed-out state.

Adding a new toolbar button

So far we have played with moving around an existing button, which already has a predefined action associated with it. Now, we'll see how to add new functionality to the toolbar. We'll add a `timestamping` function, a button that will add a date to the text.

First, we have to add the button, as we've already seen:

```
var toolbar = myEditor.get('toolbar');

toolbar.buttons.push({type:'separator'});

toolbar.buttons.push({
    group:'added',
    label:'Timestamping',
    buttons:[{
        type: "push",
        label: "Timestamp",
        value: "timestamp"
    }]
});
```

To add the button we first grab a reference to the template and then add first a separator, then a group containing a simple push button.

The button just added will have no image on the button face. To add one, we make use of the styles the RTE will generate for it. In the head of the page, we add:

```
<style type="text/css">
    .yui-skin-sam .yui-toolbar-container .yui-toolbar-timestamp
```

```
                                              span.yui-toolbar-icon {
            background: transparent url( icons/cal.png )
                                        no-repeat center center;
            left: 5px;
      }
   </style>
```

The relevant part of this CSS style is the third selector, `.yui-toolbar-timestamp`. The RTE will use the `name` given to the button as part of its class name so, for a button named xxxx, it will give it a class name of `yui-toolbar-xxxx`, which lets us associate the button with an image. We set this image as the non-repeating, centered background. Depending on the dimensions of the image we might need to align it as we've done here with the `left` setting.

The RTE will assign the button other class names to signal other possible states of the button like hovering, checked, or disabled, which we may use to further tailor the looks of our buttons.

So far, our new button looks nice but doesn't do much at all. We need to associate an action with it and to do that we can use what the RTE calls dynamic events. They are not listed in the API docs because they are created dynamically. For every button named xxxx, the toolbar will have an xxxxClick event created dynamically. So, all we need to do is listen for that event, but not before we are sure the toolbar has been loaded and is available:

```
myEditor.on('toolbarLoaded', function () {
    this.toolbar.on('timestampClick', function () {
        myEditor.execCommand('inserthtml',
                                ' [' + (new Date()) + '] ');
    });
});
```

RTE's `.execCommand()` method allows us to manipulate the text in the editing window. It will call the numerous `.cmd_xxxx()` methods listed in the API docs, but it will do some pre and post processing such as firing events, pushing the change into the undo stack, setting the `.editorDirty` property (which tells us that the text has been changed) and starting the node change process; in other words, don't bypass the `.execCommand()` method.

We could fill pages and pages with the list of the commands available but they are quite self-explanatory, for example, `bold`, `insertunorderedlist`, or `createlink`, and they simply do what the corresponding toolbar button does. Do remember to look in the API docs page for both `SimpleEditor` and `Editor` since the later adds a good number of commands of its own.

The most relevant effect of the node change process is the firing of the `beforeNodeChange` and `afterNodeChange` events, the first of which will cancel the change if `false` is returned from its listener. For example, the boldface button could listen to the `afterNodeChange` event so that it changes its state to active when the cursor is over text already in boldface. It doesn't do, so changing the state of the boldface button is hardwired into the code, which is faster, but that would be the way to do it for an add-on.

Adding CSS styles

It might look better if the timestamp is added in a different color from the rest of the text. Instead of simply having it enclosed in square brackets as in the previous sample, we might want to insert the following HTML:

```
myEditor.execCommand('inserthtml',
            '<span class="timestamp">' + (new Date()) + '<\/span>');
```

If we were to add the style definition for timestamp to our page, we would find it has no effect whatsoever on the editor. This is because the editing window is actually a separate document in an `<iframe>` within our page. Being a separate document, it has its own stylesheet different from that of our page.

To add extra styles into the editing window, we can use the `extracss` configuration attribute, like this:

```
var myEditor = new YAHOO.widget.Editor('body', {
    height: '300px',
    width: '740px',
    extracss: '.timestamp {margin: 0 1em;background-color:cyan;}'
});
```

This is not to be confused with the CSS styles required for the buttons added to the toolbar. The toolbar does reside in the same page as the rest of the application, it is just the editing area of the RTE that is actually a separate `<iframe>` and needs CSS styles set as previously shown.

Changing the available fonts

The list of available fonts in the RTE font names dropdown is quite limited. From the toolbar dump in the examples, it becomes obvious why the names of the fonts are hardcoded. Many people expect that the font names dropdown will show all the fonts installed on each machine. This is not possible; the browser environment forbids any code in it to access such information in the host machine. Besides, there is hardly any certainty that such fonts would be available on other machines.

However, if in an intranet scenario an application needs the RTE to show a particular font that is certain to be available on all the machines, then it can be easily added to the list of fonts in the toolbar template, like this:

```
myEditor.get('toolbar').buttons[0].buttons[0].menu.push(
                                            {text:'GreekC'});
```

Summary

The Rich Text Editor is an easy-to-use editor that can be added to any project that might need user input. It offers a couple of versions so you can decide where on the cost (bandwidth)/benefit (features) curve you want to be.

The RTE is also highly customizable and we've seen how to add tools to its toolbar and their associated actions, and how to customize the looks of the editor window.

Its rich set of events plus the dynamic events let you add code to capture everything that happens in the RTE and respond accordingly.

The flexibility of the RTE is reflected in the home page for the component at the YUI site, where the list of examples shows the many ways in which it can be improved or tailored for specific needs.

12

Drag-and-Drop with the YUI

I remember the excitement I felt after drag-and-drop operations on web pages first became possible with the advent of DHTML and the release of capable browsers. The feeling soon wore off, it was messy, it took an awful lot of code, and browser support was haphazard at best.

Now thanks to the YUI, that same giddy feeling of joy has returned, and this time I can't see the bubble bursting so quickly. Drag-and-drop with Yahoo!'s library is extremely easy to implement. It is completely clean, and cross-compatible with the entire spectrum of A-grade browsers.

We've already had a little exposure to the usefulness of drag-and-drop in previous chapters, as this is the mechanism that allows panels and dialogs to be dragged around the viewport or columns in a DataTable to be resized or reordered (provided the corresponding attributes are enabled). In this chapter, we're going to examine this utility in more detail, we will see:

- How to allow any element on the screen to be dragged around
- How dragged elements can interact with drop targets
- How to create draggable objects with specific behaviors

Additionally, we'll see the Slider control, the Resize utility, and the Layout manager, which are pure drag-and-drop at work.

Dynamic drag-and-drop without the hassle

When we configured our panel and dialog boxes to be draggable or columns to be resizable in previous chapters, that's all we had to do—no additional configuration was required and the library handled everything for us.

Like most of the other library components, when creating your own drag-and-drop elements, there is a range of different options available to you that allow you to tailor those objects to your requirements. These properties, like those of most other library components, can be set using an object literal supplied with the constructor, but in most cases even this is not required.

The most challenging aspects of any drag-and-drop scenario in your web applications are going to center around the design of your specific implementation rather than getting drag-and-drop to work in the first place. This utility is yet another example of the huge benefits the YUI can provide in reducing the amount of coding and troubleshooting that you need to concern yourself with.

DragDrop classes

Two classes constitute the basis for the DragDrop component. `YAHOO.util.DragDrop` is the base class for all elements that are to be dragged around. The movement itself is coordinated by `YAHOO.util.DragDropMgr`, which takes care of juggling the various DragDrop instances around. You are unlikely to create instances of either. DragDropMgr is a singleton so it makes no sense to do so; there is to be only one manager per page coordinating the motion of the other elements. You would not create instances of DragDrop either because it is what in other languages we would call an abstract class meant to be the model for its subclasses. The first of those subclasses—`YAHOO.util.DD`—allows for drag-and-drop at its most basic level. The supplied element will be transformed into an object that can be dragged around the page.

The mechanics of drag-and-drop result in a burden of fairly high processing. The library has to keep track of the mouse pointer while it is moving, the draggable object needs to be repositioned, and different events are almost continually firing while the drag is taking place. In order to minimize the amount of information that needs to be processed, especially when the draggable object is fairly complex, you can make use of a proxy element that will track across the page with the mouse pointer. When the proxy element reaches its final destination, it disappears and is replaced by the actual element.

To use such a proxy element, we can use the `YAHOO.util.DDProxy` constructor instead of the basic constructor. As the proxy element is just an empty `<div>` adjusted to the same size as the element it represents, it's much easier to track, reducing the overall processing that's required.

Personally, I think the default appearance of the proxy element is perfectly adequate; however, you can also create your own custom elements to use as a proxy. The figure below shows the default proxy-element appearance:

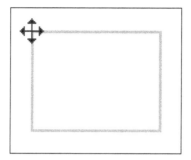

Elements can be dropped anywhere in the page; however, we may create explicit targets. These are elements that will signal when something is being dragged over them so they can produce suitable responses. We can make an element a target for dropping by making it an instance of YAHOO.util.DDTarget. All DragDrop elements can be drop targets unless explicitly prevented from becoming one by setting the .isTarget property to false. DDTargets, on the other hand, are targets but cannot be moved.

The following code, from the downloadable examples, shows how to create draggable elements:

```
var dd = new YAHOO.util.DD("DD");
var ddProxy = new YAHOO.util.DDProxy("DDProxy");
var ddHandle = new YAHOO.util.DD("DDHandle");
ddHandle.setHandleElId('header');
var ddTarget = new YAHOO.util.DDTarget("DDTarget");
var ddNoTarget = new YAHOO.util.DD("DDNoTarget",null,
                                   {isTarget:false});
```

The page has a series of <div> elements sized to make squares, each named after the type of DragDrop object it is to be turned into. The first—DD—is the plainest variety while DDProxy will have a proxy moved instead of itself. DDHandle has a header and a body and it will only respond to dragging when grabbed from the header. DDTarget will not move, but it is a drop target instead. DragDrop will fire a specific event when an element being dragged is dropped on a target. DDNoTarget, on the other hand, can be dragged but is not a drop target. All DragDrop elements are drop targets by default unless .isTarget is set to false.

Design considerations

When working with DragDrop implementations, it is useful to consider the following aspects of the design:

- Can any part of the draggable object be clicked on to initiate the drag, or should a drag handle be defined?

- Can the object be dropped on to any part of the page or should a specific drop target be defined?

- Should anything occur while the object is being dragged?

- Should anything occur when the item is dropped on an invalid target?

- Should anything occur when the object is dropped on to a valid target?

Allowing your visitors to drag-and-drop

The Drag-and-Drop utility uses tried and tested DHTML techniques, as well as some innovative new features, to allow you to easily create objects that can be dragged and then dropped. All that you need to do to make an element on your page draggable is to create a new instance of the YAHOO.util.DD class and feed in the id or element reference of the element that dragging is to be enabled for.

The constructor

The constructor for an instance of the DragDrop object can also take a second or third argument when you are instantiating objects for dragging. The second argument, which is optional, specifies the group to which the element being dragged belongs.

This refers to interaction groups—the object being dragged can only interact with and fire events with other elements in its interaction group. The third argument, which is also optional, can be used to supply a configuration object, the members of which hold additional optional configuration properties that can easily be accessed and set.

Every object instantiated with the drag-and-drop constructor is a member of one or more interaction group(s), even if the second argument is not passed. When the argument is not supplied or evaluates to false, the object will simply belong to the 'default' group instead. There is no limit as to how many groups an object can belong to.

The API provides just two methods that relate to group access. .addToGroup() is used to add the object to more than one group, so the first group membership is defined with the constructor and subsequent groups with the .addToGroup() method. To remove an object from a group, just call the .removeFromGroup() method.

Target practice

There is no doubt that drag-and-drop adds a hands-on, fun element to surfing the net that is way more engaging than simple point-and-click scenarios, and there are many serious applications of this behavior too.

But dragging is only half of the action; without assigned drop targets, the usefulness of being able to drag elements on the page around at leisure is almost wasted.

Drop targets have a class of their own in the Drag-and-Drop utility, which extends the YAHOO.util.DragDrop base class to cater for the creation of drag elements that aren't actually draggable but serve simply as a drop target.

The constructor is exactly the same as for the DD and proxy classes with regard to the arguments passed, but YAHOO.util.DDTarget is used instead. The target class has no methods or properties of its own, but it inherits all of the same methods and properties as the other two classes, including all of the events, though it never fires any.

Get a handle on things

By default, holding down the mouse button while hovering over a draggable object results in the mouse pointer 'picking up' the drag object. The pointer can be over any part of the draggable object and the drag action will still be initiated.

Handles change this default behavior and become the only part of the draggable object that responds to the mouseDown event. You can define multiple handles on a single draggable object and the handle can even be completely external to the draggable object.

To use a handle (or handles) for dragging, the draggable element itself is defined in the same way, but a child element is specified in the underlying HTML as the handle. It is then created by the library by calling the .setHandleElId() or the .setOuterHandleElId() method.

Both of these methods take just one parameter — the id of the element to use as the handle. The first method is used for handles that appear within the boundaries of the drag object, the second method is used when the handle appears outside the drag object.

There are several other useful methods (.addInvalidHandleXxxx()) that revolve mostly around allowing you to specify child elements of drag handles that should not initiate a drag interaction, or for indicating a CSS class or HTML element type that should not act as a drag handle or react to mouseDown events. This is useful for creating elements within the drag-and-drop element that react to clicks in a different way.

The drag-and-drop manager

The page-wide manager of all drag-and-drop interactions is YAHOO.util. DragDropMgr often referred to by its shorter alias, YAHOO.util.DDM. There's a lot in this class but fortunately, you don't need to take much notice of it as it works in the background during drag interactions to make sure everything proceeds as it should. There are a few helper methods that can be hugely useful however, so it is worth taking at least a quick look at the source file to see what they are.

The getBestMatch() function is useful for when a drag object overlaps several drop targets and helps you decide which target the element should actually be dropped on. This method is only used in intersect mode (see the next section) and takes an array of the targets as its argument. It returns the best match based on either the target that the cursor is over or the element with the greatest amount of overlap.

There are also a couple of properties that are used to initiate the dragging of an object. The first property is the pixel threshold (clickPixelThresh), which tells the script how many pixels the cursor should move while the mouse button is held down before a drag begins. The default is three pixels.

The second property is the time threshold (clickTimeThresh), which defines how long the button needs to be held down whilst the pointer is stationary before it is recognized as a drag. The default for this one is 1000 milliseconds.

Interaction modes

The utility supports two types of interaction in between a dragged element and drop targets, that determine when a dragged elements is considered to be over a target. The default is that the position of the cursor over the target is what counts; the alternative is that any point in the dragged object barely touching a target counts.

To switch between the different modes programmatically, the DragDropManager has a property called .mode (YAHOO.util.DDM.mode), which can be set to one of three values—YAHOO.util.DDM.POINT (the cursor counts), YAHOO.util.DDM. STRICT_INTERSECT (any point in the dragged element counts), or YAHOO.util.DDM. INTERSECT (both cursor and the element count).

Since a dragged object occupies a region while the cursor is just a point, the INTERSECT modes are a little harder to use since a dragged object might be overlapping several drop targets at once. Most events and overridable methods that signal such interaction switch from reporting a single target when in POINT mode to an array of possible targets when in either of the INTERSECT modes.

A point provides a safer means of interaction and is the default. In any case, providing visual feedback by changing some style in the drop target is recommended. In this sense, a POINT interaction is less troublesome since such a visual hint can be provided simply by using the :hover CSS pseudo-selector.

Constraints

We seldom want our visitor to drag things all over the page. We either need to limit the region where dragging is valid, or the granularity of the movement. The .setXConstraint() and .setYConstraint() methods allow us to set these limits. They both take three arguments:

- The number of pixels the element is allowed to move towards the left or the top, respectively

- The number of pixels the element is allowed to move towards the right or the bottom, respectively

- The granularity, that is, how many pixels it should jump at a time

All values are in pixels; the first two are relative to the current position of the element. Thus, for a vertical slider element we would use .setXConstraint(0,0) so the dragged knob cannot move sideways and we would also limit its vertical movement so it doesn't overshoot the caps of the slider itself.

We would use the third argument, for example, when dragging a chess piece over the board. The piece can only move a whole number of squares; it cannot sit in the border in between two of them. The granularity, then, is the length of the side of the squares.

Responding to DragDrop events

Sometimes dragging things around is all we need; in fact, it is all we usually do with a panel or dialog; wherever our visitor wishes to drop the panel it is fine. In other cases, we actually need to do something extra such as when we reorder columns in a DataTable.

HTML table columns are not contained in a single element; they cannot actually be dragged around as a single screen entity since they are cells in different table rows that happen to be in the same ordinal position and vertically aligned. In cases such as this, we drag a proxy and, when that proxy is dropped, we do the actual rearrangement of the screen entities.

DragDrop offers us two ways of responding to events (events in the general sense of "things that happen"). One is through regular events; the other is through overridable methods. For example, there is a dragDropEvent event and an .onDragDrop() method. There are also before and after versions of each. Thus, we have .b4DragXxxx(), b4DragXxxxEvent, .onDragXxxx(), and dragXxxxEvent firing in that order for each Xxxx event. Usually, the .b4DragXxxx() methods are already taken and not available to us; in fact, those are the ones that actually make screen elements move around.

Why would you have both an overridable method and an event signaling the very same thing? It is mostly a matter of preference. Events are a little slower since they carry a little overhead while methods are faster, but there can only be one override at a time while any number of functions can listen to the same event. For a drop event, that hardly matters; unless our visitor is the fastest shot in the west, a little overhead can't make any difference. For recurrent events such as those that happen every few pixels while the object is being dragged, that little difference can make the movement jumpy. Care should be taken to avoid doing any time-consuming actions in these events otherwise the user experience will be noticeably degraded.

- b4MouseDownEvent, .onMouseDown(), and mouseDownEvent: These fire when a mousedown event occurs on a draggable object. Returning false on either of the first two will prevent the dragging.

- b4StartDragEvent, .startDrag(), and startDragEvent: These all happen as soon as any of the thresholds set in DragDropMgr is exceeded and the drag actually starts.

- b4DragEvent, .onDrag(), and dragEvent: These happen while the entity is being dragged. Care must be taken not to do anything time consuming in any of these.

- .onDragEnter() and dragEnterEvent: These happen when the element being dragged first enters a drop target, according to the interaction mode set.

- b4DragOverEvent, .onDragOver(), and dragOverEvent: These fire repeatedly while the dragged element is over a drop target.

- b4DragOutEvent, .onDragOut(), and dragOutEvent: These fire once when the dragged element leaves a drop target.

- b4EndDragEvent, .endDrag(), and endDragEvent: These happen when the drag operation is finished.

- b4DragDropEvent, .onDragDrop(), and dragDropEvent: These happen when the drag is finished while the draggable object is on a drop target.

- .onInvalidDrop() and invalidDropEvent: These happen when the drag is finished while the draggable object is not over a drop target.

- `.onMouseUp()` and `mouseUpEvent`: These simply echo the native browser `mouseup` event.

Unlike other events or methods listed, `.endDrag()` is not an empty method in DDProxy, it contains the code to actually move the draggable object into the new position once the proxy is released. Overriding this method without calling its `superclass` version will prevent the object from being dropped.

The basic DragDrop example from the downloadable examples listens to all of the "after" events and logs them on the screen so you can see when each occurs. It is worth noticing that while the `dragEvent` fires continually when the element is dragged around, while it is over a valid drop target it will be followed by a `dragOverEvent` identifying the target it is over. Likewise, while `endDragEvent` and `mouseUpEvent` will always fire when the element is released, they will be preceded by either `dragDropEvent` or `invalidDropEvent` depending on whether it is released over a valid target or not. Besides not moving, `DDTarget` fires no event either, but will make a difference to what events are fired by elements being dragged or released over it.

Implementing drag-and-drop

To highlight some of the basic features and considerations of drag-and-drop we'll create a shopping basket application, which can be used by visitors to drag products they want to buy into the basket.

The page that we'll end up with by the end of this example will look like this:

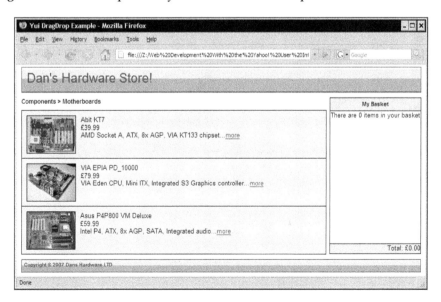

We'll need to include the ever-present `yahoo-dom-event.js` and `reset-fonts-grids.css`, to which we'll add `dragdrop-min.js`.

We'll use the `doc3` 100% fluid page layout and the `t6` template to give us a convenient right-hand side bar in the main body of the page into which we can place our shopping basket. A further CSS file contains all the decoration for this example.

Let's add the code for the product catalog first. Normally, this kind of data would come out of a database dynamically when the page gets loaded, but in this example, the database is hard-coded into the page as an array, as if it had just been JSON-decoded from a remote request:

```
var products = [
    {
        name:'Abit KT7',
        image:'prod1.jpg',
        thumb:'prod1_ico.jpg',
        price:39.99,
        descr:'AMD Socket A, ATX, 8x AGP, VIA KT133 chipset'
    },
    // … other catalog items …
];
```

We will keep a couple of variables, one to hold the number of items in the basket—`basketItems` and another for the cost of those items—`basketCost`. We will also have `<span>` elements with those same IDs to show those values to our visitor. We can add a few of the things that you'd expect to find on a page such as this, like the breadcrumb trail links and the **more...** links. Clicking on these obviously won't do anything in our example, but it helps set the overall effect of the page.

To represent the items both in the catalog and in the basket, we'll use a couple of templates:

```
var PRODUCT_TEMPLATE = '<div class="{classname}"><img id="{imageid}"
src="images/{image}" alt="{name}"><div class="info"><b>{name}<\/b><br/
>&pound;{price}<br/>{descr}...<a href="#">more<\/a><\/div><\/div>',
BASKET_ITEM_TEMPLATE = '<div class="prod"><img class="icon"
src="images/{thumb}" /><div class="prodTitle">{name}<\/div><div class=
"prodPrice">&pound;{price}<\/div><\/div>';
```

They look a little messy like this but the point is that they have curly braces enclosing named placeholders that can be filled with the named properties in the product array above, for example, {name} or {price}, or other variable information such as {classname}, which will produce the alternate green and gray backgrounds, as needed. These templates, as the product listing, are an oversimplification; in practice, we would avoid hard-coding presentation-related tags such as <b> or <br/> into the code, nor would we hard-code local matters like the currency sign (£).

We will use the first of these templates to produce the product catalog:

```
for (var output = [], i = 0; i < products.length; i++) {
    output[i] = Lang.substitute(PRODUCT_TEMPLATE,products[i]);
    output[i] = Lang.substitute(output[i],{
        classname:((i & 1)?'listing_grey':'listing_green'),
        imageid:'prod' + i
    });
}
Dom.get('productListing').innerHTML = output.join('\n');
```

For each of the items in the products array we do two string substitutions in the product catalog template. In the first, we insert the product information itself. In the second, we insert the values for the {classname} placeholder, which will produce the alternate colored bands and {imageid}, which will give us a unique ID for each draggable image. Once we have piled up all that information into output, we concatenate it all and send it into the productListing <div> within the page.

Scripting DragDrop

There are two ways that we could go about achieving our objective. We could take the easy way and create an instance of DD for each draggable screen object, listen to the events from each one and somehow associate those screen elements with a product. This would make the code simpler, at least in the beginning, but would mean that we would require a good deal more of it.

If there are just one or two objects on your page that can be dragged and dropped, then this way is fine. However, when you begin to have more than just a couple of objects that can be moved, in fact, when you don't even know how many there will be, the amount of code required to handle these objects efficiently increases dramatically.

The second way may be a little more complex and therefore will require a greater degree of understanding. However, this way allows for sharing properties and event handlers across similar drag-and-drop objects. This reduces the overall footprint of your application and saves us an incredible amount of typing.

Creating a draggable product item

We will create a DDProduct class, which will represent a draggable version of each product item. We first define the constructor:

```
var DDProduct = function(id, product) {
    DDProduct.superclass.constructor.call(this, id, undefined,{
        isTarget:false,
        scroll:false
    });

    this.product = product;
};
```

The constructor for our "drag-and drop product"—DDProduct object—will receive two arguments, the id of the screen element that will be dragged and a reference to the product information. We first call the constructor of the superclass, that is, the class we inherit from, which will be DDProxy, and provide it with the id of the element to drag. We don't care to create groups so we pass an undefined as the second argument and we further provide two configuration attributes in the last argument. We set .isTarget to false to indicate the catalog items are not drop targets (it makes no sense to drop them on each other) and that we shouldn't scroll the page when dragging. We finally store the product information into an instance property .product.

We then go to define the actual inheritance and further class members:

```
Lang.extend(DDProduct, YAHOO.util.DDProxy, {

    onDragDrop: function() {

        basketItems += 1;
        Dom.get("basketItems").innerHTML = basketItems;

        Dom.get("basketBody").innerHTML +=
            Lang.substitute(BASKET_ITEM_TEMPLATE, this.product);

        basketCost =
          Math.round((basketCost + this.product.price) * 100) / 100;
        Dom.get("basketCost").innerHTML = basketCost;

    },

    endDrag: function() {
    }
});
```

We use our customary shortcuts `Dom` and `Lang`, which we've defined as soon as we created our usual sandbox. We use `YAHOO.lang.extend()` to declare `DDProduct` as a subclass of `DDProxy` and we further define two class members— `.onDragDrop()` and `.endDrag()`. These two already exist in `DDProxy` so in this case we are overriding the original ones.

The original `.onDragDrop()` method is an empty one that does nothing at all and is meant as a hook so we can do something when the object is released over a valid target. Usually, when we override an existing method we call the original in the superclass. It would be pointless to do so here because the original doesn't do anything.

Our `.onDragDrop()` method increases the item count in the basket, uses the template for basket items to append the product info into the main body of the basket, and increases the total price of the basket contents, rounding it to the penny.

We also override `.endDrag()`. The original method is called to actually move the original object (which has not yet moved) to its new destination once the proxy (which so far moved on its behalf) is released. We don't want that to happen, we want our products to remain in the catalog to be dragged over and over again. If we let the original `.endDrag()` method stand, the draggable element would actually end up in the basket. We are using a different, smaller template for basket items than for catalog items; we don't want the original in the basket.

Why use `.onDragDrop()` instead of listening to the `dragDropEvent`? No reason at all, we could have done it either way. We could have added this code to the constructor:

```
this.on('dragDropEvent',function() {
// same code as inside .onDragDrop() above
});
```

Now that we have our `DDProduct` defined, we set everything up for dragging and dropping:

```
for (i = 0; i < products.length; i++) {
    new DDProduct('prod' + i, products[i]);
}


new YAHOO.util.DDTarget("basket");
```

For each of the products in our `products` array, we create an instance of `DDProduct` providing the `id` we generated dynamically via the product catalog template and the product information. As the template stands, that `id` corresponds to the image, via the `{imageid}` placeholder. By changing the template, whatever happens to receive that `id` would have been the dragged element.

Finally, we create a `DDTarget` instance on the `basket` element so that the `.onDragDrop()` method is actually called. If there were no targets, when our visitor releases the object we would be having the `.onInvalidDrop()` method called instead.

Visual selection with the slider control

So far in this chapter we've focused on the functionality provided by the Drag-and-Drop utility. Let's shift our focus back to the interface controls section of the library and look at one of the components that is related very closely to drag-and-drop—the Slider control.

A slider can be defined using a very minimal set of HTML. All you need are two elements—the slider background and the slider thumb, with the thumb appearing as a child of the background element. The slider thumb may contain an image or be decorated somehow:

```
<div id="slider_bg" class="yui-h-slider">
  <div id="slider_thumb" class="yui-slider-thumb">
    <img src="images/slider_thumb.gif"></div>
</div>
```

These elements go together to form the basic slider control, as shown in the following figure:

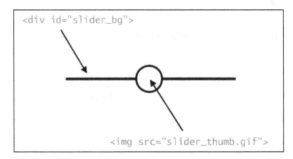

The class names are mandatory and correspond to definitions in the `slider.css` file. The "h" in `yui-h-slider` needs to be replaced by a "v" or a "region" for vertical and region sliders.

The slider control works as a specific implementation of DragDrop in that the slider thumb can be dragged along the slider background either vertically or horizontally. The DragDrop classes are extended to provide additional properties, methods, and events specific to Slider.

One of the main concepts differentiating Slider from DragDrop is that with a basic Slider, the slider thumb is constrained to just one axis of motion, either X or Y depending on whether the Slider is horizontal or vertical respectively.

The slider is another control that can be animated by including a reference to the animation control in the head of the page. Including this means that when any part of the slider background is clicked on, the slider thumb will gracefully slide to that point of the background rather than just moving there instantly.

The constructor and factory methods

Though the individual constructors `YAHOO.widget.Slider` and `YAHOO.widget.DualSlider` can be used just as in any other component, it is far easier to use one of the static factory methods, all under `YAHOO.widget.Slider`:

- `.getHorizSlider()`: Returns an instance of Slider configured for horizontal movement
- `.getVertSlider()`: Returns an instance of Slider configured for vertical movement
- `.getSliderRegion()`: Returns an instance of Slider that can move over a two-dimensional region
- `.getHorizDualSlider()`: Returns an instance of DualSlider with two sliders moving horizontally over a single background
- `.getVertDualSlider()`: Returns an instance of DualSlider with two sliders moving vertical over a single background

DualSliders are suitable for setting, for example, ranges with one slider setting the minimum and the other the maximum value. Slider regions are suitable for two-dimensional values such as saturation and brightness in a color picker.

For both the single vertical and horizontal sliders, the arguments are:

- The ID of the background element
- The ID of the thumb element
- How many pixels the thumb can move to the left or top
- How many pixels the thumb can move to the right or down
- (Optional) How many pixels it should move at a time (defaults to 1, that is, continuous)

For the slider region the arguments are mostly the same, except that arguments 3 through 6 hold the left-down-top-down limits and the optional step gets pushed to the 7th place.

For dual sliders, the arguments are:

- The ID of the background element
- The ID of the minimum (left or top) thumb element
- The ID of the maximum (right or down) thumb element
- The range, in pixels, in which the sliders can move
- (Optional) The step, in pixels
- (Optional) The initial values, as an array with two pixel values

Sliders handle all values as integers in pixels; they don't do any scaling to other units. If a 0 to 100% range needs to be represented by a slider of 150 pixels, it is up to us to convert the 150 value of the slider to 100%.

Class of two

There are just three classes that make up the slider control—the YAHOO.widget. Slider class is a subclass of the YAHOO.util.DragDrop class and inherits a whole bunch of its most powerful properties and methods, as well as defining a load more of its own natively.

The YAHOO.widget.SliderThumb class is a subclass of the YAHOO.util.DD class and inherits properties and methods from this class (as well as defining a few of its own natively). You won't create or handle objects of this class directly; it is used internally to handle the thumb or thumbs and all its properties or methods are available through the Slider or DualSlider that hosts them.

The YAHOO.widget.DualSlider class is actually a composite of two of each of the above, though they share the same background.

Some of the native properties defined by the Slider class and available for you to use are:

- animate: A Boolean indicating whether the slider thumb should animate. Defaults to true if the Animation utility is included, false if not.
- animationDuration: An integer specifying the duration of the animation in seconds. The default is 0.2.

- `backgroundEnabled`: A Boolean indicating whether the slider thumb should automatically move to the part of the background that is selected when clicked. Defaults to `true`.

- `enableKeys`: Another Boolean, which enables the *Home, End* and arrow keys to control the slider. Defaults to `true`, although the slider control must be clicked once with the mouse before this will work or receive the focus somehow.

- `keyIncrement`: An integer specifying the number of pixels the slider thumb will move when an arrow key is pressed. Defaults to 25 pixels.

A large number of native methods are also defined in the class, but a good deal of them are used internally by the slider control and will therefore never need to be called directly by you in your own code. There are a few of them that you may need at some point, however, including:

- `.getThumb()`: Returns a reference to the slider thumb

- `.getValue()`: Returns an integer determining the number of pixels the slider thumb has moved from the start position

- `.getXValue()`: An integer representing the number of pixels the slider has moved along the X axis from the start position

- `.getYValue()`: An integer representing the number of pixels the slider has moved along the Y axis from the start position

- `.onAvailable()`: Executed when the slider becomes available in the DOM

- `.setRegionValue()` and `.setValue()`: Allow you to programmatically set the value of the region slider's thumb

For the DualSlider, the thumbs values are not available through getter methods but by properties `.minVal` and `.maxVal`, which are documented as read-only and, though there is nothing preventing us from writing into them, it will have no effect whatsoever; we need to use `.setMinValue()`, `.setMaxValue()`, or `.setValues()`. All the value setting methods accept extra arguments to prevent the movement of the thumb from being animated and to avoid firing the value change events. These options are handy when setting them for the first time.

More often than not, you'll find the custom events defined by the slider control to be most beneficial to you in your implementations. You can capture the slider thumb being moved using the `change` event, or detect the beginning or end of a slider interaction by subscribing to `slideStart` or `slideEnd` respectively.

A very simple slider

What we're aiming to achieve over the course of this example is to produce a small widget that visitors to your site could use to dynamically change the font size of text on the page in a visually appealing manner.

I know that the font-size of any given page can easily be adjusted by your visitors using the native method of their browser's UI, but it's a nice effect to have directly on your own pages, it promotes usability, and would sit nicely in a "user control panel" area of your site/page.

The screenshot below demonstrates how our slider will appear by the end of this example:

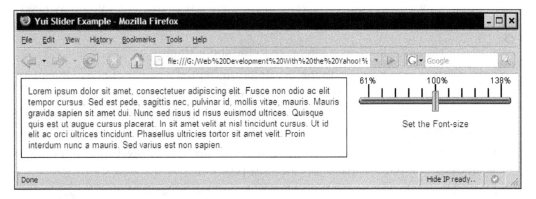

Getting started

The required dependencies for Slider are the ever-present `yahoo-dom-event.js`, `dragdrop-min.js` and of course, `slider-min.js`. We will also use the optional `animation-min.js`. You can try the example both with and without. The only way to notice it's there is by clicking in the bar and letting the thumb reach that place instead of dragging the thumb itself. Slider requires `slider.css` and we will also throw `reset-fonts-grids.css` in.

We'll use the Grid tools to have an area of text on the main body and a side panel on the right to hold the slider. The slider itself will be defined by the following markup:

```
<div id="sli_bg" class="yui-h-slider" title="font size slider">
    <div id="sli_thumb" class="yui-slider-thumb">
        <img src="images/sli_thumb.gif">
</div></div>
```

The slider thumb, `sli_thumb`, has the image making up the slider thumb hard-coded directly into it as opposed to being set with CSS, as the slider background is, and is defined as a child of the slider background element `sli_bg`. Slider really doesn't care what's inside the slider thumb, it can be an image as here, a suitable character like a vertical bar, or it can be entirely defined by CSS by giving `sli_thumb` a width, height, border, and background image.

We have given IDs and class names to both elements. The IDs are ours; the class names are required by `slider.css`, which already provides a default background, a simple bar, for the SAM skin. The **assets** folder also contains alternative backgrounds and several thumbs to choose from.

When designing a slider implementation, it is important to take into account the sizes of the slider background and thumb images when configuring properties such as the pixel distance the thumb can travel and the distance between ticks, to make sure everything looks as it should.

Adding the CSS

We might be satisfied with the background and thumbs provided along with the SAM skin but if we want to use our own, as in this case, we need to add some CSS:

```
#sli_bg {
   width:240px;
   height:50px;
   background:url(images/sli_bg.gif) no-repeat;
}
#sli_thumb {
   top:20px;
   left:10px;
}
```

These two selectors target the slider background and thumb components respectively. The main rule for the slider background is the `background` property, which is used to display the slider background image, which should not tile, and the `width` and `height` to allow enough space for it.

For the thumb we need to set the `top` position so that it fits right over the background. This is mostly a visual matter and has to be adjusted on the spot according to the size of the slider. The `left` setting needs to be there because the background has two rounded caps, one at each end, which are not an active part of the slider. We add this small offset to nudge the thumb past this dead area.

Adding the JavaScript

Now we're ready to move on to the final part of this example—the JavaScript that will turn a couple of images into a fully working slider element. Before the closing `</body>` tag, we have the following code:

```
YAHOO.util.Event.onDOMReady(function() {

    var fontSlider = YAHOO.widget.Slider.getHorizSlider(
        "sli_bg",       // the id of the background element
        "sli_thumb",    // the id of the thumb element
        0,              // the number of pixels it can move left
        200,            // the number of pixels it can move right
        20              // how many pixels it can move at a time
    );

    fontSlider.setValue(100,true,true,true);

    var sizes = {
        "0":61,
        "20":69,
        "40":77,
        "60":85,
        "80":93,
        "100":100,
        "120":108,
        "140":116,
        "160":123,
        "180":131,
        "200":138
    };

    fontSlider.subscribe("change", function (val) {

        var newSize = sizes[val] + "%";
        YAHOO.util.Dom.setStyle("content", "font-size", newSize);
    });
});
```

The `.onDOMReady()` method kicks everything off as soon as the DOM is in a complete state, which will ensure that our slider is available as soon as the page has loaded. We then create our sandbox.

The `Slider.getHorizSlider` constructor has five arguments. The first is the element with an `id` attribute of `sli-bg`, the second is the element with an `id` of `sli_thumb`. The next two arguments indicate how far the slider thumb can travel in the left and right directions; it is important that the distance does not exceed the boundary of the slider background or the thumb will be able to leave the slider background.

The final parameter sets up the tick marks for the slider, making it digital instead of analogue. The visible lines that mark each tick are part of the picture itself and are not created automatically by the control.

As soon as the slider is created, we set its initial value. We set all the options to `true` to make it quietly; we don't want the initial setting of the thumb to be animated nor do we want the events to be fired since everything is fine as originally set. The third `true` argument is to force the slider even if it was locked, which is not, but that argument goes somewhere in between the other two so we just set them all and are done with it.

We want the text size to increase or decrease depending on the position of the thumb. The slider values are in pixels and those are not suitable for setting font sizes so we have a `sizes` object acting as a translation table between slider values, from 0 to 200 in 20 pixel steps, as set in the constructor, and font sizes in percentages.

The `change` event fires every time the position of the slider thumb changes. The listener to the `change` event receives the value of the slider. We can use this value as an index into the `sizes` array and get a valid setting for the `font-size` attribute. For region sliders, the listener to `change` will actually receive two arguments, the x and y values at once. Anyway, we can always retrieve the values by using the corresponding properties or methods and, in fact, that is what we need to do with DualSliders, which doesn't give us this information in its arguments. As with any listener the `this` variable points to the very slider instance so we can access any of its members. Finally, we make use of the `.setStyle()` Dom method to physically change the size of the text contained in the content element.

It's as easy as that, no further coding is needed for the slider to work as intended.

The Resize utility

The Resize utility turns any block DOM element, usually a `<div>`, into a resizable panel. It does so by adding a set of slim handles, by default to the right, bottom, and lower-right corner of the element to be resized, and using Drag-and-Drop on those handles, it adjusts the width and height of that element. To resize an element such as this:

```
<div id="resizableBlock"><p>Lorem ipsum … </p></div>
```

this is all the code that is required:

```
var resizableBlock = new YAHOO.util.Resize("resizableBlock");
```

The resizer adds no border to the resizable block and it starts from whatever its initial size might be. It is usually better to add some styling to the block. Also, if the left and/or top edges are to be dragged, the block element has to be absolutely positioned.

```
#resizableBlock {
    height: 200px;
    width: 200px;
    border: thin solid silver;
    padding:5px;
/* required if top or left borders are handles */
    position:absolute;
}
```

The constructor can also take a second argument, an object literal with configuration attributes, several of which are passed on to the Drag-and-Drop and Animation utilities so we won't repeat them here. Among the rest, the following are particularly useful:

- `animate`: If a `proxy` is enabled, the block will use the Animation utility, if loaded, to reach its final size.
- `draggable`: This will add the ability to drag the block.
- `handles`: An array containing strings representing abbreviations of the edges and corners that can be dragged; it takes any combination of `'t'`, `'b'`, `'r'`, `'l'`, `'bl'`, `'br'`, `'tl'`, `'tr'`, or simply the string `'all'` (case-insensitive) for all handles. It defaults to `['r','b','br']`.

- `height` and `width`: The initial values in pixels instead of using the CSS equivalents.

- `proxy`: The resizer will show an outline of the element while it is being resized and will set it once the mouse button is released.

- `ratio`: The aspect ratio of the block will be maintained.

- `autoRatio`: The resizer will keep the aspect ratio of the element if resized with the *Shift* key pressed.

- `status`: If this is `true`, it will show a tooltip with the size and position of the resizable element as it is being resized and/or dragged.

- `ghost`: When `proxy` is set, a dimmer, ghost image of the resized element is shown while it is being resized.

- `hover`: Drag handles are shown only when the mouse is over them.

- `knobHandles`: Use square knobs instead of the regular handles.

- `hiddenHandles`: No handles are displayed, though the cursor will still change shape.

- `wrap`: The element is wrapped in an extra `<div>`. Some elements, such as `<img>`, `<textarea>`, `<input>`, `<iframe>`, and `<select>`, that cannot accept child elements to serve as handles are wrapped automatically. This option allows other elements, not contemplated in the original design, to be equally wrapped (for example, `<canvas>`).

- `setSize`: `true` by default, if it is `false` and a proxy is used, the element will not be resized. Instead, we need to listen to the `resize` event for the final expected value and handle it any way we want.

Most of the events the Resize utility fires are inherited from its several constituents. The only native ones are `startResize`, `resize`, and `endResize`, which provide, among other arguments, the top, left, height, and width of the resizable element.

The Layout Manager

The **Layout Manager** combines up to 5 panels or "layout units" with the central, mandatory one taking whatever space is left by the up to four resizable panels above, below, and to either side of it. Each of the layout units is in Standard Module Format, with header, body, and footer sections. This is what it looks like:

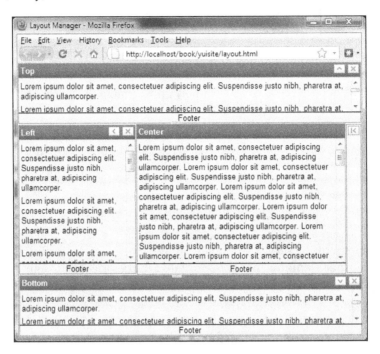

The image shows the right panel collapsed, so only a thin strip with the expand icon is all that remains of it. All the other panels are expanded and have their position as their header. The ability to resize, the collapse and close buttons, the scrollbars, the header, and footer shown are all optional and have been explicitly enabled in all except in the center panel where some of the options are not valid. The center panel will always be resized to whatever space is left by the others and it cannot be collapsed or closed. The whole page takes all the viewport. Even if the browser window is resized, the Layout Manager will adjust the panels to fit in the available space.

The content of the top panel is plain HTML:

```
<div id="topPanel">
    <p>Lorem ipsum dolor sit amet, consectetuer … </p>
    … … …
</div>
```

The other panels have similar content, each with its own id. The page was created with the following code:

```
YAHOO.util.Event.onDOMReady(function () {
    var layout = new YAHOO.widget.Layout({
        units: [{
            position: 'top', header: 'Top', body: 'topPanel',
            footer: 'Footer', height: 100, collapse: true,
            resize: true, scroll: true, animate: true,
            close: true, gutter:'1px'
        },
// the definitions for the other side panels have been omitted
        {
            position: 'center', header: 'Center',
            body: 'centerPanel', footer: 'Footer',
            scroll: true
        }]
    });
    layout.render();
});
```

Each panel or "layout unit" is defined in the `units` configuration attribute, which takes an array of object literals that are the configuration attributes for each of those units. This allows us to configure both the Layout Manager and its units at once. We have omitted the definitions for the left, right, and bottom units here for brevity.

The Layout constructor can actually take two arguments. If the first argument is a reference to an HTML element or a string with the `id` of such an element, the panels managed by the Layout manager will use that element as their container. In this case, the second argument will hold the configuration attributes. If, as in this example, the first argument is an object, the Layout manager will assume it contains the configuration options and use the whole browser window.

The Layout manager can take the following configuration attributes:

- `width` and `height`: These will default to those of the container or the viewport of the browser.
- `minWidth` and `minHeight`: The whole set of panels will adjust to its container, but will refuse to drop below these values.
- `parent`: Layouts can be nested. This attribute may point to the Layout where it is contained, so as to bind their resizing.
- `units`: An array containing the configuration attributes for each of the up to 5 layout units.

Layout methods allow you to add, remove, or get references to its layout units; render it initially or force a resize calculation. The .render() method fires the render event when completed. Resizing fires several events; beforeResize fires before starting and returning false from the listener will cancel the operation. startResize is fired echoing the same event from any of the layout units, while resize is fired when the .resize() method is called. The rest of the methods and events are inherited from the classes Layout inherits from.

Each of the layout units is handled by the Resize utility, which combines features from Element, Drag-and-Drop, and Animation utilities so most of its members come from all that ancestry. We will only mention a few of the most useful ones.

The .header, .body, and .footer properties are references to the HTML elements holding each of the three sections of the SMF panel. They should be considered read-only and may be null if that section was not set. To insert contents into those sections, it is better and much safer to use the configuration attributes of the same name.

The .expand(), .collapse(), .toggle(), and .close() methods are pretty much what we would expect. The .close() method makes the layout unit disappear and it removes it from the Layout manager. A collapsed unit can be expanded; a closed one is completely gone.

Before any of these operations is executed, the beforeExpand, beforeCollapse, and beforeClose events are fired and false can be returned from its listeners to cancel the operation. Likewise, the beforeResize event allows its listener to cancel the resizing by returning false. When the operation is completed, the expand, collapse or close events are fired. Each layout unit echoes the startResize, resize, and endResize from the resizer.

The position attribute specifies the position of the panel; it can be any of top, right, bottom, left, or "center". There can only be one panel of each.

The header, body, and footer configuration attributes let us set the corresponding section in each panel, creating it if it doesn't exist. They all take a reference to an HTML element or a string. If a string, it will first try to locate an HTML element with that id, otherwise, it uses it as the content. If false, the corresponding section will be deleted.

The collapse and close attributes let us configure whether such buttons should appear in the panel header. Do not confuse them with the methods of the same name. These do not act on the panel, they just make the corresponding buttons show. When collapsed, the collapseSize determines the size it reaches; it defaults to a size that fits the expand button.

Configuration attributes such as `width`, `height`, `proxy`, `hover`, maximum and minimum dimensions, and `animate` are sent straight through to the resizer, if the `resize` attribute is `true`.

The `.loadContent()` method can be used in conjunction with the `dataSrc` attribute, which takes a URL, to dynamically load content into any of the panels. Though the `loadMethod` attribute, which defaults to `GET`, can be set to `POST`, there is no way to send post arguments. The `load` and `loadError` events signal the completion, successful or not, of the data load. The `dataLoaded` attribute lets us check whether the data has been loaded. Layout will refuse to load a panel twice. Once `dataLoaded` is set, calls to `.loadContent()` will be ignored, and `dataLoaded` cannot be reset. As with any other panel, only plain text or HTML can be loaded; any `<script>` or `<style>` tag will be ignored.

Summary

The code required to make the images on our product listing page draggable could best be described as minimal. It's also very easy code to get to grips with. As the example highlighted, it's the mechanics of what you want to achieve with the Drag-and-Drop utility's functionality that takes far more consideration.

A close descendant of Drag-and-Drop, the Slider, is even easier to implement and can be a very effective and visually appealing addition to your pages. Although this control is relatively basic and compact, it still provides a series of custom events to hook into and a range of configurable properties.

Both the Resize utility and the Layout manager, which combines several resizable panels, allow for fluid page layouts giving our visitor full control over the size and/or position of the screen elements.

13
Everyday Tools

It would be nice if everything worked fine from the start, but that is not always so; especially when starting, whatever the environment might be, things are not likely to work as smoothly as one might have wished.

Once everything works, we need to ensure it can be delivered to our users in the most effective way. In contrast to other server-based web technologies, our scripts will be loaded in the computers of our visitors. We need to minimize the amount of code downloaded, ensure that it is of the best quality and that it runs in all likely platforms.

In this chapter, we'll take a look at tools that can help us:

- Locate and fix errors and ensure the robustness of our code
- Test across different platforms and over successive versions
- Improve the performance of the application itself and its deployment

Though we'll try to mention all tools available to us, we won't study them all as the most advanced of them are beyond the scope of this book. The table of contents for this chapter in the downloadable code bundle has links to all tools mentioned in it.

We won't talk much about debuggers either; fortunately most major browsers have debugging capabilities either built-in or that can be added, so that is no longer an issue. In the past, a whole chapter could be written on just about how to get one and make it work. Now, it is just a matter of which is the one you feel more comfortable with, all of them offering more or less the same capabilities.

Lint-free code

JavaScript is designed to be very tolerant and flexible. Some of its features allow for code that is on the edge of the abyss, ready to break down at any time. Staying away from the most dangerous features and being conservative on those we use is a good insurance against pitfalls.

As any regular at the YUI forum can attest, many problems come from fragile code. Many a question could have been spared, and the time waiting for the answer saved, if the code had been clean. When our eyes are tired after a long session of coding and we are incapable of matching braces, there are programs that do the bean counting for us, checking that the parenthesis, braces, and brackets are matched, that lines have their semicolons and all those tedious tasks.

JSLint is a free JavaScript syntax analyzer available to use online at `http://www.jslint.com` and also available to run as a command-line utility in several environments or as a Yahoo! Widget (`http://widgets.yahoo.com/`, previously known as Konfabulator) and as a plugin for several IDEs (Integrated Development Environments). It is written in JavaScript and can be easily integrated into any environment where a JavaScript interpreter is available.

JSLint can take a `.js` or `.html` file containing JavaScript and produce a listing with errors, warnings, and the symbol table for the code. Needless to say, code should go into a production environment with no errors and as few warnings as possible. This usually seems an impossible task when first exposed to its long list of errors. Running our old code through JSLint can be a humbling experience, but it is a good tool to keep us on the safe side. With a little experience it is easy to program for JSLint, which is not a bad thing at all, it encourages good practices.

The build process of the YUI Library itself includes a pass through JSLint. There is no excuse for us to be sloppy if all those hundreds of thousands of lines of code can get by JSLint with no errors.

JSLint does not modify your code, it just produces a diagnostic. It does not affect performance; none of its advice will make your code slower, but it will make it much more reliable.

It is important that our code comes out with no other global variables but YAHOO (or that of whatever library you are using), your own namespace for your in-house library components (if you hadn't placed them under YAHOO) and those native to the DOM: `window`, `document`, and those of its members that have their namespaces implicit, like `.setTimeout()` or `.location.href`. Global variables are not an error per se and are not marked as such, but they pose a risk by polluting the Global Namespace and being at risk of contagion from other sloppy code, they should be kept to a minimum.

It will also signal unused variables. If we are using our standard template, we might often find that we ended up not using all of our usual shortcuts such as `Dom`, `Event`, or `Lang`. We can make a note of it and delete them. Most often, an unused variable signals a typo: we declared the variable with a name and then used it with another slightly misspelled name.

Even the web-based version runs JSLint in the browser within the client machine, there is no code ever transmitted to the `jslint.com` site. JSLint has many configuration options to tailor it to our taste.

We also have several validators from the **World Wide Web Consortium (W3C)** (`http://www.w3.org/`) such as the HTML Validator that should also be run on our code. They also come available in several flavors that can be integrated on our build environment or run in our browsers. It is offered as a plugin for Firefox, which shows an unobtrusive green, yellow, or red icon on the status bar that can be expanded into a detailed list of errors and suggested fixes. This is handy so that we can keep our code clean as we develop and test it.

The JavaScript beautifier (`http://jsbeautifier.org/`) can also help in cleaning up code by formatting it in a standard way. JSLint has an option to issue warnings about formatting, but JSBeautifier does the changes for us. It is also written in JavaScript and can be run via its web interface or downloaded and included in our build system or as a tool in our IDE.

A quick search on the Web provides several references to XML Validators. As JSON is becoming so popular, a need has arisen for an equivalent tool for it. The JSONLint site (`http://www.jsonlint.com/`) provides one such validator. As mentioned in earlier chapters, JSON is not whatever the JavaScript interpreter can read, it has stricter rules to make it portable to other platforms: most of the JSON out there is generated by PHP or Java! Do not attempt to code a JSON encoder or parser; there are more pitfalls than it seems at first. The JSON site (`http://json.org`) lists external libraries available for most languages if they don't already have the capability built-in. Anyway, when in doubt, check it with JSONLint.

The Logger

The Logger has been built to be used directly in connection with the `-debug.js` versions of each individual library component. The Logger is primarily used to display the messages that are produced by each of the different library components at several points during their execution, allowing you to see exactly what is going on throughout the progress of your script.

Other than providing error messages to assist you with debugging and troubleshooting, each library component is configured to log informational messages when different custom events fire. This allows you to keep track of the different things that happen during the course of a particular interaction. When first beginning to use the library, this feature of the Logger can provide valuable insights into the inner workings of each component.

You needn't rely solely on the different messages hard coded into each library component either. It is very simple to log your own custom messages to the Logger Control at any point during your script so the Logger Control can help you regardless of whether you are using any of the other library components or not.

The Logger Control is different from the other controls in the sense that it is something that the visitors to your site will rarely, if ever, see. The main reason why you wouldn't have an instance of the Logger sitting happily on your application's landing page is based on the performance hit your application is likely to take when managing the interactions your visitor is making, while at the same time processing and displaying log messages. Some of the examples on the YUI documentation site are testament to this!

Additionally, the Logger is designed to work with the `-debug.js` versions of the library files, rather than the `-min.js` versions, the latter of which you should be using in a production application. The `-min.js` versions are the ones served by Yahoo! and have been optimized for quick downloading and therefore have no Logger targeting code routines in them.

Using the Logger Control when designing your pages or applications gives you an insight into what is going on in the library files you are using at different points during their execution. If you look through one of the `-debug.js` versions of any of the library files, you'll see various statements that log messages to the Logger that can help you to understand why something isn't working the way it should.

You can also log your own custom messages when building an application to help with troubleshooting and debugging your own code. I've always used the standard JavaScript `alert()` to test what information is being passed around in a function and to provide guidance when things haven't been going right. But with the Logger, you have far greater control over the format of the messages that you can output, and the interface used to view them is a lot more pleasant than an intrusive and ugly alert.

The Logger provides advanced functionality including built-in methods for easily showing and hiding, pausing and resuming, or collapsing and expanding the Logger Control. It also maintains an internal message stack into which logged messages are saved for reference, and even a buffer that can store log messages while the Logger is paused.

The purpose of the –debug Library files

Other than having all the comments, plenty of whitespace, and more sensible variable names, the -debug.js versions of each of the different library components also have plenty of additional code that outputs messages for the Logger component to display. At their most fundamental level the -debug.js and standard files are just much more human-readable and much easier to make sense of than the -min.js versions.

If you open up one of the -debug.js versions of one of the library components in your text editor, you'll be able to see all of this extra code for yourself first-hand instead of just taking my word for it. Let's look at both the standard non-suffixed and -debug.js versions of the Animation Utility:

```
YAHOO.util.Anim = function(el, attributes, duration, method) {
    if (!el) {
    }
    this.init(el, attributes, duration, method);
};
```

This is the very first function found in the animation.js file; note the empty if statement, which checks that the el object exists. Now let's take a look at exactly the same function, but this time from the animation-debug.js file instead of the standard version:

```
YAHOO.util.Anim = function(el, attributes, duration, method) {
    if (!el) {
        YAHOO.log('element required to create Anim instance',
                'error', 'Anim');
    }
    this.init(el, attributes, duration, method);
};
```

In this version of the file, the `if` statement contains a message to log to the Logger console. In this case the message alerts you (not the visitor) that you need to supply an element in order to create an animation. Each debug file is filled with additional code like this to alert you to potential problems with your code. Just for the sake of interest, let's view the `-min.js` version of the same function:

```
YAHOO.util.Anim=function(B,A,C,D){if(!B){}this.init(B,A,C,D);
};
```

Nice! Highly efficient for a browser to download and use, but not very helpful to the likes of you and me, and as you can clearly see, no log messages are generated.

Each component has varying amounts of Logger-specific code in its `-debug` file depending on each utility or control's capacity for error. The code snippets just seen from the Animation Utility are one of just a couple of lines of code related to the Logger. This is because it's a simple utility where little can go wrong.

The Connection Manager Utility on the other hand, is filled with Logger-targeting code due to its complexity, and the fact that there is a lot more that can go wrong when working with remote applications. The Logger can be extremely helpful debugging and troubleshooting Connection problems.

How the Logger can help you

Traditionally, the most primitive way of debugging your code is to use `window.alert()` calls with suitable messages. This may become quite annoying especially if the error is within a loop. As an alert box blocks the JavaScript interpreter, using `alert()` may also cause its own errors when used in asynchronous events. If an `alert()` is placed after a call to Connection Manager's `.asyncRequest()` method, you are likely to miss the reply as it will probably timeout waiting for you to click the OK button.

To create an instance of the Logger, you have to add `logger-min.js` and `logger.css` to the ever-present `yahoo-dom-event.js` and may add the `dragdrop-min.js` so the logging window can be dragged around and out of the way. Then, we can place this code at the beginning of our sandbox:

```
<script type="text/javascript">
    YAHOO.util.Event.onDOMReady(function () {
        var myLogger = new YAHOO.widget.LogReader();
        var Dom = YAHOO.util.Dom, Lang = YAHOO.lang;
```

That is enough to get us this logging window up in our screen:

The window will float above the page and, if `dragdrop-min.js` was included, it can be moved out of the way or, otherwise, the **Collapse** button will reduce it to the title bar itself.

The main window contains the time-stamped messages from the application with the newest on top. They are color coded, as shown in the checkboxes below. Those checkboxes can reduce the clutter in the logging window by showing the messages of just one particular category. If you are trying to locate some undefined fatal error, it is a good idea to enable just the red errors first to avoid being flooded with too much information.

Finally, the logger lets you see messages related to a particular source. Each YUI component will identify its own messages as in the screenshot just seen; we have messages coming from the YAHOO global object and from the LogReader itself.

The Logger is not limited to messages issued by the YUI components, we can also send our messages by using the `YAHOO.log()` method:

```
YAHOO.log("The div's class is " + el.className);
```

This would print the text in the first argument under the `info` category for the `global` source, which are the defaults. You can add your own category, source, or both:

```
YAHOO.log("Component X has loaded!", "info", "my source");
```

There is no need to create a source or category beforehand; if any message comes up from a particular source, Logger will add a checkbox for that source. Likewise, there is actually no limit for the categories; you can add your own category:

```
YAHOO.log("Component X has loaded!", "mine", "my source");
```

The `"mine"` category will not have any color assigned as the built-in ones do, but that can be easily fixed with a little CSS:

```
.yui-log .mine {
    background-color: magenta;
}
```

The Logger is actually made of several classes. `YAHOO.widget.Logger` is a static class that cannot and need not be instanced; just one will be available for any application as soon as the `logger-min.js` file is included. It contains the queue of messages being logged. The size of this queue, initially 2500, can be configured via the `.maxStackEntries` property.

The `YAHOO.widget.LogReader` class can be instanced, as we've just seen, and is the one that will read the queue and show the messages in it. You can actually create the LogReader at any time and it will show whatever has been logged since the beginning.

The `YAHOO.widget.LogWriter` class is a helper that makes it shorter to write messages to the log. Its constructor takes a string as its only argument and that will become the source for all messages sent from it.

Finally, the `LogMsg` class is for internal use mostly and is how the Logger stores messages in the queue.

The `YAHOO.log()` method is located in the `YAHOO` global component, so it is always available. It does not require the `logger-min.js` file to be included; if there is no Logger available, it won't do anything and it won't generate an error either. The worst that can happen if you leave a `YAHOO.log()` statement behind is that your code will have more dead weight.

The `YAHOO.log()` method in fact calls `YAHOO.widget.Logger.log()`, if present. This static class offers a couple of interesting options. Instead of logging to a LogReader window, you can log into the browser console, if available, by calling the `.enableBrowserConsole()` method. You can also try to log native JavaScript errors, when supported by the browser, by calling `.handleWindowErrors()`.

The Logger window will usually float above the page but it is easy to fix it to a particular place, if so desired. You can provide a reference to an empty element in the screen, usually an empty `<div>`, and the LogReader will draw itself in it. It can still be dragged out from that place, but the gap will remain.

We can have some control of the Logger itself by using some of its methods. To reduce the clutter, we might not want the logging to start before a certain point. We have no control over what the YUI components log or when they start; if you have a `-debug` version of the component, it will log everything. However, you can clear the console at anytime, dropping what had been logged so far. You can also show and hide the LogReader window or specific categories or sources. The static Logger class offers:

- `YAHOO.widget.Logger.reset()`: This clears all the messages from the logging buffer.

While LogReader provides these methods:

- `.clearConsole()`: This clears the LogReader window but does not destroy the messages in the queue. Any refresh will bring them all back.

- `.showCategory()` and `.hideCategory()`: These produce the same effect as clicking on any of the category checkboxes. They refresh the console so anything cleared from it, but not reset, will show up again.

- `.showSource()` and `.hideSource()`: Same as the above for sources.

- `.show()`, `.hide()`, `.collapse()`, and `.expand()`: Let you take it out of the way totally or partially and restore it.

- `.pause()` and `.resume()`: Pause and resume the rendering process; the messages will still be queued, but not shown (saves time in time-critical operations).

One interesting aspect of the LogReader and the Logger is that the queue of messages is a separate internal structure from the logger window, so messages can be shown or not, but they will still be saved. Hiding a category or a source simply prevents that category or source from being shown, the messages are still there and can be shown at any time; nothing is lost.

Debugging

If we can't get things working, we need to go to our debugger. Most major browsers have their debuggers. The most popular for quite some time and, perhaps, the most evolved is FireBug (`http://getfirebug.com/`) a free debugger for the equally free Firefox browser (`http://www.mozilla.com/`) available for most operating systems. Internet Explorer has recently incorporated a debugger and Safari has had one for some time now.

Most of them are pretty intuitive and, anyway, each has its own documentation. We'll just mention a few things as they relate to the YUI Library.

JavaScript always tries to carry on in spite of errors. Sometimes an error that is not immediately fatal allows the interpreter to keep going until it really gets messed up and stops. At that point, the error is long past and hard to find. It is better to run all debuggers with the "break on all errors" (or however it might be called in each debugger) option on. This makes the interpreter stop at the first hint of an error and, thus, closer to its actual source.

Usually, we will load the minified versions of YUI files. If the debugger stops with an error within the minified YUI code it will make no sense neither to you nor to anyone else; please don't paste any such errors in a message to the YUI forums nor expect a reply, miracles just take too long. Instead, find out how to look at the "Call Stack" in your debugger and trace the stack of function calls until you get to your own code. Some debuggers let you inspect the variables as they were at that point in the stack trace; if they do, check the arguments of the function call that got you in trouble; otherwise, put a breakpoint there and re-run the code and see what is it that you are passing as arguments to the function in the YUI Library. Check against the API docs and see if they match. Chances are that some variable has gone out of scope or has not been yet initialized and is undefined or `null`. Perhaps you didn't wait for the DOM to be ready and an HTML element is not yet where you thought it would be.

Asynchronous events are particularly hard to debug. If you are stepping through a sequence of instructions and arrive at an asynchronous call such as Connection Manager's `.asyncRequest()` or DataSource's `.sendRequest()`, the debugger will never catch up on the callback. You need to place explicit breakpoints in the callbacks. Also, don't step over an asynchronous call, it will distract the debugger from listening to the reply and it will miss it. When you get to a call to an asynchronous function, place breakpoints in the callbacks and give the debugger a go, do not single step, so the interpreter is ready and listening when the reply comes back.

For repetitive events, such as those triggered by interval timers, you just might need to use the logger. While the debugger keeps the interpreter on hold, the timer events will be ignored, and there will be too many of them. Likewise with `mouseover` events, you can't capture what goes on in a `mouseover` listener without disrupting the sequence of calls. The Animation and Drag & Drop utilities are particularly hard to debug by single stepping and the interpreter won't queue the events for you to look at them at leisure, they will simply be dropped; you have to log them instead.

Most browsers find some way to log into their console, but that is not standard. Calls to Firebug `console.log()` method will break in IE versions 7 or earlier. That is when the YUI Logger comes in handy because it works in all browsers.

If you really feel like stepping into YUI's code, load the raw or debug (`-debug.js`) versions of the files, not the minified (`-min.js`) ones. All aggregates are minified so to step into `yahoo-dom-event.js` you actually have to load `yahoo.js`, `dom.js`, and `event.js` separately.

Watching bits go by

Sometimes the interaction with a certain server is not what we expected. A typo on a URL might get us a 404 – Not Found error. At other times, when we assemble URL arguments via code, we miss one or forget to encode them properly, the server, totally baffled, might reply in ways we didn't expect. It often happens that the server returns a nicely formatted HTML page explaining the error when we were expecting an XML or JSON reply. The receiving code on the client side gets confused by such a message intended for humans not for code.

It is good to check out what actually gets sent and received. Firebug already shows that in the Net tab; other browsers may or may not have similar features. In those cases, a tool such as Fiddler (`http://www.fiddler2.com/`) or Wireshark (`http://www.wireshark.org/`) is a good choice; both are free.

Fiddler works only on Windows and it is oriented towards web traffic (mostly HTTP) so it is an easier tool to use. Wireshark works on Windows, Mac, and Unix and it is a far more capable tool but also very generic as it often shows too much information. If you are using a Windows machine, go for Fiddler.

First of all, check that everything you assumed loaded got loaded. A frequent message is **YAHOO is not an object**. As anything in the YUI Library is under `YAHOO`, it is the first thing that is likely to be accessed, so if it is not found it signals that you tried to load the library from the wrong source. Bad URLs also cause missing images or scrambled layouts for lack of the proper CSS files. Any of these tools will highlight such an error in red as they produce a 404 – Not Found error.

Other errors are more subtle; a bad argument in a URL may get a reply from the server, even if it is nothing more than an error code. It is important in those cases first to check the reply; there might be an error message there. Otherwise, it is important to check both the arguments on the request, which must be properly encoded, and whether the format of the reply is really what we expected it to be. For XML or JSON replies, it is easy to use any of the validators mentioned earlier.

Sometimes a request does not come out at all. The browser has a cache and some browsers, notably IE, cache more than they should. The YUI Library can't do anything about that, but it can certainly be fixed. The wrong way to do it is to add random arguments to the URL. This makes each request unique and non-cacheable. In fact, the reply will be cached, but each cache entry will be associated to a unique URL that will never be repeated, so it is a waste of cache space. As the cache space is limited, filling it up with unique replies floods the cache and makes it overflow, dumping valid cached pages and, in general, degrading the overall performance for the user.

A much better alternative is to use proper headers at the server side. For example, the following will work in PHP:

```
header('Cache-Control: no-cache, must-revalidate');
header('Expires: Mon, 26 Jul 1997 05:00:00 GMT');
```

This will prevent any browser from caching any reply, wasting neither time nor memory. Make sure the date is valid and well past or it can also be a -1. Other environments will have other means of setting the HTTP reply headers but the content is basically the same.

Seeking performance

Once everything works, we want to make it faster to improve the user experience. The first stop should be Yahoo!'s Exceptional Performance team site (http://developer.yahoo.com/performance/) and, in particular, reading their recommendations at: http://developer.yahoo.com/performance/rules.html.

YSlow

Those recommendations are quite easy to follow thanks to a tool the team has made and is available as an add-on to Firebug. You can actually have it loaded all the time and forget about it. When you want to try it you just click on its tab in the Firebug panel and let it try a page; it will provide you with an overall grade and a detail for each of the categories, with links to the particular entry in the team's site explaining what the problem is and how it can be fixed.

The website for YSlow reports improvements of 25% to 50% in performance. The best part of it is that we can incorporate many of its recommendations as a standard coding practice (for example, `<style>` tags towards the top, `<script>` tags towards the bottom) so we don't actually need to fix anything on each web page; once we adopt these practices, which are hardly onerous, the performance benefits come already included.

YUI Compressor

To make your code load fast, it is a good idea to compress it. This is the same tool used for the YUI Library; all the `-min.js` files have been produced by the YUI Compressor. It takes either `.js` or `.css` files and compresses them while still keeping them reliable. The YUI Compressor is a Java program so it needs a Java runtime. It can also be used in a build environment. (In fact, the whole build environment used to build the YUI Library is available as YUI Builder, though we won't discuss it in this book.)

The Compressor strips off all comments and unnecessary whitespace (space, tabs, and new lines), it drops most semicolons and, whenever it can, it renames variables to short one letter names. Global and globally accessible variables cannot be reduced, so working within a sandbox and using shortcuts gives us a further advantage, the Compressor will shorten our `Dom`, `Event`, and `Lang` aliases even further, something it cannot do with their full names as they are global.

The YUI Compressor has a verbose option that will produce several warnings that might help you further reduce the size of the code; things that it could have reduced but was unable to. A call to `eval()` or a `with` statement will prevent the Compressor from doing its job. As the argument to an `eval()` might contain references to variables in the scope, it cannot risk renaming any variable just in case the string being evaluated references them. The effects of a `with` statement can't actually be predicted until the statement is reached at runtime, so the Compressor can't predict what can be safely renamed and what not. Anyway, neither of these statements should have passed a check with JSLint.

It is easy to make aggregate files out of compressed files, they can simply be concatenated. Though they look awful, the compressed files are still valid JavaScript or CSS files and can be concatenated (each with its own kind) as their originals can. JSLint will certainly doubt whether those files are valid, it will flood the screen with errors, but you don't need to be concerned about them. Run JSLint on your source files, not on the compressed ones.

Perhaps the most important consideration when using the YUI Compressor is: make your code clean and verbose. There is no point in scrimping a few spaces or new lines here or there, using cryptic variable names or avoiding comments. You can't outsmart the Compressor in making your code smaller, so better don't even try. Make your code clean, nice to read, well commented, and let the Compressor make the production version.

Images and Sprites

Even the smallest image requires a full transaction to load. In those cases it is not so much the image size itself but the latency, the time for the request to reach the server and for the image to come back that takes the longest. Browsers have a limit on the number of requests they can have queued up, and waiting for an image is not the best use of time.

There are several things we can do about that. For larger images, compressing them can be a good idea. The first thing, however, is to select the correct file type. You should not save icons, which usually have a small palette, as JPEG files, a format that is more oriented to preserve the various hues from an actual picture. PNG files support both types of compression and it is easy to pick the wrong one. PNG also supports various sizes of palettes and using the larger palette will increase the file size. Smush.it, now a Yahoo! product (http://www.smushit.com/), can process your images and give you smaller versions of them without sacrificing quality.

You may also consider using images as CSS background images instead of as `<img>` tags. From a performance perspective, it is good because they get loaded later. Second, background images don't force a reflow of the page. If the `<img>` tag does not have the `width` and `height` attributes set, the browser has to wait for the actual image to find out its size and how to float things around it. With a background image, the size is determined by the object that contains it so the page can be laid out well before the image gets loaded.

From the point of view of the graphics designer, the look can be fully controlled from the CSS; there is no need to touch the HTML to change the references to the images. It also means that simply changing the style of the document body from, say, `yui-skin-sam` to `.yui-skin-pancho`, the whole page is changed, including icons.

The following two lines are visually equivalent:

```
<p><img src="icons/myclose.gif" /> … Some text …</p>
<p id="myclose"> … Some text …</p>
```

When the second line of code is supplemented with the following CSS style declaration:

```
#myclose {
    background: transparent url(icons/myclose.gif) no-repeat 0 0;
    padding-left: 30px;
}
```

The padding is necessary to prevent the text from overlapping the image

We can further improve this. A component like the Rich Text Editor that has so many images in its toolbar, each of them possibly in active, inactive, and disabled states, you would think would take lots of individual images. In fact, it takes very few because the images are piled into what is called a "Sprite", like a roll of photographic film containing a separate image in each frame. The browser can load the whole strip in one connection to the server and you can then use the frame you want; the browser will deliver all the frames requested from that single loaded copy. The downloadable examples contain a sample of this technique that uses the `background-position` CSS attribute to slide the correct frame under the area where it is to be shown. Sprites are very handy and they can easily be created in a batch process using a tool such as ImageMagick (`http://www.imagemagick.org/`).

YUI Profiler

The YUI Profiler is an advanced product, which we shall only mention. It captures the calls to the functions you explicitly want to monitor, or all the methods in an object, and counts the number of times each was called and how long execution stayed in it, reporting minimum, maximum, and average times in milliseconds.

This information is good when you want to evaluate where the bottlenecks in your programs are and where you might want to focus your optimization efforts. The tool itself is not hard to use and it is further complemented by the Profiler Viewer, which displays this information graphically. However, interpreting the information and deciding what can be done about it requires some experience and, in the end, it has little to do with the YUI Library, the subject of this book, but with application design and plain JavaScript coding.

YUI Testing

Testing an application is quite tedious; it gets worse because your application has to run in several different browsers with different behaviors. Later on, there comes a new version either of your application, the libraries you use, or of any of the browsers you are expected to support and all the testing has to be redone. In practice, most testing is replaced with very devoted praying.

YUI Test is a very simple library that lets you run tests automatically. You can define tests and test suites, ask it to perform some actions and then check the results. Those actions, besides explicitly calling functions and methods in your application, can be User Interface events. You can ask YUI Test to simulate mouse events such as clicks, double-clicks and mouse down, up, move, over, and out events as well as key ups, downs, and press. Thus, YUI Test is not limited to test functions but the whole behavior of the UI.

It can also test asynchronous functions such as DataSource's `.sendRequest()` by delaying the final checks until after a given delay.

YUI Test reports its results in the YUI Logger. It is very easy to build a test suite, which can be optionally included in your application.

Once written, the test can be run in all supported platforms and, when a new version comes out, it is easy to test that everything is still fine.

The test suite is not something static. Every bug report is an opportunity to add a new test to the suite for that bug, which obviously went undetected the first time. It is also a good way to ensure that a patch doesn't produce an undesired side effect. Running the tests after the patch is applied assures us that nothing got broken and no behavior changed.

In writing this book I wanted to try the JS beautifier before recommending it. I used the sources for the DataTable and RTE components, which are the largest ones in the whole library and are written by different team members so they have different coding styles. I checked the results with JSLint, but that still didn't assure me that the resulting code actually run. Fortunately, the RTE has a good test suite so I ran the test suite on the beautified code and it passed with all green info messages in the Logger.

Testing in multiple platforms

Sometimes the problem is how to test on different versions of the same browser. It is possible to install all browsers at once and run them, the problem comes when you want to test something in different versions of the same browser, as the newer one will replace the older one.

If you don't want to have extra real machines running the older versions, you can have virtual ones. Products such as VMWare, Portable Ubuntu, or MS Virtual PC let you create a virtual machine that can run a completely separate set of programs. The last one is particularly important because it lets you run several machines with the same license of Windows and the Microsoft Developer Network has articles on how to install the old versions of its browsers. While other browsers can run on multiple platforms, IE is relatively restricted; you can have two different versions of Firefox one on Windows the other on a Linux virtual machine. It is harder with IE so MS Virtual PC offers a solution for this.

API Docs

The tools that build the API documentation for the YUI Library are available to us. We can produce the same documentation for our applications as Yahoo! does. This is particularly important for libraries, as that is the main source of information for their users. The YUI Doc tool extracts the documentation from comments in the source code itself, so it is easy to document the code as you go. Those comments will be deleted by the YUI Compressor so no trace remains to bulk up the delivered code. The documenter does not actually read the executable code, so it cannot check that what you document is true. On the other hand, this is good as, for example, calling method `.createEvent()` to create a custom event is not required, we may document an event we never create, though we do fire it.

The HTML pages produced use a CSS file that is very easy to modify to give your docs your own look. The source code is available, including the templates for the generated pages, for further customizing. These pages can be placed online as they are made of plain HTML and some JavaScript code to support searching.

Summary

The focus of this chapter has been on the tools that help us in the production of reliable, fast, and compact code, on how to test across multiple platforms, and how to document it.

These tools will never be visible to our visitors, unlike our bugs which normally stand out to haunt us. Our reputation and careers might depend on them. They can help us solve in minutes, issues that would require an uncertain wait if we asked in the forums. They let us see what really goes on and confirm our assumptions or, dispiritingly often, squash them.

They let us compress, squeeze, and arrange our code, styles, images, and other elements in the most efficient way, detect bottlenecks that bog our applications down and, thus, improve both the delivery of the application and its execution.

The YUI Documenter is able to extract information about our programs from comments embedded in the source code itself. This is especially valuable if we develop libraries to be used by other members of a development team. It is easy to keep the documentation in sync with the code and it doesn't add any bulk to our delivered code as the comments can be stripped out by the YUI Compressor.

They were created as a consequence of real needs by very experienced people; we would be fools to assume we can do better without them. They help us develop code of the highest quality and provide the best user experience.

The index for the downloadable examples has linked references to all the tools described here.

Index

B

E

processing 133

K

Konfabulator 350

L

lang attribute 34
layout constructor 345
layout manager
  .close() method 346
  .collapse() method 346
  .expand() method 346
  .render() method 346
  .toggle() method 346
  about 344, 345
  configuration attributes 345
  constructor 345
  layout unit 345
  methods 346
layout unit 345
lazyLoad property 213
left attribute 143
levels, DOM 72
linkClickEvent 282
loadError event 347
load event 347
loadMethod attribute 347
Locale object 47
Logger
  about 351, 352
  features 352, 354
  instance, creating 354-357
Logger.reset() class 357
log() method 356
LogMsg class 356
LogReader class
  about 356
  methods 357
LogReader class, methods
  .clearConsole() 357
  .collapse() 357
  .expand() 357
  .hide() 357
  .hideCategory() 357
  .hideSource() 357
  .pause() 357

.resume() 357
.show() 357
.showCategory() 357
.showSource() 357
LogWriter class 356

M

menu classes
  about 201
  ContextMenu class 201
  ContextMenuItem class 201
  MenuBarB class 201
  MenuBarItem class 201
  Menu class 201
  MenuItem class 201, 203
  MenuItem subclasses 203
  MenuManager class 201
  subclasses 202
menu control
  about 200
  menu classes 201
  navigation menu 200
  right-click context menu 200
  style menu bar 200
MenuItem class
  about 203
  configuration attributes 203
MenuItem subclasses
  about 203
  ContextMenuItem 203
  MenuBarItem 203
MenuNode 236
menu subclasses 202
metadata 262, 263
methods, Button class
  .addHiddenFieldsToForm() 221
  .blur() 221
  .destroy() 221
  .focus() 221
  .getForm() 221
  .getHiddenField() 221
  .getMenu() 221
  .hasFocus() 221
  .isActive() 221
  .onFormKeyDown() 221
  .submitForm() 221

Thank you for buying
YUI 2.8 Learning the Library

About Packt Publishing

Packt, pronounced 'packed', published its first book "*Mastering phpMyAdmin for Effective MySQL Management*" in April 2004 and subsequently continued to specialize in publishing highly focused books on specific technologies and solutions.

Our books and publications share the experiences of your fellow IT professionals in adapting and customizing today's systems, applications, and frameworks. Our solution based books give you the knowledge and power to customize the software and technologies you're using to get the job done. Packt books are more specific and less general than the IT books you have seen in the past. Our unique business model allows us to bring you more focused information, giving you more of what you need to know, and less of what you don't.

Packt is a modern, yet unique publishing company, which focuses on producing quality, cutting-edge books for communities of developers, administrators, and newbies alike. For more information, please visit our website: www.packtpub.com.

About Packt Open Source

In 2010, Packt launched two new brands, Packt Open Source and Packt Enterprise, in order to continue its focus on specialization. This book is part of the Packt Open Source brand, home to books published on software built around Open Source licences, and offering information to anybody from advanced developers to budding web designers. The Open Source brand also runs Packt's Open Source Royalty Scheme, by which Packt gives a royalty to each Open Source project about whose software a book is sold.

Writing for Packt

We welcome all inquiries from people who are interested in authoring. Book proposals should be sent to author@packtpub.com. If your book idea is still at an early stage and you would like to discuss it first before writing a formal book proposal, contact us; one of our commissioning editors will get in touch with you.

We're not just looking for published authors; if you have strong technical skills but no writing experience, our experienced editors can help you develop a writing career, or simply get some additional reward for your expertise.

jQuery 1.4 Reference Guide

ISBN: 978-1-849510-04-2   Paperback: 336 pages

A comprehensive exploration of the popular
JavaScript library

1. Quickly look up features of the jQuery library

2. Step through each function, method, and
   selector expression in the jQuery library with
   an easy-to-follow approach

3. Understand the anatomy of a jQuery script

4. Write your own plug-ins using jQuery's
   powerful plug-in architecture

Joomla! 1.5: Beginner's Guide

ISBN: 978-1-847199-90-4   Paperback: 380 pages

Build and maintain impressive user-friendly web
sites the fast and easy way with Joomla! 1.5

1. Create a web site that meets real-life
   requirements by following the creation of an
   example site with the help of easy-to-follow
   steps and ample screenshots

2. Practice all the Joomla! skills from organizing
   your content to completely changing the site's
   looks and feel

3. Go beyond a typical Joomla! site to make the
   site meet your specific needs

Please check **www.PacktPub.com** for information on our titles

www.ingramcontent.com/pod-product-compliance
Lightning Source LLC
Chambersburg PA
CBHW062035050326
40690CB00016B/2947